The *Parents*™ Magazine Baby and Childcare Series combines the most up-to-date medical findings, the advice of doctors and child psychologists, and the actual day-to-day experiences of parents like you. Covering a wide variety of subjects, these books answer all your questions, step-by-important-step, and provide the confidence of knowing you're doing the best for your child—with help from *Parents*™ Magazine.

Titles in the *Parents*™ Baby and Child Care series
Published by Ballantine Books:

PARENTS™ BOOK FOR NEW FATHERS
PARENTS™ BOOK FOR RAISING A HEALTHY
  CHILD
PARENTS™ BOOK FOR THE TODDLER YEARS
PARENTS™ BOOK FOR YOUR BABY'S FIRST YEAR
PARENTS™ BOOK OF BABY NAMES
PARENTS™ BOOK OF CHILDHOOD ALLERGIES
PARENTS™ BOOK OF CHILD SAFETY
PARENTS™ BOOK OF DISCIPLINE
PARENTS™ BOOK OF INFANT COLIC
PARENTS™ BOOK OF PREGNANCY AND BIRTH
PARENTS™ BOOK OF TOILET TEACHING

Parents™
Book of
Discipline

BARBARA R. BJORKLUND, M.A
and DAVID F. BJORKLUND, Ph.D.

BALLANTINE BOOKS • NEW YORK

A Ballantine Book
Published by The Ballantine Publishing Group
Copyright © 1990 by Gruner + Jahr, USA Publishing

Cover photo © Augustus Butera

www.randomhouse.com/BB/

Library of Congress Catalog Card Number: 90-93029

ISBN 0-345-43640-7

Manufactured in the United States of America

First Edition: August 1990

10 9 8 7 6 5 4 3 2 1

To all our children,
Debbie, Allen, Derek, Heidi,
Nick, Cheri, Glenna,
Michelle, Nicholas, Brittany,
Jeffrey, and Benjamin

Contents

Acknowledgments		ix
To the Reader		xi
1.	Discipline and Your Child: Some Things to Keep in Mind	1
2.	The Disciplined Life-style	11
3.	Tools for Changing Behavior	32
4.	Discipline and Development	53
5.	Parents as Models of Discipline	83
6.	Know Your Child	97
7.	Independence	119
8.	Discipline in "Nontraditional Families"	141
9.	The First Year	158
10.	The Second Year (Twelve to Twenty-four Months)	185
11.	Twos: Terrible and Otherwise	209
12.	Discipline with Three- and Four-Year-Olds	231
13.	The Early School Years	249
	Index	265

Acknowledgments

One of the things that makes writing so difficult is that it is one-way communication. This book was an exception. We were fortunate to have parents of young children help us out all along the way. We would like to express our appreciation for the hundreds of mothers and fathers who talked with us and responded to our questionnaires. The love and concern they expressed for their children made us feel that we were writing to close friends, and their wisdom and insight into family discipline issues are evident throughout this book.

Ironically, we signed the contract for this book a week after our youngest child turned eight, leaving us with no children between birth and seven. We would like to express our thanks to our siblings and their spouses for their thoughtfulness in providing twelve nieces and nephews whose ages range from birth to seven years and who served for us as examples of happy, well-adjusted, loving children. Furthermore, we would like to thank them for passing out questionnaires to their friends, coworkers, kindergarten parents, preschool parents, and perfect strangers in the supermarket. They are Rose and Ron Carlson, Patty and Dave Hall, Sandy and Joe Ladika, (of Bradenton, Florida); Bruce and Pam Bjorklund, Steve and Kathy Bjorklund, (of West Boylston,

Massachusetts); and Lynne and John Kiritsy (of Oxford, Massachusetts).

Much of the work on this book was done in the summer of 1988 while we were guests of the Max Plank Institute for Psychological Research in Munich, West Germany. We are grateful to Drs. Franz Weinert and Wolfgang Schneider for providing a real "home away from home" for us as well as a comprehensive library, energetic work atmosphere, and state of the art communiation systems so that we were able to stay in touch with our students, colleagues, and family members at home.

And finally, we would like to acknowledge Elizabeth Crow, current President and Editorial Director of Parents Magazine, who started this project with us as Editor-in-Chief, Ann Pleshette Murphy, current Editor-in-Chief of Parents Magazine, who completed this project with us, and Ginny Faber, Senior Editor at Ballantine Books. It was a pleasure to work with all three.

Barbara and David Bjorklund
Ft. Lauderdale, Florida
April, 1990

To the Reader

This book is about discipline with children from birth to age seven. It has a different focus, however, from other books you may have read on family discipline. The main reason for this is that we are developmental psychologists. Our interests are in the normal changes children go through on their way from birth to adulthood. We believe that adults who have an influence on children's lives—especially parents—need to be aware of these changes in order to do an effective job of child rearing. For this reason we have written an entire chapter on development (Chapter 4) and have included additional information on development throughout the book where we judged it relevant.

We believe that the primary goal of parents (and teachers and baseball coaches) is to help children along the path to becoming independent, well-adjusted adults. We believe that the goal of having obedient, well-behaved children is short-sighted and that when parents concern themselves too much with "quick-fix" remedies, they lose sight of their long-term goals. For this reason, we have included only one chapter on this topic, "Tools for Changing Behavior" (Chapter 3).

Our focus in developmental psychology is on children's thinking processes—cognitive development. We believe that the key to family discipline is found in internal attitudes, not external behavior. Adults lead the family because of their superior thinking abilities, not because they are physically stronger or can yell louder than their children. Adults can plan ahead, schedule time, prevent problems before they occur, model behavior they want their children to imitate, and adjust their communication level to fit the limited understanding of their young children. This book emphasizes these parenting tools in chapters on "The Disciplined Life-style" (Chapter 2), "Parents as Models of Discipline" (Chapter 5), and "Know Your Child" (Chapter 6).

Discipline is something that develops out of the parent/child relationship, and emotional attachment, beginning in infancy, is the foundation of this relationship. Children identify with their parents and other important adults in their lives because of this internal influence, not because of external influences such as allowances, gifts, and stars on behavior charts. Attachment begins in infancy when children learn that they can depend on their parents to be protectors and providers, and it continues throughout life, changing in form as the adult and the child change.

We believe that adults should use this influence wisely. When parents use their love as cheap prizes to hand out when children perform clever tricks (such as making good grades, winning swim meets, or cleaning their rooms) and take it away when the performances fall below par, they may gain in the short run, but it is at the expense of their children's future senses of security and self-esteem. The truth is that when the grades are high and the ribbons are plentiful, the praises abound from many sources. But when the grades fall and the meets are lost, children need and deserve the reassurance of their parents' bond. We believe that using parental love to enforce household chores and school grades is like winning a tennis match by dropping a nuclear bomb on the opponent's side of the court— it's overkill, it's counterproductive, and it's just not fair.

This book emphasizes the importance of parent/child attachment and de-emphasizes the adversarial role of parent versus child that often appears in discipline books. We believe that parents and children should feel that they are on the same side in this often-stressful world, and that fostering this feeling is frequently more important than making a "disciplinary" issue of every misstep. This book gives parents permission to use their judgment and sometimes choose to change their rules, back off of highly emotional issues, and sometimes let misbehavior go with no comment if they feel the family relationship is at risk.

Many family battles are fought over independence and control. When parents view their role as making short-term, external behavior changes, these problems increase as the child grows and soon become the focus of family interactions. But when parents take a long-term view and are more concerned with their children's internal attitudes, they realize that children who seek independence and control over their own lives are signs of parents' success rather than a threat to their authority. When a fourteen-month-old girl clamps her jaw shut at breakfast and refuses to eat unless she can feed herself, it makes a big difference whether Mom views this angrily, thinking that her daughter is scheming to make her harried morning even more stressful, or if she views it proudly with some amusement, thinking that she has done a good job of fostering confidence and self-sufficiency in her daughter. Parents who take a long-range view of their role realize that their control and their children's dependence is only temporary, not the major issues of family discipline. They can shift their thoughts and energy to helping their children develop abilities that will make them independent, self-controlled, and self-disciplined. We devote an entire chapter to independence in preschool children (Chapter 7), a discipline issue that is often not considered important until the teen years.

During the months we were writing this book, we talked with parents about their discipline problems. We asked what solutions they had tried and which were successful and not successful. We sent batches of questionnaires out to friends and relatives around the country, asking them to pass them out to parents of preschoolers they know. We received hundreds of responses. We intended to use our questionnaire as a poll, tallying the various types of problems, dividing by ages, and being good scientists. But so many parents had turned the "short-answer" format into an "essay" format that we decided not to turn their answers into statistics, but to let them speak directly to the readers. The boxed items throughout this book are comments from parents. Some are problems, some are solutions they have found helpful (and not), and some are words of wisdom or encouragement they wanted to share. Following each problem, we have given our comments and suggestions.

The first eight chapters form the core of this book. We write about discipline in the context of family structure and child development, with the goal of raising a self-disciplined child. The last five chapters cover specific discipline questions parents commonly report with children of different ages, from birth through seven years.

We believe that there are seldom set answers to family discipline problems. Instead, parents must weigh the alternatives and select the answer they believe is best for their children and themselves. We hope that our suggestions are helpful for these particular problems, but more to the point, we hope that our ideas will give readers a long-term view of their role as parents and help them establish a disciplined life-style for their family, making their home a pleasant, secure sanctuary for all members, and a good training ground for the future.

1. Discipline and Your Child: Some Things to Keep in Mind

What Discipline *Is* and What Discipline *Is Not*

Usually when parents think of discipline, they think of problems. "What can I do to *discipline* my child when he persists in calling the next-door neighbor doo-doo head, or when he threatens his little sister with physical violence." "How can I get my daughter to go to bed at night without fussing or stop her from making a scene in the grocery store when we pass through the candy aisle?" Handling these situations involves doing something to remedy an immediate crisis. When parents think of discipline only in these terms, it's what we refer to as "crisis parenting."

True discipline, however, entails much more than dealing with behavioral emergencies. In fact, discipline is most effective when it is viewed as the result of a continuous interaction between children and parents over time. We teach our children to *become disciplined*—to develop self-discipline—by dealing with them lovingly and consistently on a day-to-day basis and by setting good examples for them to emulate. Discipline should be viewed as "rules to live by" and not simply as a bag of tricks to make a child comply in specific, problem situations. Discipline is part of a life-style. Disruptive and problem behaviors have a history—they don't arise out of the blue. Understanding that problem behavior is often the result of pat-

terns firmly established in infancy can help parents avoid problem situations, modify undisciplined life-styles, and handle
immediate crises with a minimum of strife.

Developing a disciplined life-style sounds like a lot of
work—for both children and parents—and it is. But it also has
its rewards. Children who have structure in their lives feel
secure and in control of themselves. They are able to make
plans and predict future events. Because their lives run on
schedule, they can apply more physical and mental energy to
social pursuits and fun. Disciplined children are by no means
sticks-in-the-mud or wimps. They are not to be found dressed
in velvet suits with lace collars taking tea with their grand-
mothers while other children are having fun on the playground.
They are very likely on the playground, too, enjoying life to its
fullest and knowing that they are an important functioning part
of a healthy family.

Developing a disciplined life-style requires considerable effort on the part of parents. It involves thinking about the kind
of life you want to live and the kind of children you want to
raise. It involves evaluating your own childhood, keeping what
you think is valuable, and weeding out or updating the rest. It
involves firming up your adult life so you can be a positive role
model for your children. It involves many long talks with your
spouse about making definite family rules. It also involves the
risk of ''looking human'' to your family when you fall short of
perfection. And once all that is in place, it involves periodic
checking to make sure everything is running smoothly and to
make the inevitable corrections when everything is not.

This book is concerned with discipline during the first seven
years of life. Many of you are in search of solutions to specific
problems, problems which have been faced by thousands of
parents before you. Problems are facts of life when raising
children, and it is surprising to realize how common some of
these problems are. In this book we provide many such examples of children's misbehavior and ways of dealing with them.
These examples come from scientific studies of parent/child
interaction, from the writings of other experts in child psychology, from hundreds of interviews with parents, and from our
own experience as parents and teachers of child psychology.

But we're attempting to do more—much more—than provide parents with a few tricks for coping with specific prob-

lems. We try to show how to raise a disciplined child—a child responsible for his or her own actions and in control of his or her own behavior. We believe that the goal of parenting should be to raise a competent, independent adult, and that this process begins in infancy. One of the greatest gifts parents can give their children is self-discipline—control over their own lives. Such a gift is most easily given with warmth, love, and respect for the child as an individual.

Two Views of Parenting

Parents too often view child rearing, and discipline in particular, as imposing their will upon their children. They feel that as parents, it is their job to shape a child's personality and character—to teach the child the ways of the world and to mold him or her into the type of person they can be proud of.

How else can we prepare our children for life? After all, as experienced adults we've been through it all. From this point of view, children are little lumps of clay and parents are the sculptors. Such a view places all the responsibility on the artist and none on the raw material.

On the other hand, some parents believe that child rearing is more like gardening. Nature provides the necessary sun and soil and seed, and the parent is little more than the attentive gardener whose job it is to water them and watch them grow. This view places most of the responsibility on the child, leaving parents hopeful that they have been entrusted with a well-bred seedling who won't grow out of control.

Not surprisingly, the truth lies somewhere in the middle. Parents are truly the most significant shapers of children's lives. Yet the child comes into the world with a unique biology that forms the basis of his or her personality. Some babies are easily soothed, whereas others must be danced around the living room most of the evening before calming down; some love being held, whereas others tolerate cuddling only long enough to be fed. These dispositions—personality traits if you will—influence how children interpret and respond to their world, and to their parents in particular. Yet children, regardless of their biology, are influenced by the efforts of parents. Children and parents have a relationship that is like a continuous dance, with one partner adjusting his steps to the moves of the other.

What has all this to do with discipline? Basically the origins of a disciplined life-style can be found in early parent-child interactions, and these interactions are a product of the unique characteristics of both the child and the parents.

Sarah and Elizabeth: Similar Beginnings, Different Outcomes

Consider the early months of Sarah and Elizabeth, two infants from different families in different cities. Both were born prematurely, and although healthy, they were slow to develop. Their cries were high-pitched and unpleasant to the ear for the first month or so. Each spent the first two weeks in the protective environment of an incubator, and neither set of parents had much opportunity to interact with their child. When their parents took them home, both babies were sluggish. They didn't smile or make eye contact with their parents and didn't make the cooing and babbling noises that their siblings had as babies. Basically for the first five months, Sarah and Elizabeth were both sickly and unresponsive babies, who did not provide the social cues of smiling, eye contact, and vocalizations that make babies endearing to their parents. Yet the outcomes for these children were vastly different.

Highly anxious, Sarah's mother was desperate for a little girl to love. But when Sarah was born, she was kept at the hospital, and once home, she seemed unloving and did not respond to her mother's pleas and efforts to play. To top it off, Sarah's unpleasant cries were highly irritating. Over the first three or four months, the mother's disappointment grew. Her baby became not the beautiful, loving infant she had hoped for, but a demanding, unappealing burden. The mother held Sarah responsible for her husband's lack of communication and her own feelings of desperation and low self-esteem. Sarah and her mother were developing a pattern of interaction that was not conducive to a healthy development for either the child or the mother. Even after the symptoms of her prematurity were gone, Sarah would continue to be viewed, albeit unintentionally, as a difficult and unloving child. Unlike her older brother, she would constantly upset her mother and would be difficult to control.

On the other hand, Elizabeth's high-pitched cries and general lethargy were signals to her mother that she had a sick baby on her hands. Elizabeth's mother provided her with extra physical contact and made a special effort to talk and sing to a baby who wasn't quite ready to talk and sing back. Her sickly child was her major topic of conversation, and she considered herself the one to "make my baby better." By five months, Elizabeth, like Sarah, *was* better. Not that everything went smoothly for Elizabeth and her mother over the next three years, but they developed a comfortable and loving interaction that has resulted in a close and understanding relationship.

Who is responsible for the poor interaction between Sarah and her mother? It's easy to lay blame at the mother's feet. Obviously if she had been more sensitive and caring, she and her daughter would have developed a closer and, from the point of view of discipline, a more successful relationship. Yet Sarah's mother got along fine with her older son. But the problem isn't only with the sickly baby, either, as we can see from the example of Elizabeth. The source of the problem lies in both the mother and the child.

From birth, children signal their parents concerning their wants, needs, and desires. Often they seem to be saying, "This is how I want you to treat me." A parent's job is to read these cues and to respond accordingly. This requires immense sensitivity and flexibility, often more easily said than done. Sometimes the needs of the parent just don't match the needs of the child, as in the case of Sarah's mother, who could not adjust her feelings and behavior to deal with the special needs that her baby presented.

Sarah's case is extreme. Yet perfect matches between parents and children are rare. Because it is the parents who are more mature intellectually, socially, and emotionally, the task of adjusting one's behavior so that a smooth interaction can occur falls to them. But infants and children also do a good deal of adjusting to meet the demands of their parents. If we let children determine exactly how parent/child relationships developed, we would end up eating at fast-food restaurants every day of the week.

Obviously what we have here is a two-way street. To become civilized members of society, children must adapt to the rules and special characteristics of their parents. Discipline is not something that develops "naturally." But if parents are to raise a child with self-discipline, they must consider his or her special needs and characteristics. Each child is different and will develop in his or her own way, though general patterns will apply. Parents must truly get to know their children as individuals in order to provide the special attention and discipline appropriate to each child's personality and temperament.

Children are shaped by their parents, but they also come into the world as biologically unique individuals who will do as much shaping as being shaped. Parents who see child rearing and discipline only as imposing their will on a malleable child will have their hands full. Likewise, parents who "accept the child as he is," making little attempt to alter a child's "natural inclinations," will also have a rough time of it. Children need structure and guidance, but not all children respond in the same way to parental discipline. What works for one parent/child pair may not work for another. Raising disciplined children involves teaching children self-control and respect, both for themselves and for other people. This process is by necessity an interaction between a child with his or her own biology and that child's parents, who have their own special way of viewing the world. Making this interaction "work" is the key to raising a self-disciplined child.

Discipline and Development

Children at different ages require different types of behaviors from their parents. They have different ways of understanding their world and thus different ways of perceiving what their parents do. The techniques used to control the behavior of a one-year-old will simply not be adequate for controlling the behavior of a two- or three-year-old. Children change over time and this requires that their parents change.

We are reminded of sad cases when parents are unable to change to the demands of their developing children. It is all too often that a two- or three-year-old child is placed in foster care because his or her teenage mother just can't handle the kid anymore. What is also common is that the young mother quickly finds herself pregnant again, delighted that she is about to have another *baby!*

Such young women are often excellent mothers of infants. The demands of the little, highly dependent ones are met with joy. They love singing to their babies, and carrying them wherever they go, and feel competent to handle the needs of their tiny wards. Yet despite the needs of their mothers, babies begin to grow up. They crawl and walk and attempt to escape from their mothers' clutches to discover the wonderful world that surrounds them. They decide that they don't want to go for rides, or shopping, or to hangout with mother's friends, and they let their displeasure be known. They require intellectual stimulation that goes beyond baby talk. They become unmanageable. They won't conform to their mothers' schedule and their mothers seem unable to adjust theirs to their children's. The mothers see no way of recapturing control because they are unable to adapt to the increasing demands of their growing children. The requirements of an eighteen-month or two-year-old child are vastly different from those of a six- or twelve-month old. Parents must make the transition with their children. When they don't, the seeds of a difficult relationship are planted.

Some of the most persistent problems in child rearing during the early years can be traced to parents' difficulty dealing with or understanding the developmental level of their children. Children become more competent and demand more independence, but parents frequently have difficulty dealing with children's newfound abilities. Some of the fiercest battles are fought in children's "war of independence." On the other hand, parents often expect *more* of children than they are capable of producing. Such overestimation of children's abilities is another frequent source of conflict and one that can be avoided if parents are alert to the developmental level of their children.

Discipline, Love, and Respect

Raising a disciplined child is best accomplished in an atmosphere of love and respect. Discipline is an act of love when it provides children tools for coping with life. This is not akin to what many parents say while spanking their child: "This is going to hurt me more than it hurts you." Discipline is not synonymous with punishment. Discipline is a set of rules to live by, tools for solving life's problems. Discipline is learned more by example than by instruction. When loving parents are disciplined in their actions, their children find it easy to develop in a similar way.

Imposing discipline on children—developing a self-disciplined child—requires respect for the integrity of the child. Children have feelings and thoughts that are different from those of their parents. Children's thoughts are immature and their feelings difficult to articulate and difficult for adults to understand. Nonetheless, they are real and children need to know that what they think and feel is considered worthwhile. Children who are rarely taken seriously—whose ideas are not listened to and who are repeatedly told without justification to comply—do not see the merit of discipline. The child whose rationale is, "I'll behave so I don't get into trouble," does not develop respect for adults. When the opportunity comes to break the rules without being "caught," he or she will do so.

On the other hand, children whose ideas and feelings are respected, who are listened to and who sometimes get their way when their arguments are sound, see their parents as reasonable people worthy of respect. The rules laid down by their parents are not always agreeable, but they are not capricious either. As all children do, they will argue and disobey, but they will also develop an appreciation for their parents' judgments and the merits of a disciplined life-style. Of course, they can't articulate this, but children who are accorded respect will learn respect for others in the process, and are more apt to internalize those "rules to live by."

The Myth of Perfect Parents and Perfect Children

Parents are not perfect. We have good intentions but we have our failings, too. We don't always put our tools away after working in the garage and so find ourselves cursing the loss of our three-quarter-inch wrench. We don't have the patience to save our money before purchasing a new set of golf clubs, so we add the cost to an already overburdened credit card account. Similarly we know we should respond warmly and consistently to our children, but some days we just don't. You've probably read dozens of "how to" books on how to raise children, how to deal with a cranky baby, or how to survive two children under two years of age, and they all sounded good. But you always seem to fall short and you sometimes feel like a failure.

Well, you're not alone. You're not a perfect parent, but neither is anyone else—including the authors of all those "how to" books. But take heart. Perfection is not all that it's cracked up to be. Children are amazingly resistant to lapses in parenting. Children tolerate our mood swings, our inconsistencies, and our occasional tantrums. What is important to children is the general day-in and day-out home environment. Children who are loved and respected are secure enough to put up with a parent who is less than perfect.

The other side of this coin, however, is that we should not expect perfect children. Despite their very best intentions, they, too, will stray from what they have been taught is right. They will have *their* moods, *their* inconsistencies, and *their* tantrums. We as parents must expect this and accept this occasional misbehavior as part of childhood. Just as we don't expect our children to stop loving and respecting us because of our misdeeds, we should not withdraw our love from them, even temporarily, for *their* misdeeds. What we should strive for is a reasonably consistent, loving household, with rules that are enforced *most* of the time, and with people, both children and adults, who are considerate of one another *most* of the time.

Difficulties and conflicts in raising your child are inevitable, and you have not failed as a parent just because life with Junior is not problem free. Becoming civilized is not something the human animal does naturally. The child is not pre-wired to learn good table manners or to be respectful of the property of others. The presence of problems is not a sign that things are going wrong, but rather a sign of growth and development. And there is not a single best way to handle these problems. You and your family have unique wants, priorities, needs, traditions, and personalities. Only you can decide the best way to raise your children. However, regardless of your values and what you wish for your children, there are tools and attitudes that will make that job easier, and that, essentially, is what this book is about.

In the course of writing this book, we have collected comments from hundreds of parents concerning their discipline problems, solutions, and words of wisdom. These comments will be offered throughout the book in boxes.

Being a parent gets better in some ways, but there is always *something challenging*. Raising children is a life of contradictions. It's exhausting, expensive, scary (being responsible for three lives) and still exhilarating, challenging, fulfilling, and just plain fun. No one can make me smile like my kids.

2. The Disciplined Life-style

The key to effective discipline is to view it not just as "things to do to keep your children in line," but as a way of living—as a life-style. Children will behave thoughtfully and responsibly if their lives have structure and are predictable. It is parents who provide the structure and predictability for young children, and this takes work. It requires having well-articulated rules, schedules for meals and bedtimes, and consistency. It requires relinquishing to your child some control over small things. But the effort is worth it. Living a disciplined life is not only good for children, but also for adults. Being disciplined and having disciplined children can reduce the stress of everyday life for families and minimize the conflicts that are inevitable.

In this chapter we concentrate on four important aspects of raising a disciplined child: 1. *Giving children some control over their lives;* 2. *Providing schedules;* 3. *Building children's feelings of usefulness;* and 4. *Making children feel responsible for their own actions.*

Giving Children the Feeling of Control

The roots of control are planted firmly in infancy. From their first month on, children seek to gain control over their world. In fact, the development of a newborn into a full-fledged adult can be viewed as the development of a totally dependent creature into a fully independent one.

During the first year, infants learn control by communicating their needs and wishes to their parents and having parents respond. Babies send signals: they want to eat, need to have their diapers changed, wish to play. When parents understand and respond, babies perceive that their actions make a difference. They have some control. "I'm important here. When I speak, people listen to me. What I have to say makes a difference."

As children get older, parental understanding of and response to their signals remains important. But their increased physical and mental abilities require that they be given greater control over their circumstances. Of course, you can't expect two-year-olds to make many decisions for themselves, but there are areas in which control can be given.

Giving Children Choices

Perhaps the simplest way to give children the feeling of control is to give them choices among a few alternatives, any of which is acceptable to Mom and Dad. For example, three-year-old Mary may choose cereal or scrambled eggs for breakfast most mornings. She likes both, and Dad is willing to fix either. If she doesn't decide by the time the first egg is cracked, however, she gets the eggs because that's what Dad is having. All in all, it's much better to *give* children control by allowing them choices than to have them *take* it through tantrums and stubborn behavior.

I give my children choices, but both choices must be agreeable to me. The children feel like they are in control. Sometimes it doesn't work—neither choice is agreeable to the child. Then *I* decide, and the *child* has a problem. This is where consistency is important—not to give in to a child's demands if he didn't make a choice when he had a chance.

Dad drove five-year-old Kristina to kindergarten every morning, and she was expected to dress herself. This she did without complaint, because Kristina had specific tastes in clothes and enjoyed picking them out in the morning. But she rarely dressed herself to her mom's or dad's satisfaction. Kristina would pick out clothes from the hamper ("But I like this dress. It isn't *really* dirty."), or wear combinations of clothes that drove her mother up the wall ("You look like a ragamuffin! Now go back in your room and put something halfway decent on!"). Kristina's parents wanted to encourage Kristina to take care of herself in the morning, but felt frustrated when they didn't like the choices Kristina made for clothes.

The solution was a relatively simple one. Before bed each evening, Dad would go through Kristina's clothes and select two or three outfits that she could wear the next day. From that selection, Kristina chose one, and it was left on her chair to be put on the next morning. The other outfits were returned to the closet or drawers. This way, Kristina was allowed to make a choice, but among alternatives agreeable to her father.

Kristina's mom and dad also let Kristina have a say in the type of clothes they bought for her. When Kristina and her mom go clothes shopping, they have a rule that if Kristina doesn't like it, they don't buy it. Mom, of course, has absolute veto power, so there have been times when Kristina falls in love with an outfit that her mother hates. At age five, Kristina knows that she doesn't necessarily get everything she wants.

Keep the Options Real

As kids get older, the decisions they are allowed to make can become bigger. However, offering choices is important at any age. If the options are realistic (as opposed to something like choosing between sushi and escargot for lunch), children will have the feeling of some real control, while parents will be offering alternatives that they can live with.

It may seem easier just to impose our will upon our kids; After all, our decisions are in their best interests. However, the inconvenience of coming up with two or three alternatives and letting children decide between them is probably easier in the long run. Children who are given choices *do* have some control, although probably not as much as they *believe* they have.

And, in the long run, children who feel that their parents take their decisions seriously, are children who will give their parents little trouble.

Sometimes, the Kids Are Right

Oftentimes, the first word children learn to use effectively is "no," and they give their parents this one syllable response everytime they are asked to do something. However, the reverse holds true in some families. We know parents whose first response to any request made to them by their young children is "no." Basically the philosophy is, "If I haven't told you it's okay before, don't bother asking if it's okay now." Letting children have their way is seen by some parents as a sign of weakness.

In less extreme cases, many parents are unwilling to reconsider a decision, despite pleas and new evidence from their children. "Consistency" is viewed as stating a policy and then sticking with it through thick and thin. Many parents are deathly afraid of losing control of their children, and giving in to children's requests is viewed as a first step on the road to chaos. "Once we give these kids an inch, they'll take a mile. It's us against them."

As we hope we've made clear to this point, however, giving children some control over their lives does not mean "giving in" to unreasonable demands. It may mean giving in to "reasonable" demands (or, hopefully, reasonable polite requests). Sometimes the best thing parents can do is to listen carefully to their children, evaluate their requests, and then go along with what they ask for. However, this means granting some control to your children and having the flexibility to change your mind when the evidence in that direction is sufficiently strong. This also requires that parents be secure with themselves and their role as parents.

My son is three years old, almost four, and the problem that I encountered with my son was that he was very persistent in wanting to have his way. There were some things that he could do for himself without assistance. He would say, "I can do it!" and would push me away if I tried to do it for him.

I've learned to let him do some of the things that I know he enjoys doing, such as helping to wash the car, running the VCR, playing with his great-aunt's dogs, pulling pots and pans out of the pantry, and staying over at his uncle's some weekends because he enjoys playing with his cousins.

We will talk more about the issue of parental security and changing rules and plans to meet unexpected situations in Chapter 7. For now, let us only say that giving children some control over their lives sometimes means changing our minds and being less than one hundred percent "consistent."

Consistency doesn't mean always doing things the *parents'* way. It means doing things the *best* way.

When children are allowed to have some control of their own behavior, there are potential problems. If children are in control, by definition, parents are not. Of course, parents can always step in and reassert control, and this is often necessary. Yet children will seek control, striving to be independent from their parents and to do things "on their own." This is not so much insubordination, but rather the natural course of development.

Establishing Rules

Children aren't the only ones who need to feel in control of their lives. So do adults. Many self-help books on the shelves of local libraries and bookstores deal, in one way or another, with people attempting to be in control of their own lives—to "pull their own strings," to feel "Okay" about themselves, or to act assertively in certain situations. We have no intention of entering this arena, but we would like to say a few words about taking control of one's *family* life, and how this greatly affects child rearing and discipline.

Most of us don't really know what we're getting into when we become parents. Babies are planned, nurseries readied, and college accounts started only days after conception. But few of us enter parenthood having a clear idea of how we want to run our families—of what is important to us as parents and how, precisely, we want our children to behave in certain situations. In other words, few of us become parents with an easily stated philosophy about how we plan to raise our children.

What most of us do instead is develop a philosophy of child rearing as we go along. We watch our kids grow and we realize what sort of people we want them to be. We come to recognize that certain things are important to us and others are not, and this is fine.

Yet many parents never develop such a philosophy. They are guided by some unspecified set of rules and follow them when they are convenient. When problems with their children arise, they are often surprised. They didn't know having a five-year-old crawling into bed with them every night would be so troublesome! (It wasn't when the child was two.)

Parents need to develop a philosophy of child rearing—a system of beliefs to live by. This does not only mean opinions about values such as honesty, compassion, and loyalty, but also ideas about specific behaviors. Is a bedtime schedule important? How do you feel about manners? Should children say "please" and "thank you" all the time, keep their elbows off the table, and never horse around when they are eating? Or should there be some leeway? How do you feel about profanity, about sharing with other children, about fighting (when it involves sticking up for your rights rather than unnecessary aggression), about making beds and picking up toys?

It may seem that the easy answer is, "Yes, we care about all of these things. We want our children to be well behaved." But there is more than one way of being "well behaved." Parents who have considered the alternatives, who have deemed some aspects of their children's behavior worth worrying about and others not, will be less surprised when "problems" do arise and will have some notion of what to do about these problems.

Most crucially, parents must communicate their ideas to each other. Too frequently parents disagree on an issue of discipline and don't even know it. Their children do, however, and often will make the most of this lack of communication.

Households need well-defined sets of rules to live by. These rules need not be written in stone, but they should be upheld by both parents and understood by the children. This requires discipline on the part of parents, and, above all, communication and planning.

HOUSE RULES OF THE BARTON FAMILY

- No hitting by anyone.
- Everyone wears seat belts all the time the car is moving.
- If you don't eat at mealtime, then *no* snacks later and *no* dessert.
- No yelling in the house by anyone.
- No food in Mom's car.
- Kids ask before using phone.
- Say "please" and "thank you" to grown-ups *and* to children.

The Importance of Schedules

Control is important for children because, among other things, it gives them some predictability. If children feel in control, they know pretty much what's going to happen to them in the short term. Of course, events just happen, but if possible, we like to know *when* they're going to happen. We have to pay our taxes every year. We have no real control over whether we pay them or not. But at least we know *when* they're due and can make the necessary plans to make the experience as painless as possible. Kids are no different. In fact, children tend to like a bit more routine than the average adult. Perhaps it's because they have less direct control over things, and that in its absence, they like schedules.

Napping and Sleeping Schedules

Preschoolers who get along pleasantly without daily naps are few and far between. Yet some of the biggest discipline problems with young children arise because they are tired and cranky.

But how do you get a three-year-old to take a nap who

doesn't want to? "I am *not* tired! And I *won't* take a nap. You can't make me!" Well, maybe you can't this time, but enforcing a quiet period at a specified time during each day is a great starting point.

When establishing a nap schedule, it might be necessary to lie down and take a nap with your child. This may seem counterproductive, as one reason you want your little darling to take a nap is so you can get some work done. But you've got to start somewhere.

Nap times are good times for stories. Lying down for a while isn't so bad if you get a story. (Don't be surprised if your child wants one of the same three stories every day. Young children like familiarity.) As the days go by, keep the story, but leave after it's over. For previously unscheduled children, this is apt to be accompanied by pleas of "Don't leave me!" or "But I'm not tired. I don't want to sleep!" Good responses are that you're only going to be in the next room and that they don't have to sleep if they don't want to. All they have to do is rest. They can look at their books in bed if they like or play with their stuffed animals. But it is quiet time for the next hour. (One advantage parents have here is that few preschoolers can tell time.)

After a few difficult days, children typically consent to the routine and begin to complain less vociferously when nap time comes around. (Don't expect the complaining to stop completely. Young children seem to think it's their duty to complain about naps, even if they're agreeable to taking one.) And by the end of the week, most children actually fall asleep. If they don't, you may have chosen the wrong time of day for your child (maybe he or she really isn't tired), or you may have one of the rare ones—the preschooler who really doesn't need regular naps.

Chances are, once a schedule of naps is established, life will go easier. The five-o'clock grumpies that typically arise just before supper may be eliminated. Suppertime itself may be more enjoyable, especially if that, too, occurs on a regular schedule.

A related problem that many parents report is getting children to go to bed peacefully. Here again, a regular schedule can help reduce the nightly conflict. For example, one mother writes: "The biggest problem in our home is bedtime. I have two boys, ages four and five. Unless they are exhausted, they balk at bedtime. Everything from wanting a drink, to getting out of bed several times, to sneaking books under the covers. These are their tactics. The household is tired and short-tempered by then, and many times shouting ensues."

How to solve such a recurring problem? This mother found the answer in establishing a regular evening schedule.

"Routine was the answer for us: supper, bath time, book reading, then bed. I try not to let them get overtired and I find if they give me trouble, I threaten to take something away (a trip to the park, a picnic, etc.). This works better than spanking or yelling."

Of course, nighttime schedules are easier to start before problems with bedtime begin, but they can be instituted at any time. Don't expect the going to be easy at first. A child who has never gone to bed on a schedule will not welcome the change. However, when an evening routine can be established, much as the mother of the two boys described above accomplished, children know what to expect and when to expect it and, eventually, they learn to comply with it.

One critical aspect of a schedule, however, is that it be followed regularly. We know one mother who insists that her four-year-old son has a nine o'clock sharp bedtime. Yet he still fusses about going to bed, despite the routine. A closer look reveals, however, that the schedule is more in the mother's mind than in the child's routine. Although the nine-o'clock rule is the rule of the household, it is not enforced on nights when Mommy or Daddy works late, when Mom and child stop to visit with Aunt Alice after work, nor on weekends when family activities often run well into the evening. The result is a schedule that is in force less than half of the time. No wonder the child balks going to bed on schedule. His four-year-old mind cannot discern any regular pattern, and rightly so. His parents want the benefits of a schedule for their son's bedtime, but the freedom to make plans as they go, depending on what the day happens to bring. As this mother has found out, you can't have it both ways.

We don't mean to imply that families on a schedule have no flexibility. No schedules are unchangeable. But when changes in routines are the rule rather than the exception, young children cannot be expected to conform to a schedule that is enforced in name only. Parents must decide between real schedules, which can be modified from time to time, and spontaneity. In our experience, life with children runs more smoothly with schedules. Little is sacrificed, particularly if parents can tell the difference between bending schedules and breaking them.

Two at Once

Schedules are perhaps more important for parents dealing with two or more preschoolers simultaneously. It is often difficult to keep track of one child, but two (or three) undisciplined children at once can really be hair raising. Take, for example, the plight of this mother of three:

My children are ages five years, four years, and four months. My biggest challenge was how to go to the store and manage not to act like "Mommy Dearest." How many times I used to just run to the corner for a missed item on the grocery list or a little necessity that I really needed? Almost daily before the children were born. But to get two kids (three now) into socks, shoes, and car seats, then to keep track of them while they played hide-and-seek or grabbed everything in sight, was an insurmountable problem.

I lost one in a department store for thirty minutes one day. A clerk found her in a dressing room sitting in front of a mirror playing little people with her fingers as puppets.

What was this mother to do? The answer she found was in establishing routines and in planning the day to avoid, whenever possible, those situations that would leave her a bundle of nerves.

I gave up going to the store for the first four years. Even now I am limited.

I arrange for quick stops on my way to and from work while the baby-sitter was still available.

My husband began calling from work to see if he could pick up anything I needed on the way home.

I reserved every other Saturday or maybe Sunday to shop for me, maintaining a "wish list" in the interim

Dealing with two (or three) young children at a time could mean having to deal with two (or three) different schedules. Is one child ready for a nap while the other is raring to go? Is one hungry for lunch while the other wants to play some more? Does one get tired in the afternoon and fussy about going out, while the other is refreshed and easy going in the P.M.? In such cases a schedule becomes a must.

The first thing that should be done is to think of what a reasonable schedule is apt to be. If one child is a morning person and the other is a night person, whose sleeping pattern is likely to be most adaptable? Some kids are more flexible than others regarding sleeping and eating patterns, and evaluating this is a good first step.

What would *you* like the schedule to be? Do you want some free time in the morning, before supper, in the early evening? Are your children best "in public" in the morning or in the afternoon? Does one or the other play with children in the neighborhood, and if so what are those children's schedules? Are there times when one or both of the children is willing to "keep out of your hair," such as an hour in the morning when they watch Sesame Street, or a half hour in the afternoon when "Ghostbusters" is on television? Will naps on schedule work better if the two children are put to bed at the same time, or should you get one down before you deal with the other? No single schedule is best for all multichild families, and the more people you have to consider, the more complicated it becomes.

Once a schedule is decided upon, it has to be implemented. Here is where things can break down. At first, your children are likely to resist its imposition, and you may begin to wonder whether getting these kids into some kind of routine is worth it or not. Do your best to stick to the schedule you've planned. Be mindful, however, that if you and your children are having difficulty maintaining both the peace *and* the schedule, you may need to reevaluate the schedule. This does not mean going back to an unscheduled life-style, but merely that another schedule may work better.

Schedules also help others who deal with the children, such as grandparents. For example, one grandmother reported to us that she always has difficulty when her two granddaughters, ages three and six, visit. "Individually they are darling children," she said, "but together there are always problems.

They are so jealous of one another that if I do anything for one, the other gets very upset. The three-year-old gets so mad that she won't speak to me or even look at me." Do they act this way at home, we asked? "No," she said, "their parents don't tolerate it. One of them will get sent to her room or scolded. But I'm their grandmother. I don't *want* to discipline them."

The grandmother's problem can be overcome by scheduling. She can see the children one at a time, leaving the other home with Mom or Dad. This may cause some distress at first, but chances are the complaints of the left-behind child will quickly die down. (Young children can easily be distracted and seem not to dwell on past injustices for long.) Or she can schedule her grandchildren's visits when Grandpa is also around. *Two* adults should be able to give enough attention to *two* preschoolers to keep the complaining to a minimum.

Schedules Are for Parents, Too

Children are members of a household, and, in many instances, a child can be on a schedule only if the parents are on a similar one. Of course, it's ludicrous to think that a nap and bedtime schedule would be the same for all members of a family. But other schedules are truly family affairs.

For example, mealtimes are often occasions when the entire family gets together (sometimes the *only* times). Getting children to eat on a regular schedule means getting the rest of the family on that same schedule. Also, regular naps must be taken at regular times, usually in a regular place. What this means is that Mom and Dad have to get their acts together so the children can stay on schedule.

Nap and mealtime routines easily disappear in families whose members are constantly running in and out of the house for all kinds of "necessary" errands. We know of several families whose car engines barely cool off between trips. A trip to the mall is necessitated in the late morning, followed by lunch at home, and then a quick trip to the local convenience store for the missing ingredient for the evening meal. Then it's home again until the older children call for rides home from soccer practice or Mom decides to visit with a friend across town. There is nothing wrong with this fast-paced life-style. It's just difficult to keep kids on any kind of a meaningful schedule when Mom and Dad can't predict with any degree of certainty where they are going to be when nap time or mealtime hits.

Before I became a full-time Mom of twin girls, I worked as a receptionist in a doctor's office. It came very naturally for me to schedule the family routine with an appointment book. I even found one with evening hours listed, too.

On Sunday nights, my husband and I plan the week. We schedule nap time and mealtime, doctor's appointments, and shopping trips. We also try and schedule a few hours for each of us to get out alone, and some time for us together, without the kids.

We have found that grandparents and family members are happy to help out if we can call Sunday evening and ask for help with a pediatrician's appointment at two o'clock Thursday.

I have never had "just one," but I think this might be a good idea for *any* family. Friends laugh about my "appointments," but I don't know how we would survive any other way!

The solution, of course, is to establish a schedule for the adults. Being on a schedule does not mean staying tied to the house all day long. Actually we are convinced that people on schedules can get more done in their waking hours. Schedules require planning, and the task can get difficult when you're planning schedules not only for yourself but also for your child. But the outcome, in terms of raising a disciplined child and of greater domestic tranquility, will be well worth the effort.

Keeping Things Stable

Children have their rooms, their baby-sitters, and their nursery schools. These are familiar, and children feel comfortable in familiar surroundings. Despite the predicaments they often get themselves into, most young children are not thrill seekers. They may venture out into the neighborhood, climb the tree in the backyard, or race their tricycles down the driveway, much to the chagrin of parents, but they do their exploring and adventuring when they are secure and in familiar surroundings.

In general, young children prefer familiarity to change. Parents should think twice before changing day-care centers, hiring a new baby-sitter, or redecorating the nursery, especially if there are other changes going on or stress in family life. In fact, when unexpected discipline problems arise in a child, parents would be wise to look for instability in some part of their child's life. Take, for example, the experiences of one mother with her four-year-old son.

> Justin was moody and irritable. I didn't think much of it at first and just attributed it to missed naps. But by the third day, I realized that he just wasn't himself, and the little tiffs we were getting into constantly represented more than a sour mood from tiredness. He's never been much of a talker about his feelings, but I finally dragged out of him that he had a new teacher at his preschool and, apparently, things weren't quite what they had been before. He didn't like the new teacher, he said, although he wouldn't say why, and he was mad that he couldn't have his old teacher back. I told him that I would talk to his new teacher the next day and see what I could do. Well, the new teacher seemed perfectly nice, and she assured me that she would keep a careful eye out for Justin. Apparently that was all that was necessary, because Justin's mood and behavior improved immediately. I was glad I found out what was bothering him when I did, because we were heading into some first-class trouble. I was glad I found out that his problem behavior had an understandable cause.

When change is inevitable (for example, when a family moves, or a change is necessary from day-care to kindergarten), don't be surprised if temporary behavior problems crop up. Parents who can pinpoint the source of these problems will have an easier time dealing with them and getting the family back on track.

One additional thing to keep in mind about stability is that some children are more susceptible to change than others. For example, five-year-old Derek came home from kindergarten one afternoon to find that his mother had rearranged the living room furniture. This just didn't sit right with him, and he let his mother know about his discomfort immediately. Derek liked stability. He liked things where they "belonged" and didn't like her moving things around just for the sake of change. His older siblings, on the other hand, had no problem with such inconsequential changes. They seldom noticed much about the living room furniture at all. What does this mean? Mainly that different children react differently to change, and parents must recognize this. The moral? Know thy children. This will be the focus of a later chapter in this book (Chapter 6).

Enhancing Children's Feelings of Self-Esteem and Usefulness

Perhaps the thing preschool children hear most from parents is, "You can help by staying out of the way!" Ten minutes later, that "useless" four-year-old is found splashing in the bathroom sink, water and shaving cream covering the floor.

This may only be true in the mind of the adult. Young children have an overly inflated notion of their own abilities and believe that they truly can make a contribution. And most children really want to do something to help. They are aspiring to be adults and are emulating the most important people in their lives—Mom and Dad.

Children who feel important are less apt to get into things they shouldn't just to prove to their parents what "big kids" they can be. And when children know that they are valued by their parents—that Mom and Dad think they're smart and can be helpful—the entire parent/child relationship runs more smoothly. Showing respect for your children and commenting on their worth contributes to a positive family environment, one that is conducive to living a disciplined life.

When children insist that they can help with a job, it is often easy to dismiss their request, knowing that the job will be more easily done without them. Most of the time, little harm comes from letting children help out, but it usually seems to be more trouble than it's worth.

> Michael (age three and a half) insisted that he could help me clean the bathroom. I'd just as soon he would play in his room, but he was insistent and so I reluctantly let him give me a hand. While I was washing out the shower, I turned around and found him "washing" the floor with a sponge that he had covered with Ajax. I was so mad! Mad at him and mad at myself for letting a three-year-old talk me into "helping" clean the bathroom. I should have just said *no* when he asked, I thought. Michael did get very upset when I yelled at him and kept repeating that he was only trying to help and that I didn't let him finish. I just put him in his room and cleaned the mess up myself.

This mother certainly had a problem, but just saying no to his request would probably not have been the best solution. Michael wanted to help and believed that he could; what he lacked, in this case, was proper supervision. Not that his mother should have stood over him, ensuring that he did not make a mess, which would have taken as much of her time as cleaning up did. Rather, she could have designed a special job for her son, one that afforded him some sense of accomplishment, but that would result in little damage even if done incorrectly.

It's not difficult to think of examples in this situation. She could have given him a damp sponge and asked him to clean the pipes under the sink, or to polish the door handle, or to wipe down the tile on the side of the tub. With specific instructions, and a job that is involved enough for mother to complete *her* task and return to monitor her son, everyone could end up being happy. The bathroom is clean and Michael has contributed to this job, as he insisted he could.

Since he was a toddler, Jimmy always wanted to help me when I was building something. He loved tools and knew the names of everything. After a while I knew if I was building something, Jimmy would be there to "help." So, beginning when he was about three and a half, I had him get all the tools for me. He'd go in my toolbox and get me a screwdriver or hammer or whatever. He wasn't always right, but I never told him so, just sent him back for another tool. I'd let him tighten a nut or screw when he could, and have him hold things for me like bolts. I told him he was my special helper and that when a project was finished, "we" did it together. It made him feel important and, although it sometimes took me a little longer to finish a project, it was fun working with him. Jimmy's eight now and can build some things all by himself. He will sometimes ask for my help and once he even asked me to hold some nails for him while he hammered! What a kid!

The trick is giving children things to do that let them feel important, without making extra work and hassles for the parents. This, again, requires a knowledge of your child's abilities. What exactly is your child capable of, and what activities require close supervision?

Children feel useful and important when they are asked to do certain jobs by their parents. It's not necessary to wait until a child asks to do a job (or just jumps in and "helps" out without being asked). Parents can take a little control themselves and select jobs for their young children to do.

Of course, there are nuisance jobs such as picking up one's toys or putting one's clothes away, and children of all ages (*and* adults) need to be reminded periodically about these daily chores. But "useful" jobs are those that children see as being important to someone else—important for the running of the household or for the proper execution of a particular task. For example, a three-year-old girl may be given the important job of getting the mail each day and placing it on the dining room table. It's *her* job, and obviously an important one. A four-year-old can have the responsibility of folding Dad's socks when they come out of the wash, emptying the wastebaskets, dusting the living room, or putting away certain items of groceries. Any job that is usually done by an adult is seen as a high-status job, and therefore desirable. (We know of one four-year-old who asked for the privilege of cleaning the cats' litter box. It's a job his Grandpa did, and one that, to his way of thinking, carried much prestige.) Don't underestimate what young children may find interesting, and don't miss these opportunities to let them perform a task that will give them feelings of mastery, control, and usefulness.

Sibling Rivalry and Useful Children

Sibling rivalry often arises when children feel they are competing with each other for the same place in the family. A new baby doesn't have to signal competition if the older child is pleased with his or her new role as older sister or brother and helper. Depending on children's ages, they can be very useful by fetching diapers, pulling baby wipes from the container, singing songs to the baby, "reading" stories, pushing the stroller, etc. Parents can comment on how nice it is to have a *big* child who is so much help with the baby. And they can tell the older child how the new baby watches and learns from older sisters and brothers.

> I expected a sibling rivalry problem with five-year-old Holly when her new brother was born, but it never happened. In fact, she is almost too devoted to the new baby. She has abandoned her dolls and wants to help me at every feeding. This week she wanted to take him to school for show-and-tell! This may be some extra work for me, but I'm glad she is so pleased being a big sister.

Making Children Feel Responsible

When children feel useful, they feel responsible. It is difficult to distinguish "useful" children from "responsible" children. When parents give children jobs to do, even if those jobs have been simplified, and praise them for a job well-done, children are learning pride in their accomplishments and are learning to become responsible.

For most people, the word "responsible" has serious overtones. We're never responsible for enjoying ourselves, for feeling good about ourselves, or for achieving some goal. We rather think of responsibility as a necessary burden—the fulfillment of obligations. Self-discipline is most certainly involved. But young children often see it differently. Responsibilities are important assignments that make them feel useful, which they like.

Raising children who are independent and responsible for their own actions should be one of the major goals for parents. When children are responsible for their own actions, fewer discipline problems will arise. But how do you *make* a child be responsible? When do you start? When do we let children take the consequences of their own, perhaps unwise, decisions and when do we step in and take responsibility ourselves?

As parents, we must start teaching children responsibility as early as we can. The eighteen-month-old can be responsible, to a moderate degree, for the mess she made in the kitchen, and the two-year-old can take the (not too drastic) consequences of throwing mashed potatoes at his older sister. As children get older, their responsibilities should increase in proportion to increased liberties. Responsibilities and liberties must be age dependent. Knowing what your child is capable of doing and of understanding will determine how much responsibility he or she is able to take.

Again, responsibilities are not always something that children see as a burden. Many children come to this conclusion because it is the message their parents communicate. Responsibility, these children are told, is something you cannot avoid. That, for some children, is an immediate challenge to see if it can indeed be avoided. Parents' attitudes are contagious. Children will learn to face their obligations to their families happily or begrudgingly, depending to a large extent on their parents' views of responsibility.

Remember, children like to feel useful, and parents who can take advantage of this knowledge are off to a good start. Whether jobs are requested or assigned by a parent, it's important not to expect more from children than they are capable of doing. If your five-year-old daughter has the responsibility of making her bed everyday, expect a five-year-old job of bed making. If it's your four-year-old son's job to put out the silverware for dinner, don't be surprised if the forks outnumber the knives some evenings. And don't be overly critical. The tasks themselves are important, but if it's just the end product you care about, you could probably do it better and quicker yourself. What's more important are the jobs your children *think* they are doing and the feelings of competence, self-worth, and self-control that such work affords them.

SUGGESTED RESPONSIBILITIES FOR CHILDREN

One- and two-year-olds

- Putting toys *back* into containers, toy boxes, shelves, bins.
- Placing napkins on the table, one for each family member.
- Watering outdoor plants with small watering can or hose.
- Dusting furniture (or anything) with feather duster.
- Spoons—putting them in the dishwasher, taking them out, washing them, drying them, or putting them in the silverware drawer.
- Help wash the car (on a warm day, wearing a bathing suit).
- Help give the dog a bath (on a warm day, wearing a bathing suit), help with cooking (pouring, stirring, tasting).
- Remind Mom or Dad to pick up ice cream on the way home (if Mom or Dad asks "what was I supposed to remember?")

Three- and four-year-olds

- Clean patio doors and low windows with spray cleaner and paper towels, clean glass-top tables as above.
- Put letters in post office mail slot while Mom stands a discreet distance away.
- Watch for the mailman and bring mail inside to designated place.
- Bring in newspaper and put it in designated place.
- Set table with place mats, spoons, and napkins.
- Help with cooking (open packages, pour contents of measuring cups into bowl, grease cake pans using a paper towel, help with assembling sandwiches, decorate finished product with garnishes—parsley, lemon wedges, sprinkles of paprika, Lifesavers on cake, etc.).
- Help with yard work—pulling weeds under supervision and instruction, planting seeds, putting leaves and tree cuttings in trash, holding trash bags open while parent fills them.
- Dusting furniture with spray and cloth.

Childproofing

The idea of childproofing will likely be a familiar one to modern parents, and one about which they are usually conscientious. But childproofing is usually thought about in terms of safety (as well it should be). Parents are less apt to think of childproofing as a form of behavior control and a tool for discipline, yet it can be one of the most valuable tools for avoiding problems with a young child that a parent can have.

The first step in childproofing is to locate potential unsafe areas in your home. This process needs to be done early and repeated periodically as children grow and develop new abilities and interests (and as the household changes). Potential problems can be areas that are truly dangerous (electrical outlets, insecticides, medication, cleaning products), merely dirty or distasteful (dog food, kitty litter, toilet bowls), and things that are valuable to others (fragile antiques, mementos with sentimental value, important papers).

> We childproofed our home when Brett was a baby. I packed up my crystal collection and put it away for a while. As he got older I would think about putting it out again, but there was always some reason not to—clumsy walking at two, rough-and-tumble play at four, then the baseballs, footballs, and basketballs. When he went away to college, I put a few pieces out on the bookcase. My husband broke one while rushing to get the dictionary in a heated Scrabble game. I broke another while dusting. Now we have grandchildren. I think a better term for it would be "people proofing." If you want to enjoy your fragile valuables, put them in a glass front case—even if the kids are grown and gone.

Now that you've checked the house for safety hazards, what about discipline hazards? Are there things lying around that, although not dangerous, are likely to attract your child and invite damage? What about older siblings? Has your child been warned about taking big brother's or big sister's prized possessions? Think of situations that a preschooler might get into around the house and try to structure your home to avoid the disastrous ones. A little planning with regard to childproofing can help avoid many problems.

Yes Times

Another side to childproofing that may help you avoid problems is "yes times." These are special times when you can share your valuables and collections with your child. If you want to pass on your love for beautiful things or your interest in objects from the past, they should be more than no-no's to your children.

> I have a china doll collection and as my daughter got older, it seemed silly to keep telling her not to touch Mommy's dolls. One day when she was three, she was sick and I had run out of things to keep her entertained, so I decided to show her some of my dolls. I took her in my room and we sat in the center of the bed. I took the dolls out one at a time and told her the story of each—where I had gotten it and what kind of doll it was. She touched the faces and the clothing gently and we admired how pretty each was. I was afraid she would begin to think of them as playthings and get into them herself, but she never has. Instead, she asks me if we can look at "Mommy's dolls." It's nice to share my interest with her, and when she is a little older, I think I'll begin a collection for her.

Such experiences help children to realize the importance you place on your possessions and will lead to children who are more respectful and careful with the possessions of others. By relaxing the rules during supervised times, children are learning what, exactly, their limits are. They learn that they may be allowed certain privileges when an adult is there to watch, which will make them more apt to ask for such privileges than just to take them when nobody is watching.

Communication

Another way to prevent misdeeds is to make sure the instructions you are giving your children are in a form they can understand. It is estimated that seventy-five percent of mistakes made in businesses are the result of poor communication. If this is true for adults, then it applies doubly for parents and children. Below are suggested ways to avoid six major communication problems parents have with their young children.

1. Use Words Children Can Understand

Children's communication skills increase rapidly from the age of about eighteen months on, language, of course, being the main form of communication. But children as well as adults make use of gestures and tones to understand messages. What this means is that children often understand what an adult *means*, even if they don't understand what the adult actually *said*. This is usually good, for we can communicate some complex ideas to our children, even if they don't fully comprehend the words we use.

But sometimes our words are crucial, and, because they seem to understand so much most of the time, we expect our children to understand us *all* of the time. Even if they don't understand us, children rarely ask for an explanation. All this can lead to a situation in which the parent thinks the child is misbehaving and the child is unaware of what is going on.

Being a single, working parent, I need all the help I can get. I used to ask my five-year-old to sort the laundry while I did the breakfast dishes in the morning—whites in one pile, colors in the other. I'd run in the utility room ready to throw a load of wash in the machine before leaving for work and find a pile of clothes containing everything from jeans to pink lace underwear. I would get *so* angry. My daughter is supposed to be so smart in school, but she couldn't handle a simple chore like that! Finally it dawned on me. She *was* doing what I asked, *exactly* what I asked. She was putting white clothes in one pile and colors in the other. but to her, pink lace was a *color*! What I should have said was to put "light" clothes in one pile and "dark" clothes in the other. I feel embarrassed about this, but it taught me a lesson. I watch what I tell her now.

There are many times, of course, when we want to teach children new words and concepts. If we continued to speak baby talk to our children, their rate of language development would be greatly slowed. Although our children increase their vocabularies when we use words a little beyond their comprehension, giving instructions to do something (or *not* do something) is not the time for vocabulary enrichment.

2. Use Terms That Mean the Same to Children as They Do to You

This is related to the communication problem listed above. Often times we know that children know the words and phrases we use (we even hear them using the same words and phrases themselves), but the meanings may differ slightly.

Young children are often very literal. For example, when a parent says to a three-year-old, "Wash your hands," the child is likely to return with clean hands but covered with dirt from the wrists up. Other examples are "pick up your toys" (you didn't mention putting them away), "give your brother some cereal" (you didn't say to put it in a bowl or add milk), and "wash your hair while you're in the shower" (you forgot about the rinse). Preschoolers who make these mistakes aren't being wise guys; they are just learning the language.

When Allen was three, he could put on his own shoes (thanks to the miracle of velcro). I would hand them to him one at a time and point to which foot they went on. One day we were late for a doctor's appointment and he came out of his room showing me proudly that he had put on his shoes without any help. I looked at his feet and said quickly, "Allen, you have them on the wrong feet. Sit down right there and put them on the other feet while I lock the doors." When I came back he was still standing there, looking thoroughly confused. "But Mommy," he said, "I don't have any other feet."

---

3. Give Instructions That Are Clear—Never Vague

Admonishing young children to "behave," "be good," "be polite," or "quit acting like little hoodlums" leaves a lot open to interpretation. Imagine getting your tax form from the IRS in January and having it say only, "Pay up what you owe or else." Or imagine trying a new gourmet dessert recipe that says only, "Mix ingredients and cook until done."

We often assume that a general instruction, such as "Behave yourself," will cue children to shape up immediately. Maybe such a meaning is clear to the adult who gives it, but not necessarily to the child who receives it. Those commands are often given in public places or when company is present—that is, under unusual situations. Young children often have a lot of leeway in how they are expected to behave at home. Sometimes it is all right to wrestle with Daddy or tickle Mommy, so when company calls and a child is told to "behave yourself," he may not realize that horsing around with Mom and Dad is now not allowed.

Being explicit about what children are expected to do in upcoming situations can help. It doesn't mean that your children won't misbehave, but it at least lets them know what you want them to do, or perhaps more importantly, what you *don't* want them to do. And it gives you more confidence in evaluating the reasons for their misbehavior.

We take our four- and six-year-old daughters out to dinner on special occasions. While we are getting them dressed, we review the rules in a positive way—quiet talking, good manners, napkins in lap, please and thank you to the waiter, and so forth. Then we talk about them again on the way to the restaurant, making a game of it. "Do you yell and scream in the restaurant?" No! "Do you jump on the chairs like monkeys?" No! "Do you put the napkin on your head?" No! It gets silly sometimes, but it's getting the message across without nagging. Of course, we always go early and make reservations so there is no wait. I wish I could say it works perfectly, but it does work *most* of the time.

---

4. Be Specific

Some rules are intended to be wide-ranging, all-purpose, under-any-circumstance laws. When you tell your two-year-old daughter not to eat dirt from the flower bed by the front door, you also mean that she should not eat dirt from the back-door flower bed, the potted plants in the house, and the vegetable garden at Grandma's. Other rules are intended to be more specific. If you tell the same two-year-old not to touch Daddy's leather-bound, first-edition volume of Shakespeare's sonnets, you certainly don't mean that she should not touch the storybooks in her own room, the picture books at preschool, or the old copy of *Reader's Digest* in the bathroom. With repeated instructions and maturation, children will come to understand better how specific or how general you mean your rules to be.

But in the meantime, what looks like misbehavior might just be misunderstanding.

5. Children Need Reminding

Saying "I forgot" has recently become a popular defense among some grown-ups who need to avoid perjury charges. They "forget" that they approved a questionable deed by their underlings, "forget" that they gave away valuable information to unauthorized persons, and "forget" that they have large sums of money in foreign bank accounts. Forgetting has gotten such a bad reputation that we often don't remember that preschool kids really *do* forget things frequently. It's not just a defense maneuver.

Kids forget over an extended period of time. This is especially true if that time is filled with distracting activity. An example would be telling your four-year-old son on the way to school in the morning that he has to put away his race car set when he gets home after school or he can't watch TV. We'd be willing to bet that even little Albert Einstein would goof up on that task.

Kids also forget when asked to remember too many things. Instructing your two-year-old to go in the bedroom and ask Mommy for the nail file is asking for trouble. So is expecting a six-year-old to remember to do her homework, brush her teeth, feed the dog, *and* get ready for bed, especially if that is not part of a nightly routine.

Parents need to give preschoolers frequent refresher courses and not expect them to remember too many instructions over too long a time.

6. Try Not to Yell, Nag, and Threaten

Many years ago we overheard a mother in a department store threaten to throw her whining son "out in the street where a big truck would hit him" if he didn't shut up. We were horrified, especially when the son continued whining. Fortunately we learned what her young son already knew—her threat was an idle one, so he no longer paid attention.

Humans make good use of their attention, and children are no exception. If some signal in our environment loses its meaning for us, we learn to block it out. Our old but favorite car has a faulty dashboard light that signals frequently that our engine is overheating. This bright red light used to cause a great deal of alarm, but after several panicky trips to the mechanic, we no longer see it, just like the whining child no longer heard his mother. It has no useful information for us. Sometimes a passenger in our car will say, "Look, your engine is overheating!" and we say "What?" Then we realize what he is seeing and we say "Oh *that*—it's on all the time, it's no big deal, it doesn't mean anything." If we had interrupted the child's whining and said, "Did you hear what your mother said? She just threatened to throw you into the traffic," his response would probably be as calm as ours to the passenger in our car. "What? Oh, that. She says that all the time, it's no big deal."

The lesson in this is for parents to use words sparingly. Make each one count. Don't rant and rave or lecture to a preschooler. Don't yell and swear and threaten. Because, aside from all the possible psychic damage and moral implications, it *simply doesn't work.*

> Staying calm in a time of crisis (which is sometimes almost impossible) has proven to be the best way to handle discipline with my children. When I stopped yelling at my children, they finally *heard* me!!!

In talks with hundreds of parents over the years about discipline, perhaps the leading vote getter for "things that don't work" is *yelling* (although spanking is a close second). A loud and authoritative voice can get a child's attention and result in speedy compliance. But when yelling is the customary form of communication in a household, The Voice loses its special power and is apt only to make the yeller hoarse.

Rewards for Nonproblem Behavior

Behavior Modification

One popular and time-tested technique of controlling children's behavior is granting rewards when they do something good. These rewards increase the chance that the child will repeat those positive behaviors. Star charts, gifts for good behavior, praise, hugs, increased privileges, money, trips to fun places are all examples. The systematic use of such rewards is referred to as *behavior modification*.

Although in reality behavior modification can refer to any means of altering children's behavior by varying the conditions in the physical environment, most "behavior mod" systems for children emphasize rewards as an alternative to punishment. Basically the idea is to catch kids doing good, and to reward them, which makes them more apt to behave in that way in the future.

We don't mean to quarrel with behavior modification in its entirety. Use of positive reinforcement is a far superior way of controlling behavior than is frequent use of punishment. However, we do quarrel with the use of behavior modification as a major family discipline tool, because use of rewards such as money, food, toys trip to the park or beach, and even stars on a chart, reflect ways of *parents controlling their children*; such techniques do not necessarily foster ways in which *children learn to control themselves*. As we mentioned in Chapter 2, children who feel in control of their own behavior are less apt to misbehave.

One major drawback to the rewards system is that once the rewards cease, the good behavior often stops. For example, studies have shown that children who receive rewards as they learn a new skill are less likely to practice that skill later than children who learn the skill without such rewards.

In this way, children are no different from adults. We will modify our behavior in order to receive certain rewards. Most of us would soon quit going to work, for example, if our employer decided to withhold our paychecks. However, the things we do willingly and repeatedly are typically motivated by our desire to do what we find intrinsically worthwhile or what we perceive to be "right." We perceive ourselves as having free will—of behaving as we do because we are in control of ourselves. We do things that are consistent with our beliefs. We *can* be coerced or encouraged to do many unpleasant things, but only if the rewards of compliance (or drawbacks of noncompliance) are great enough.

Since the same applies to children, the persistent use of tangible rewards is not the best way to teach them to control themselves. Most young children will work very hard for praise alone. They want to be perceived as good boys or good girls, and the parents' approval or dissatisfaction is often powerful enough to guide their behavior.

To the extent that they are intellectually able, children incorporate their parents' beliefs as their own and feel good when they behave according to these beliefs and bad when they knowingly violate them. Children learn to control their own behavior and to comply with parental rules, because their behavior matches a belief system developed over years spent in a loving household.

Love as a Reward for Good Behavior

Love is a potent motivator, and not just for children; but parents must be cautious. When we tell our children that we love them when they are good, what message do we send them when their behavior is less than perfect? Withdrawal of love is a threat that can keep children in line, very effectively indeed, but it's a dangerous game to play.

Children deserve unconditional love from their parents. Mom and Dad are the foundation for a child's emotional development. They are the solid base that can be depended upon when things get difficult. They are the people who will love them and protect them no matter what. For a young child, with no other source of emotional support, the threat of its loss can be devastating. The consequence is often a child who is unsure of his parents and thus unsure of himself.

This does not mean that we must face obnoxious and stubborn behavior with a smile. We can and must disapprove when appropriate. But we must remember to be critical of the offending *behavior* and not the *child*. We should not promise love in exchange for good behavior, nor threaten removal of love for misdeeds.

A lot of touching and kissing and saying, "I love you" is important. Also letting them say "I hate you"—expressing themselves without fear. I always ask, "Do you hate me forever or just right now?" Then they laugh, but it also gives me the freedom to say "I'm not too fond of you right now either." This lets them know that even when they are creeps, I still love them; I just don't like what they are doing now.

Remedies for Problem Behavior— Nonpunitive Alternatives

What do you do when the preventative measures fail no matter how carefully you plan? Having children who are less than perfect is to be expected and parents must deal with a misbehaving child. Once misbehavior is in action, parents have several choices.

One option, of course, is to stick your head in the sand and hope the unpleasantness goes away. This should not be a serious option, however. By this we don't mean that every time a child strays from the straight and narrow, a parent should do something immediately to put the child back on course. Sometimes a minor infraction of the rules can be tolerated, at least for the time being, as it is often more troublesome (and embarrassing) to set a child straight then and there. Sometimes the best thing to do is to ignore a misdeed temporarily, and to discuss it in private with your child at a later time.

But most of the time you know when your child has gone too far. So what do you do? Most parents have enough stories to fill a book with things that worked and things that didn't. Many have shared stories with us, and we would like to outline some of the ways to change the course of a misbehaving child.

Removing the Child

We've discussed childproofing your house and thus minimizing the number of problem situations young children can get into. This is especially important for children three years of age and younger, who are thereby protected from such danger as poisons, sharp instruments, and electric sockets. But you can't protect your house and possessions totally from your child, nor vice versa.

Kitchens and bathrooms, offering running water and gooey soap and shaving cream are very attractive to an inquisitive youngster who is just learning about the world. Likewise, fancy electronics are fascinating to young children. A simple twist of a knob or a push of a button can cause all sorts of interesting things to happen. Particularly troublesome in our home are dog and cat food, kitty litter, and chess pieces.

Perhaps the best way to handle problems that childproofing

can't solve is simply to remove the children from the offending situation. This sounds too easy to be true, and in a way it is. But the first thing parents should do when their toddlers get into things they should not, is to say "no" firmly (yelling is not necessary) and to pick up the child and remove him or her from the immediate environment and place the child somewhere out of sight from the scene of the potential crime.

This technique will work fine for most children under one year of age because of children's short memories. With only minor modification, it will be successful with slightly older children, working best when accompanied by the substitution of something equally attractive. Splashing water in the sink, (and over the floor) is likely to be very enjoyable for a two-year-old, for example, and being set on the living room floor and told to "play with something else" will not likely be satisfying for the child (nor as a result, for the parent). Parents should try to provide some substitute activity, often just a few minutes of undivided attention. Simply talking to young children, playing simple hand games, or reading a two-minute story, can cause the formerly captivating activity to be forgotten.

For children two years of age and older, you can acknowledge that splashing in the sink *is* fun, but that they cannot do it now while Mommy is putting on her makeup. But later on in the day, they can go outside in the wading pool and splash around all they want. Of course, such promises should be kept, and they should not be made with younger children. The reason is that children younger than two are likely either to forget the promise, or, to ask every five minutes whether it's time yet. In other words, they do not have the mental capacity to understand exactly what is involved in a promise, and so, as a discipline tool for younger children, it will not work.

Removing young children from problem situations is amazingly simple and effective. And if you can hold your temper and avoid unnecessary shouting or lecturing to children too young to appreciate the lesson, it will work well and without the often negative consequences of punishment.

Warnings

Once misbehavior begins, parents can often curtail it by issuing a warning. This has to be used sparingly and has to offer real information to the child. In other words, the child has to take your warnings very seriously.

When my kids cross over "the line," I let them know by speaking to them in Spanish. My mother did this to me and always reminded me of my stern grandfather. My kids never knew my grandfather, but they know when I speak to them in Spanish I mean business. It's especially nice when we are in public and they get out of hand. I can just whisper a few words to them and they behave beautifully. I don't have to yell or make a scene.

The most valuable disciplining tool I have is counting to three in a very stern but calm voice. When my son misbehaves, I say "One . . . two . . . t-h-r-e-e . . . spells . . . three!" It gives him time to think things over, and as importantly, it gives me time to get control of myself and size up the situation instead of flying off the handle immediately. I started it when he was crawling and continued it until he was eight or nine. What happens after three? If he hasn't complied, he got spanked, which I believe has happened only two or three times. He is now thirteen.

The reason the topic of warning is separate from that of punishment is that the warning in itself serves to short-circuit the problem behavior. Although the actual punishment needs to be very real in the child's mind, it doesn't necessarily need to be applied. In fact, we questioned a group of college students about their childhood memories of discipline, and while all could remember being warned by their parents about ensuing application of a belt, paddle, stick, or hand, only three in the class of twenty-four reported the dreaded event actually happening. Five students remembered a certain tone of voice their parents used that meant "do this or else . . .", but none could remember what the "or else" referred to, just "something awful."

Changing Plans

For some reason, parents changing their plans or their minds is often seen as a sign of weakness. In every other aspect of our adult lives we have the freedom to make plans, proceed with them, and make corrections along the way. However, as parents we somehow expect ourselves to make a plan and stick to it, come hell or high water. Yet, as it is in the rest of life, changing plans with respect to your children can also be a good idea. Our plans and rules for our children must change, eventually, as they get older. Sometimes situations change sooner than we expect, and, when this happens, we should feel comfortable making changes ahead of schedule. At other times, our plans and ideas about child rearing or our children turn out not to be as good as we initially thought they were. Rather than sticking with a bad plan, we can have the wisdom to modify what we once thought was right, to what we now think is better.

This, however, requires security. We must feel comfortable with ourselves and with our role as parents. Parents who fear that they will lose the respect of their children by changing their minds, are parents who are insecure about themselves.

- Secure parents are able to listen to a child's objections and to change their minds about some particularly troublesome rule.
- Secure parents are able to give themselves time to consider problem situations and not act on them immediately. Indecision is sometimes a sign of maturity and wisdom.
- Secure parents are able to talk to their own parents or to other parents when a problem arises and decide to change their plan of action.
- Secure parents allow themselves to reevaluate a problem situation and decide to do what the child wants after all.
- Secure parents can put themselves in the place of the misbehaving child and evaluate the child's point of view.
- Secure parents can back off from a tense situation and decide that the matter at hand is not worth the hurt it is causing.
- Secure parents can recognize the danger of losing control and take some time out to cool off before they do or say things they don't really mean.
- Secure parents can act calm when children seem out of control, realizing that little of value can be learned under such conditions and saving their words of wisdom until later.

Secure parents, in other words, are able to change their minds when the situation warrants it. However, the last part of that sentence is as important as the first—"when the situation warrants it." By this, we mean that secure parents will evaluate a problem situation and consider the child's point of view. Many times they will decide that their original ideas and plans are still appropriate, but when a change is called for, secure parents will make that change and problem behavior will often diminish.

Punishment

We use the term punishment here to refer to unpleasant things parents can do to their children when the children misbehave or fail to do what they are told. When used effectively, punishment decreases the chance that the negative behaviors will occur again.

Two types of punishment will be discussed: letting natural consequences occur (or helping them along), and parent-inflicted punishment.

Letting Nature Take Its Course
(More or Less)

Natural Consequences

If the behavior you expect from your child is important, there are usually some natural consequences. That is, we want our children to behave in a certain way so that they will avoid the unpleasant outcomes that their behavior is apt to bring about. Many of these consequences are the very things we are supposed to protect our children from, such as getting hit by cars, becoming malnourished, and being truant from school. Obviously letting nature take its course is out of the question in these cases. However, there are a few opportunities parents have to step out of the way and let Mother Nature do our jobs in our place.

For example, two-and-a-half-year-old Nicholas was playing with a jar of soap bubbles on the patio one day. His mother told him repeatedly to put the jar up on the table or he'd knock it over with his foot. Nicholas had responded repeatedly with his favorite word, "No!" His mother surveyed the situation and saw that the soap bubbles cost forty-nine cents and the patio was outdoors and overdue for cleaning. She sat down in the lounge chair, put her feet up, and started reading a magazine article. In no time at all, Nicholas has accidentally spilled the jar all over the patio. He wailed and cried and stomped his feet. "Mommy!" She looked up from her magazine and asked innocently, "What happened, Nicky?" He said that the bubbles had spilled. Being a smart mother, she comforted him and took him inside for lunch and a nap. She resisted the urge to say "I told you so" (a quality her husband also appreciates). The next time Nicholas put the jar on the table after a single suggestion by his mother.

When children must bear the consequences of their own actions, it teaches them a lesson that lectures rarely can: In a way, it teaches them that they have some control over situations and that they are responsible for their actions. We wrote much of control in the previous chapter, mainly in terms of letting children feel that they are capable of making some important decisions in their lives. But taking the negative consequences for their own actions is the other side of control—being responsible when things don't go as planned.

As our example above suggests, oftentimes parents must remind children that they indeed are responsible for the outcome of their behavior. The lesson Nicholas learned about being careful with soap bubbles (and about the wisdom of his mother's advice) might be lost without a well-worded reminder from his mother the next time the situation arises. This is not the equivalent of "I told you so." In fact, showing compassion at the time of the child's loss may actually help the lesson sink in.

What is important is that children be aware that they are responsible for what they are doing. Thus, parents need to anticipate some problems, decide that the negative consequences would not be too serious, and then warn their children of what their behavior is apt to produce. If children still insist on following this course, let them. When your prediction comes true, gloating is not necessary.

The importance of warning children ahead of time about the possible consequences of their behavior lies in the fact that many young children will not be aware of the connection between what they do and an unhappy outcome. For example, if a three-year-old left her bowl of ice cream where the family dog could get it, and five minutes later found it gone, it might be unfair to hold her to the same degree of responsibility had she been warned about the four-legged ice-cream thief ahead of time. Three-year-olds, even those who have grown up around ice-cream-eating dogs, may not be aware of the connection between a low table, ice cream, and Fido. Thus, when the ice cream disappears, they are crushed and really don't understand that they could have prevented it.

But three-year-olds who are warned of this possibility can certainly make the connection. Young children often have greater cognitive abilities than they show spontaneously. Thus, although three-year-olds may not put two and two together themselves to produce four (or more appropriately, put *ice cream*, *low table*, and *dog* together to produce *misfortune*), they are capable of understanding those connections if they are explicitly warned of them. If after being fairly warned, the ice cream is still left on the table and the dog does his part, the natural consequence of "No more ice cream" is quite reasonable.

Perhaps all of us learn lessons best when we experience them directly. Children are no different. We do not want our children to suffer severe consequences for their immature and faulty decision making. We must be careful and not let children learn "almost everything" from the consequences of their decisions. We remain the responsible people in the parent/child relationship and must not pass that responsibility onto our children on the grounds that we are teaching them discipline through "natural consequences." And we must be cautious never to let the consequences of children's decisions be dangerous to them. But when we can, letting children learn from their own mistakes is a good idea. We must always take the age and ability of the child into consideration and be sure that we do not lose control of the situation ourselves. But few things teach discipline so well as the consequences of undisciplined behavior.

Parent-inflicted Punishment

When all else fails, parents sometimes need to inflict punishment on their misbehaving child. There is a lot of controversy about this, and we don't pretend to have "the" answer.

It depends on the parent and the child. But we recommend four basic rules:

(1) It should not be used on very young children (under a year or so).
(2) It should be delivered immediately, as soon after the precipitating event as possible.
(3) Children must realize what they are being punished for.
(4) It should fit the misdeed.

Examples are taking away privileges and toys, time-outs, isolation, and spanking, as follows:

1. Taking Away Privileges (and Toys)

After a warning, parents can intervene and take away some pleasant object. Make sure the child knows what's going on and try to make it as logical as possible. For examples, taking cookies out of the cookie jar when told not to should result in no dessert that day, not in having the child's tricycle taken away for a week. This does not have to be accompanied by yelling, hitting, or other displays of anger. The punishment is the loss of the toy or privilege.

2. Time-outs

After a warning (or two), parents can suspend the ongoing activity for a given length of time in hopes it will result in better behavior when it resumes. For example, two children playing with blocks who have been warned to stop arguing can have the blocks taken away for three minutes (a portable timer is nice for this) while they think about playing nicely. Then the blocks are given back, and, if all goes well, they resume peaceful and pleasant play. If they don't the blocks are taken away (see above).

Or a child who persists in yelling while Mom is trying to balance the checkbook and has asked for some quiet time can be placed in a chair (The Chair) for five minutes of silence and then allowed a chance to play again without yelling. Time-outs are done quietly and calmly with minimal anger and lecturing. The are also done once per offense and no more than once a day. The time should be roughly equivalent to the child's age. Three to five minutes can be an eternity to a preschooler (and longer time-outs can become fun when children forget they are being punished and start playing exciting games with their shoelaces).

3. Isolation

Sometimes sending a child to his or her room is a wonderful device. Although many folks argue that kids' rooms today are so full of toys and diversions that it is like sending them to Disney World for punishment, they miss the point. Sending young kids to their room is punishment because you say it is. And they may be having a great time in there, but they are still *in there*, and you're *not*. This is especially good when you're tired and cranky and your child is, too.

4. Spanking

Very controversial. Many parents *never* spank their children and have adorable, well-behaved little angels. Others do spank their children frequently and also have little dears. In other words, whether parents spank or not doesn't seem to make much difference in whether their children behave well or not.

Parents usually spank when they have lost control of the situation with their children, and often feel guilty about it later. When parents are able to anticipate discipline problems and take early action to prevent them, they find that they remain in control and the spanking decreases.

Note: When we use the term "spanking," we are talking about a whack on the backside, a smack on the bottom, a swat on the behind—not slapping, punching, hitting, or beating. These types of punishment *do* have clear-cut effects on children's behavior. Children who are physically hurt by their parents often grow up to be resentful, abusive adults with little self-esteem. Children learn best by watching us. If we model abusive behavior directed at our young children who depend on us to protect them, we are destroying their sense of security and trust. Think about it.

I spanked all my kids when they misbehaved, but looking back now I realize that it only produced the behavior I wanted once or twice. Usually is just made me feel more in control. Now I'm not sure if that was the kind of control I wanted. I don't think it damaged the kids, who are fifteen, twelve, and eleven now and happy and well-behaved. I just don't think it really worked.

I spanked my first child a lot, but with my second one, I learned smarter tactics. He was stubborn and defiant. The more I spanked him, the worse he got, Once, when he was two, I spanked him for spitting. The more I spanked him, the more he spat. Finally I realized that *he* was in control, even though *I* was doing the spanking. I couldn't keep him from spitting, but I *could* keep him from spitting in the house. So I picked him up and put him on the back porch and told him he could spit out there, but that I didn't want to see it. He did for a while, but the fun wore off quickly. I did the same thing with "bathroom words." When he went through his "poo-poo, pee-pee" stage, I calmly carried him to the bathroom and told him that those were "bathroom words" and if he was going to say them so much he should do it in the bathroom where I didn't have to listen to him. Then I pretended I couldn't hear him. It didn't last long.

We slapped our kids because our parents slapped us. I never thought about it too much. Then one day my son hit his sister and as I slapped him, I heard myself say, "I told you a hundred times, don't hit!" It sounded so strange that I was punishing him by doing the same thing to him that he had done to his sister. I thought about it and decided there are better ways. My husband and I attended a class for parents at our son's preschool and now we use other types of discipline. Once in a while we use a "smack in the diaper area," but when I do, my words come back to me and I feel a little foolish.

At the two-year mark I resorted to spanking to make my rules clear. This was futile and I felt (once I looked at what I was doing) that I was a poor example of how one should deal with a difficult situation. The more I lost control of myself, the less I was able to think of alternative situations and creative ideas to remedy the situation (or avoid it completely the next time). My child is far from perfect, but we have peace in our family. That, I believe, is the hardest part of being a parent.

Parents need to realize that a child's misbehavior is not a personal attack on the parent or a reflection that the parent has somehow failed. Neither is it a sign of lost parental control. The thought of a six-foot-tall C.P.A. (who actually understands the Tax Reform Act of 1986) "losing control" over a two-foot-tall toddler who thinks that three pennies in a long row is "more" than five pennies in a shorter row is absurd. Especially when you keep in mind that the little guy thinks of the big guy as the most important person in the world, the provider for all his needs, and so powerful that one angry thought from the big guy could make the little guy cease to be. This is how preschoolers see their parents. The thought of children this age being engaged in some sort of devious "power-struggle" is a product of the adult's imagination. With this in mind, parents can view misbehavior in a less-threatening way.

Kids forget. They misunderstand. They make mistakes. They make bad decisions. They don't hear words and loud noises that have no real messages for them. They want our approval, our attention, our admiration. They want to be part of our activities, our interests, and our loving relationships. They struggle to be free of our protection, not because they reject us or want to leave us; they just love us so much they want to *be* us.

4. Discipline and Development

Children develop. This obvious fact has important consequences with respect to discipline. Some of the greatest conflicts arise out of misjudging children's developmental abilities. As children progress from infancy through toddlerhood to school age, they change not only physically but also in how they understand and respond to the world around them. Parents must recognize these changes and adjust their thinking about their children accordingly.

On one level, this is obvious. An infant restricted to a crib must be treated differently than a three-year-old who is free to roam the house and who, within limits, can communicate verbally with adults. On another level, however, responding to developmental changes is much trickier than it may appear. We all have certain ideas of what we consider to be appropriate behavior. We wish to start our children on the course of responsibility early and believe that we should behave toward them in a consistent manner, often from the crib onward. Yet, as children grow, they develop a different perspective of their world and thus of their parents' behavior toward them. Effective discipline requires that parents develop along with their children.

Perhaps the source of most parent/child conflicts throughout childhood centers around children's quest for independence. This is often thought to be a major problem only in adolescence, but it is the source of many disagreements and battles during the early years as well. We become accustomed to our children's dependence. They are just little children, after all, and need our constant care and supervision. It just so happens that most children act as if just the opposite is true. Parents are barriers to get around so that they can explore the wonderful world that surrounds them and experience the joys that "freedom" brings. Obviously some compromises are needed.

In this chapter, we will look at some of the problems that are apt to occur just because children change with age. As we stated above, perhaps the most persistent difficulty in child rearing revolves around children's increasing quest for independence. Even parents who sometimes misjudge children's increasing abilities, other times demand more than children can handle. Realizing both children's abilities and limitations at any age will help to avoid problems and help to resolve difficult situations when they do occur.

Overestimating Children's Abilities

Not long ago, we overheard a mother making an arrangement with her two-and-a-half-year-old daughter: "Today is *your* day. You and Mommy will do what you want today. We'll go to McDonalds for lunch, bake some cookies, and go to the park. But tomorrow will be *Mommy's* day. You'll stay at the baby-sitter's while I go to aerobics and when we're home you can watch TV or play in your room while I work. Okay?" The child quickly agreed to the arrangement and probably had a wonderful day with her devoted mother. However, come the next day, it is just as likely the child was unusually disagreeable about being left with the sitter and leaving Mommy alone to do her work. Reminders that the child had *her* day yesterday and that a deal had been made would do little to improve the situation.

Making deals with two-year-olds just doesn't work. Young children concentrate on one thing at a time, and deals require the ability to keep at least two things in mind at once. This is particularly difficult when one part of the deal happens at one time and the second part of the deal happens much later—such as the next day. Simple deals such as "I'll give you a cookie now if you put your dirty clothes in the hamper," or even "You can have a piece of cheese now but only if you stop pestering your sister," have a greater chance of success. But real negotiation is out of the question with two- and three-year-olds. They just don't have the mental abilities to hold up their end of the bargain.

Similarly, we often expect more of children than they can easily produce. How well can we expect a three-year-old to share? How much temptation can we expect a four-year-old to resist? Do we really believe that a two-year-old will remember to brush her teeth every morning or to pick up her toys after play without having to be reminded?

> I have found that many of the problems I had in raising my daughter came when I attributed her often difficult behavior to her *personally* and not to the fact that it just might be reflecting her particular stage of development. When I stepped back and asked myself whether she was misbehaving because she just wanted to be a little brat or because she was only acting her age, I could handle her behavior much better, and took it less personally.

Changing as Children Change

How and when should parents change their discipline toward their children? Take your cue from your child. Children don't "think" about changing their behavior or attitudes—these changes are dictated primarily by biology. They become increasingly mobile, able to roam around the house and yard and to discover many marvelous things that heretofore were unknown to them. Their thinking changes nearly as rapidly as their actions. With age, the simple explanations that satisfied the two-year-old are no longer enough. They want to know *why* they can't go in the backyard now, or *why* they can't have a snack at five o'clock in the afternoon. A simple "no" just isn't enough.

Parents should take these changes in their children's abilities as signals to change their own behavior. A nine-month-old who chances into Dad's shaving cream can be quickly removed from the site of the crime, spoken to nicely, and, chances are, won't fuss too much. This child has little recollection of the events leading to the shaving cream, and merely removing her from the situation will, in all likelihood, be sufficient "discipline" to cure the problem. An eighteen-month-old who makes a similar discovery may not be so easily assuaged. The older child will seek out the white, gooey stuff again, and will not be pleased with Mom for limiting his exploration so unfairly.

The older child's displeasure is a cue for Mom to change her behavior. The eighteen-month-old is able to remember the discovery and the fun of the shaving cream oozing through his fingers, and he wants to do it again. Mom and Dad can say no and repeatedly remove junior from the shaving cream, or they can try something different. For example, instead of merely removing the child from the offending situation, his parents can provide him with some equally attractive alternative, distracting the child's attention from the forbidden activity. Or they can admit that playing with shaving cream in-and-of-itself is not so terrible; it's just spreading it all over the bathroom walls and floor that is disagreeable, and schedule some "shaving cream play" during bath time. The child has the motor and intellectual skills to handle a can of shaving cream and to get a lot of fun out of the activity. Setting aside a time when such fun is okay and other times when it is not is something an eighteen-month-old can understand.

Since taking the lead from our children is not always easy, its helpful to know what to expect as they grow. In the remainder of this chapter, we will provide a brief description of child development from infancy to age seven, along with some age-related problems and solutions.

The First Year

Although people don't usually think of discipline in reference to infants, this is when discipline begins. Infants develop rapidly during the first year. They form attachments, learn to recognize familiar people and places, and gain some control over their surroundings.

Perhaps the most important part of discipline in the first year involves establishing schedules. Infants are born with their own schedules—biological clocks that tell them when it's time to eat and sleep. Over the course of the first year these clocks change, due both to biological changes in the child and to the scheduling demands of parents.

Physical and Motor Development

Changes in Locomotion in the First Year

Babies don't do much in terms of motor behavior at birth. They are born with well-developed reflexes such as grasping and sucking, but for the most part, when they are put somewhere, that's where they'll stay until someone moves them. This immobile period doesn't last long, however. By four or five months, many infants are able to move from place to place by lying on their stomachs and pulling themselves along with their arms. This is not a very efficient form of locomotion, and few infants who move in this way travel far. However, within several months, most infants are on their hands and knees, crawling to where they want to go. Not all infants crawl. Some "scoot," propelling themselves as they sit upon the floor; others roll; and still others "walk" on hands and feet, not letting their knees or elbows touch the floor.

Regardless how it is done, this increased locomotion presents new opportunities to children. Their world is no longer restricted to what they can see and hear while sitting in one spot, nor must they limit themselves to the toys and objects that Mom or Dad has given them. This can be truly exciting for the infant, but it is the beginning of a whole new set of problems for the parents.

Sleeping

The amount of time a baby sleeps per day is variable (as it is for older children and adults), but, on average, a newborn will sleep sixteen hours a day—of course, not sixteen hours straight. Some parents have babies who are sleeping through the night within weeks after birth; other parents feel they may never get a full night's sleep again. Over the course of the first year, baby's sleep needs decrease, so that by one year most infants are happy with about twelve hours of sleep per day.

But even for "average" sleepers, the distribution of the sleep can vary widely. Some babies are "night people," no problem if Mom and Dad are too, but often they aren't, and adjustments must be made. Some twelve-month-olds are tired, but throw a fit when put to bed, which is usually as distressing for the parents listening in the next room as for the infant. Other infants will fall asleep according to a reasonable schedule, but every precaution must be made so as not to wake up baby. Phones are taken off the hook, notes to "knock quietly" are taped to front doors, and the entire household is required to speak in whispers.

Clearly many problems arise surrounding baby's sleeping habits. The point is that both family and infant need to do some adapting. For example, many parents *avoid* the silent nap time; from the earliest days, baby's bedroom door is left open and conversation is kept to a normal level. Initially the baby may have difficulty getting to sleep, but many parents end up with a baby who can sleep through a hurricane.

Sometimes solutions to sleeping problems are not that simple and compromises are necessary. For example, one mother tells us of her seven-month-old son who fought tooth and nail each night when they put him in his crib. She had followed the instructions of baby books and friends, letting her son cry until he fell asleep. Still it continued and she felt uncomfortable with his distress. The solution? She and her husband bought an adult-sized mattress and placed it in the corner of the room, padding the walls around the bed with fabric-covered foam rubber. They then put their son down for the night at the regular time, but not in his crib. Rather, the mattress gave him a much larger surface available for sleeping and this seemed to solve the problem. His mother writes, "Our son was thrilled at the space he had in which to sleep. He was safe and happy. So were his Mom and Dad."

Mental Development

Infants' abilities to make sense of their world develop rapidly over the first year. Cognitive abilities are very limited, yet, within twelve short months babies are able to recognize dozens of familiar people and places, realize that their behavior affects others around them, and understand some of the rudiments of cause and effect.

Baby's Perception

At birth, all of an infant's senses are working to some extent. In fact, a baby's sense of smell, taste, touch, and hearing are functioning reasonably well.

While it's an old wives' tale that infants can't see at birth, their vision is admittedly not very good, most having the equivalent of 20/400 vision. During the first several months of life, most like to look at things that move and that have high contrast. Older babies also find these things to be attractive, but by four or five months also like to look at things that are slightly novel—things that are new but remind them of something they already know. For example, a five-month-old is apt to be fascinated with the face of his mother's sister. Chances are his aunt resembles his mother, and the resemblance is interesting. Babies will even look longer at the slightly novel face than they will their own mother. This means that babies are learning important things about their world, such as features of significant people.

Learning to Have an Effect on Their World

During the first half year or so, babies learn that they can have some effect on things that surround them. For example, when our daughter Heidi was four months old, she was lying in her playpen with a "crib gym" strung over her head. While flailing her arms and legs she hit the mobile, causing it to spin. She suddenly stopped and stared intently at the moving object above her head. When it stopped moving, she began to squirm, to shake her arms and legs, and finally to cry. Again she hit the mobile and again she quieted and stared ahead at the wonderful event she had caused. This may not seem exceptional at first blush, but it is the beginning of children realizing that they personally cause something in their environment to happen.

Once babies discover that they can cause things to happen, they start trying new things, though nothing too drastic at first. Four- or five-month-olds can make the connection between their cries and their parents' appearance at their doors, and may use this newfound knowledge to get what they want in ways that never occurred to them before.

Out of Sight Is Out of Mind

Until about eight months of age, babies believe that objects that are out of their sight no longer exist; including even Mom and Dad. Out of sight is literally out of mind. Mom and Dad apparently are viewed as pleasant, recurring events and not as things that are permanent in time and space. And when babies find interesting and forbidden objects, merely removing them from their sight will usually be enough to stop their interest in them. Older infants realize that an object still exists even though they can't see it, and simply removing the object from them may not be as effective as it is for the younger baby.

Simple Language

Beginning around this time, children start to understand simple language. Nothing too complex, mind you, but by nine or ten months or so, "yes" and "no" and "juice" and "milk" and "Mommy" and "Daddy" can be understood. By ten or twelve months, many babies can speak a few recognizable words. They don't put them together into sentences yet—that feat is about six months down the road—but they begin to use words to communicate verbally and can understand some of the simple speech that is directed to them, especially when accompanied by gestures or familiar objects.

Learning by Association

Infants' learning abilities are simultaneously remarkable and limited at the same time. By twelve months of age, infants have acquired a lot of knowledge, yet their learning ability is still restricted. Infants much under one year need repetition before any particular event will sink in. And if babies are to learn to associate two things together, those things must follow very closely in time. For example, in studies with six- and nine-month-olds, babies had to associate something they did (pulling on a string, for example) with some pleasant event that closely followed their action (for example, someone smiling at them and talking to them). Infants typically had no trouble learning this association, frequently pulling on the string in order to see the smiling face. However, when the smiling face followed the string pull by as little as two seconds, infants had difficulty learning the task. They seemed to have forgotten what it was they did a few seconds earlier (pull the string) that was responsible for the pleasant outcome (the smiling face). In other words, babies can make associations easily, but the associations have to follow very closely in time if any learning is to occur.

This limited learning ability has important consequences for discipline during the first year. A slap on the hand is a common punishment for infants who get into things they should not. But such punishment will not work because of the limited learning and memory abilities of babies. By the time Mom moves across the room, the child will probably be unable to associate the slap with the action that caused it. The parent may thus unknowingly be punishing infants' exploration or their pride in crawling, not the undesirable behavior itself. A better response is to quickly remove children from the offending situation. By the time they are ten feet away and out of sight from the forbidden object, they are apt to have forgotten it. Such a simple solution won't work for an older child, of course, but it will work quite well and with minimal distress for the young infant.

Social and Emotional Development

The greatest joys of being the parent of an infant revolve around baby's social responding. There's something special about a baby who makes eye contact with you, smiles, and coos. Adults—even those who profess not to care much for babies—can't resist responding to these social signals of infants by making silly faces and sounds, all to keep baby happy.

Becoming Socially Responsive

Babies do not start out so social. For the first two months or so, they do more taking. This can be discouraging to many parents, especially when the baby is fussy or "difficult to handle." An important thing to keep in mind during the baby's first two or three months is that it gets better. Babies become truly social around this time, building on the interaction parents provided them during their earlier "nonresponsive" months.

Babies, of course, have individual personalities. Many five-
and six-month-old infants are all smiles and will go to anyone
with out-stretched arms, while others are more reticent and a
little less smiley. Nevertheless, in general, babies between
about three and eight months tend to like people, and although
Mom and Dad are treated warmly, babies this age seem not
really to care whom they spend their time with.

This "all welcome" attitude often changes beginning around
eight months. Infants who weeks earlier thought nothing of
being dropped off with a sitter, may now have a fit under
similar circumstances. Even Grandma may not be an adequate
substitute for Mom and Dad. Babies at this age frequently
show great distress when separated from their parents, even if
the substitute is a familiar person. This is normal, but the range
of reactions can vary from a little whimpering that lasts only
seconds after Mom and Dad leave, to violent tantrums that
persist until the child cries himself to sleep. Even within a
given range of behaviors, reactions will vary from one day (or
hour) to the next. And some well-adjusted babies seem never
to show this distress for strangers or from separation from
Mom and Dad.

Becoming Attached

The most significant social accomplishment of infants during
the first year is becoming attached to their parents. Attachment
begins at birth and continues to be modified over the course of
infancy and beyond. Also, all attachments are not created
equal. Some children develop *secure* attachments to their parents, whereas the attachments of others are described as *insecure*.

Psychologists have developed tests assessing one-year-olds'
reactions to being separated and later reunited with their mothers. Mother and child are together in a small room, when
Mother unexpectedly gets up and leaves. Babies stop what they
are doing, cry for their mothers, and generally show signs of
distress. Two minutes later Mother returns. What the psychologists are interested in is how children respond to the return of
the mothers. Most one-year-olds greet their mother warmly;
they run to her, jump in her lap, and in a matter of seconds

cease their crying. Soon, they climb out of Mom's lap and continue to play with the toys in the room, frequently looking back to make eye contact with Mom. These children are described as being *securely attached* to their mothers.

Other children respond quite differently. Some run to Mom, but never stop crying. They whimper and cling to Mom as if they are afraid that if they let go, they will be abandoned again. Others are hostile, refusing to look at their mothers, and staying in a corner far away from Mom. Some actually strike their mothers, punishing them for leaving. These children have been described as being *insecurely attached* to their mothers.

The significance of this is that babies who are securely attached to their mothers at twelve months are apt to be more independent, more cooperative with their parents, and show greater self-control years later. In other words, the nature of a child's attachment influences subsequent parent/child interactions and the incidence of behavior problems. What is equally important is that security of attachment is largely determined by the way in which parents interact with their children during the first year of life.

What Is It That Makes for a Securely Attached Child?

Perhaps the most important factor is the parents' sensitivity to their infant's signals of physical and social need. Babies get hungry; they want to play; they are bored; they are tired; they are really interested in this toy; they need help fitting a block into the box; they want a spoonful of banana pudding now and not a spoonful of string beans; they want their socks off and their hat on. How well do parents read these signals? To what extent do parents operate independent of their babies' behavior? In other words, do parents respond *to* their babies' needs, or do they basically ignore their babies' efforts at communication and do to baby what *they* think should be done?

When parents are sensitive to babies' physical and social signals and respond promptly, babies develop a sense of control. "What I do makes a difference in what happens to me." This sense of control helps infants develop a sense of autonomy and independence. It also teaches them that parents can be depended upon and will respect their needs. This leads to children who are more competent and who are apt to have more positive interactions with their parents. (The development of attachment and its consequences for discipline, will be discussed in greater detail in Chapter 7.)

Having a securely attached child does not mean that your discipline problems will be over, but it does help. As noted earlier, children who feel they have some control over their lives, who can depend on their parents when they get into situations that they cannot handle, and who feel that they are respected by their parents, are apt to be in control of their own behavior and to respect the wishes of their parents. Infancy, of course, is only a beginning. Once patterns are established, they must be continued and adapted over time. The sooner one starts, the easier time one will have of parenthood.

Toddlerhood (Twelve to Twenty-four Months)

Motor and Intellectual Development

"Nothing Can Stop Me Now!"

Sometime during the second year, babies begin to walk (and run). This new ability increases their exploration of their world and provides them with greater independence—and also with the opportunity to get into more trouble.

Along with their newly acquired walking skills, toddlers' fine motor coordination improves, too. Their hands are no longer merely the chubby extensions of their arms, but finely coordinated tools that can turn televisions on and off, pick up pins from the carpeting, and hold small objects and toss them yards away. Toward the end of the second year they can hold a crayon and make lovely circular marks on paper, floors, and walls. Toddlers are able to do many marvelous things, and this often means that parents have their hands full trying to keep up with the many activities of their youngsters.

How Toddlers Understand Their World

Along with increased motor abilities come increased mental abilities. The Swiss psychologist Jean Piaget described babies during the teen months as "little experimenters." Now for the first time they invent slightly new behaviors to achieve their goals. They no longer have to wait until chance provides them with an interesting event (such as the example with our daughter Heidi mentioned earlier). They can make interesting things happen themselves, and, given the opportunity, they do exactly that.

Toddlers are continuing the process begun months earlier. They want to know what makes things tick and, more importantly, how *they* can *make* things tick. They are explorers and adventurers. ''Is it possible to unravel the toilet paper, getting it all into the toilet without tearing the paper? How does one get into the bathroom sink? Isn't it interesting that one knob makes the music so much louder?'' Adults are perplexed as to why fifteen-month-olds find dog food and kitty litter so fascinating, why they are so interested in electric sockets and wastebaskets, and why they insist upon climbing out of their high chairs and manipulating and mouthing everything that's on the kitchen table.

Although children at this stage are wonderful problem solvers, their knowledge is still limited to their actions on objects. Toddlers know things by acting upon them. They cannot yet make mental comparisons or represent objects and events symbolically. So, for example, if a fifteen-month-old girl wants to see if her brother's Big-Wheel tricycle fits beneath the coffee table, she'd have to do it by physically attempting to place the tricycle under the table. It makes no difference that the big wheel rises a foot above the table; she cannot simply examine the two objects and discern that one is too big to fit under the other. She *can* learn this, however, by *doing* (although it may take several attempts before she concludes what to an adult is obvious). Her intelligence is one of action and not one of covert ''thinking'' characteristic of the older child.

Negativism

Infants during the first year of life do get angry, but it is typically not until the teen months that truly negative behavior is first seen. Toddlers are developing a greater sense of self and are able to differentiate themselves from their parents. They know now that what they do and what their parents do are independent. They need not comply with every wish of their parents—it is not necessary because they now perceive themselves as separate from their parents. This negativism, which is found more in some toddlers than others, is a potential source of problems for parents during the second year.

Language

Children's ability to understand language increases dramatically at this age. As children begin to put words together into sentences sometime around eighteen months, they become much easier to communicate with than one-year-olds. However, there is so much more to communicate to a toddler than to an infant.

Parents of toddlers sometimes feel that they could be replaced by a tape recording that says, "No-no," "Don't touch," and "Come back here." How parents respond to children's increased locomotion, mental abilities, and negativism sets the stage for discipline during subsequent years.

Living with Toddlers

How can toddlers be "kept in line" without "keeping them down?" Restricting children to cribs, high chairs, and playpens for long hours is one way to protect your child and your possessions. But this method has serious drawbacks. First of all, some children will not *allow* themselves to be so confined; they will holler and squirm and eventually learn to escape. These are "high-activity" children who are happiest when they have room to roam. Other children are more complacent and will spend long hours in their playpens, playing with a couple of favorite toys. In fact, when these children *are* "let out," they may limit most of their exploration to one room and be happy staying in a single location for long periods of time.

The Exploring Child

But explore children must, and even toddlers who are reluctant to leave mother's side should be encouraged to do so. It is through exploration that children learn a sense of mastery—a sense of control over their world. Yet a toddler cannot be given free reign over the household. Toddlers may have the curiosity and abilities to get into everything, but they do not have the knowledge about what is safe and what is not. They also have little sense of private property. Anything within their reach is fair game, regardless of how valuable it is to Mom and Dad.

Some middle ground must be found. Restrict a child too much, and parents and child will be in a constant battle for freedom. Discipline should never be used to "break" children—squelching their curiosity and preventing them from asserting their independence. But restrict too little and children fail to learn that there are limits on their behavior.

For example, we know of one family who permitted their toddler daughter to write on the walls of their house with crayons. They feared that preventing her artistic expression would stifle her development. Not surprisingly, this toddler was also given great latitude in other areas. This child had great difficulty when visiting the homes of other people (such as us). She was unaware that her artistic endeavors were not appreciated by everyone, and did indeed become quite frustrated (and downright nasty) when the crayons were taken away from her. The child knew no limits and she and her parents were rarely invited back for visits. Some years have gone by, and this child has not gotten any easier to deal with. She talks back to her parents in public places, pouts and sometimes screams when she doesn't get her way immediately, and is generally unpleasant to be around. This is not to say that permitting this child to scribble on the walls *caused* her unruly behavior years later; but the pattern was set. Discipline is something that is acquired continuously over childhood, and the longer one waits to impose discipline on children, the more difficult a task it will become.

Other parents we know faced a similar problem with a toddler who loved to scribble and was constantly being reprimanded for writing on the walls. To solve this problem, these parents installed a three-foot-high blackboard in the child's room that extended over the entire wall. Multicolor pieces of chalk were provided and the child was free to draw whatever she liked on her chalkboard. At first there were mishaps. When the toddler was writing on forbidden walls, she was quickly removed to her room and instructed to do her artwork on her "blackboard wall." Before long, everyone was happy, and the blackboard wall remained for this child and later her brother to enjoy through their childhood years.

The Childproof House

What does one do with a toddler with wanderlust—with a child who fights any restriction and who wants to leave no stone unturned, so to speak, as he explores his surroundings? The first thing is to childproof one's house. Place harmful and precious objects out of reach. Conflicts are minimized when parents feel confident that there is little of danger or value for their toddler to get into. Let children explore as much of the house as possible and try to share some of their excitement in the discoveries they are making. Let children know you are interested in what they are doing, and they will continue to share their discoveries with you.

But there is really no such thing as a perfectly childproof house. There must be some limits on what your toddler does, and these limits must be enforced. One of the easiest techniques for stopping children from doing something they are not supposed to be doing, is to remove them from the situation and give them something else to do. These children have reasonably good memories by now, and simple removal alone will not be enough. However, they are also easily distracted, and their distress about being removed from one "fun" activity can often be alleviated simply by being introduced to another, more acceptable, "fun" activity.

The Special Toy

There will be times, of course, when this strategy will not work, even with the best tempered toddler. One thing that some parents have found successful is to have a special toy that is pulled out only for emergency circumstances. When your twenty-month-old demands something to eat thirty minutes before supper, or the Swedish Ivy hanging in the den is just too attractive to be ignored, it's time for the "special toy." Many parents report that this trick works well most of the time.

The problem is, of course, that the "special toy" strategy must be used sparingly, and that access must sometimes be denied. Some parents find this difficult, reasoning, "If the kid wants the toy and we have it, there's no reason why he shouldn't have it." This technique involves denying a child something he wants. It teaches discipline to children but also requires some discipline on the part of the parent.

The "Not So Terrible" Twos

The changes that occur over the first two years are substantial. Beginning around two years of age, they become even more dramatic. The differences are not so much in terms of physical or motor development (although toilet training is usually accomplished during this period), but primarily in terms of intellectual abilities. The thinking of the two-year-old is vastly different from the thinking of the toddler. Somewhere between the later teen months and their second birthdays, children become symbol users. They are able to make mental comparisons between objects; they are able to retrieve memories from the past and anticipate the future. They are no longer dependent upon their own, direct actions to understand things. They can know the world via symbols, most notably language.

This new intellectual ability transforms how children understand their world and also transforms parent/child interactions. The thinking of the two-year-old resembles the thinking of his or her parents more closely than that of an infant. Children now require explanations. Their understanding of language is reflected not only in what they comprehend but also in what they say. Many children are speaking in complete paragraphs before their third birthdays.

New Abilities, New Adjustments

Parents must make the adjustments to these new abilities, and sometimes this is difficult. Children move even farther away from parents now. The negativism that was budding during the teen months often blossoms in the "terrible twos." These children have real likes and dislikes and often resent adults telling them what to do. They want to play with a certain toy at a certain time and in a certain way. They want to order for themselves at restaurants, and will sometimes refuse to eat merely because *Mom* and not *they themselves* placed the order with the waiter. Yet the two-year-old's newfound independence is more imaginary than real. They actually are capable of taking only little more responsibility than the toddler; the point is they *believe* they are very responsible and want to exercise some of this responsibility.

These can be trying times, but they need not be. The child's increasing independence must be acknowledged, but remember that two-year-olds (as well as older preschoolers) *know* more than they can actually do. They believe they are capable of making decisions and expect to be able to do so. Letting them make some decisions and feeling that they are in control of complex situations is important for children of this (and later) ages. The trick is to let them make decisions that can only have a positive outcome, and, in other situations, to let them *think* they are in control when in fact you hold all the cards.

Giving Two-Year-Olds Some Control

Many parents are reluctant to give their children any real control of a situation, feeling that this constitutes "giving in" to the child's demands. In fact, for the most part, two-year-olds can be allowed to make their choices in some situations and *feel* in control in others.

For example, deciding what clothes to put on in the morning or what to have for lunch are decisions a two-and-a-half-year-old can make. But don't give young children open-ended options. Don't tell your two-year-old to wear anything she wishes or to select anything she wants for lunch. There is a distinct possibility that her choices will be so outrageous that you will feel compelled to veto them, ending up with a disappointed child and a broken promise. Instead, give your child a two-choice option. "You can wear your pink shorts and Disney World T-shirt today or your yellow jumper and ruffled blouse"; or "You can have a peanut-butter-and-jelly sandwich or soup for lunch." The options must be kept simple. Children get confused when there are too many things to consider or the options become complicated (for example: "If you wear the jumper, you can wear your sneakers; if you wear your shorts and T-shirt, you can wear either your sneakers or your pink sandals, and you can wear that pink headband that goes with the shorts").

Another trick to keep in mind with the "two-choice option" is that if you have a preference, mention it last. Two-year-olds have limited memories, and although, if push came to shove, they probably *could* remember both alternatives, the last one spoken will stay in their minds longer and, more often than not, will be the one they choose.

Sometimes these children will refuse to make even the simplest decision. They display an ability, also found in older children, of being able to stay awake and function at some level despite extreme fatigue. In fact, they will argue, often vehemently, that they don't need a nap, and that they won't fall asleep even if they are made to lie in bed. Parents often give into this, for they think it is easier to live with a grouchy kid than to develop a schedule for naps. But most two-year-olds still need naps, and naps are best done on a schedule.

Problems With Two-Year-Olds

Two-year-olds present parents with new sets of problems. Their increased language and intellectual abilities require that parents take them seriously, yet these children are not nearly as competent as they think they are. Sometimes we must treat two-year-olds much as we do older children, asking their opinions and getting their input. At other times we must treat them more like toddlers, doing things for them, despite their claims that they are quite capable of doing things themselves. We must still impose schedules, for two-year-olds do not have the maturity to stick to one themselves (nor do three- and four-year-olds, for that matter). All this calls for careful and sometimes quick judgment on the part of the adult, and the ability to respond flexibly and to make changes in one's plans when necessary. Because of the complexity of dealing with a two-year-old, it is easy to understand why matters sometimes get out of hand.

Here's one detailed example of a major conflict between a two-year-old and his mother. A woman in her early thirties entered a Florida Turnpike fast-food restaurant with her ten-year-old daughter and her wailing two-year-old son. It was three-thirty on a Sunday afternoon. The family had been traveling since early morning and they were tired and hungry. We have never before heard as much noise from a child with a pacifier implanted firmly in his mouth. The mother pulled the boy behind her as she walked because whenever she let go, he'd drop to the floor, his crying uninterrupted.

When she pulled him into the food line, he slipped away, climbed over a railing and into the nearest seat. She calmly ignored him, walked down the line a few steps, selected a roast beef sandwich for herself, turned to her son and said in a normal speaking voice (as if nothing unusual was happening), "What would you like, Jonathan?" Jonathan, of course, only shook his head and increased his wailing. She asked again, this time in a louder voice, followed by a demand to, "Come over here right now!" When this was ignored the mother stormed over to her child, grabbed him by the arm, and hoisted him over the railing back to her place in line. "What do you want to eat, Jonathan?" Again, only the persistent crying.

A few feet down the line it was time for drinks (Mother had apparently selected a sandwich for Jonathan). "What do you want to drink, Jonathan?" "Jonathan," she asked in a reasonably calm voice, "do you want Coke or Sprite?" The cries now increased, as Jonathan escaped a few feet before being recaptured. The cries continued for about a minute, until the boy broke free again and made his way, only whimpering now, to the exit. Taking his ten-year-old sister's hand, he pushed against the door.

From the cash register came a call: "Jonathan, don't you go outside. Julie, make sure he doesn't go out." Jonathan's cries escalated again, and within the minute his mother was by his side with a tray of food. Mom tried calmly addressing Jonathan, but he wanted nothing to do with talking. He threw his pacifier to the floor and hit a new all-time record for decibel output from a child under three.

His mother dragged him to the ladies' room on the other side of the restaurant, from which only a "whack," presumably on Jonathan's bottom, was heard. However, the intensity or quality of Jonathan's cries never varied. We left before Jonathan and his mother returned from the restroom (assuming they ever did), and so we don't know exactly how this episode ended.

What's a Mother To Do?

What options did this mother have? To her credit, the temper tantrums were mainly from her son. She did not scream at her son (two people yelling in a small restaurant would have driven most of the customers to the vending machines outside). Yet her son was obnoxious, behaving as only an angry two-year-old can; she had lost control of him and he showed little evidence of self-control.

For one thing, posing serious questions to a crying belligerent child was counterproductive. He was in no mood. Asking once might have been appropriate, but not once it was clear that giving him a choice was not going to modify his behavior. Giving a two-year-old a choice of food is a privilege not a right.

What other alternatives were there? Actually this mother had several. She was fortunate to have a well-behaved daughter who was old enough and presumably capable of being some help.

Option 1

As the family enters the restaurant and Jonathan's crying persists, mother could have given some money to her daughter and asked her to go through the lunch line for the three of them. Mother and Jonathan would wait at an appropriate table. The whimpering Jonathan might even have selected the table, giving the child some modicum of control early on. So what if it's in the 'Smoking Section.' At the table Mother could have attempted to console her distraught son. Chances are, some improvement would have occurred, mainly because little but quiet was being requested of Jonathan. He *didn't* have to follow where he didn't want to go. He *didn't* have to make decisions he wasn't in the mood to make. Or Mother could have held him on her lap, not attempting to engage him in conversation, and hoped that the crying would subside soon. Chances are it would have, but of course such a rational approach to an irrational child might have had no positive results at all.

Option 2

Either after or instead of Option 1, Jonathan could have been removed from the situation. "This constant fussing has got to stop. I am not taking you in this restaurant when you are acting like this!" Such a statement would not have changed Jonathan's behavior one bit, but it would have set the groundwork for what was to follow. What should have followed was removing Jonathan from the restaurant. His mother could have given money to her daughter, as in Option 1, and waited outside with Jonathan. If Jonathan stopped fussing, the two of them could have returned to the restaurant and eaten inside. If not, Julie could have brought the food outside and the three of them could have eaten on the bench. If the crying persisted, there's nothing wrong with eating in the car. And what if Jonathan refused to eat? Well, it's his stomach. Eating while parked or driving are tricks of the trade when traveling with children.

Option 3

When traveling with young children, fatigue often sets in. Even two-year-olds get excited about a trip, and excited kids don't sleep. However, nonsleeping, excited kids still get tired, cranky, and hungry. Knowing this, a schedule for the trip is important. Many travelers like to drive as far as they can before stopping. Fine, but can the kids take it? A three-thirty lunch is pushing it for a tired two-year-old. His frustration (and thus his temper tantrum) could probably have been avoided by better planning.

These are things to keep in mind when traveling with children of any age. However, some plans are easier said than done. For example, it is difficult to "make" kids nap in the car. We have found that imposed quiet time often works. The radio goes off, the children's tape recorder playing "Winnie the Pooh" stories goes off, and conversation is limited to a minimum (even among the adults). Long trips with young children require entertainment. However, some imposed quiet time can result in naps and rested children. Rested kids, who eat on schedule, are less apt to explode in a rage than tired and hungry children.

Three- and Four-Year-Olds

There's an old saying to the effect that the "terrible twos" are followed by the "trusting threes." Of course, not all parents would agree. The twos are not so terrible for many parents, and for others the threes are not so great. In general, however, much of the turmoil parents experience between their children's second and third birthdays diminishes in the years that follow. Some of this might be attributed to the parents, who have had a year or so to learn how to deal with a thinking and sometimes stubborn child. But much of the change can be attributed to the child.

Children's Language and Humor

Language skills, that began to explode during the previous year, continue to develop. Three- and four-year-old children can talk your ear off if you'll let them, and they've learned enough of the world to have some interesting things to talk about.

Bathroom Humor

Children also have learned to play with words, and some of their humor is apt not to meet the approval of their parents. For example, three-year-olds find great mirth in using "bathroom" language. They are apt to call another child (or a parent) "pee-pee head," or state that Aunt Mary's chocolate pudding looks like "doo-doo." This can be quite shocking to unexpecting parents.

One reason for their interest in bathroom language concerns the recent accomplishment of toilet training. Most parents put a lot of emphasis here, and in the process children learn that terms relating to their elimination process are reserved just for that. But humor at this age includes simply using a wrong name for something (for example, calling a cat, "doggy"), and when the wrong name also is emotionally charged, it is doubly funny.

The shock of your sweet little angel using the preschool equivalent of locker-room language is lessened if it is expected. The best first response is not to act shocked and not to laugh. This can then be followed by a calm statement that, "We don't call people that," or "That's not a nice thing to say about Aunt Mary's pudding." However, there is usually someone in the crowd who is cracking up over the comment, and this reinforces the habit. Parents should express their displeasure with these statements (but not shock), and ask others to do the same. It will only confuse children to laugh at their little bathroom joke when it is directed at a careless driver and then to admonish them for the same joke when it is directed at Grandpa. Three-year-olds are not sufficiently sophisticated to understand when some jokes are okay and when they are not. Children's humor does change over the preschool years and, unless supported by adults or older siblings, the bathroom jokes will disappear. Most children will make such jokes, and parental overreaction is likely the best way of keeping such humor in their repertoire as they grow older.

Intellectual Skills and Deficits

Children's intellectual skills continue to increase over this age period, but most of their thinking is qualitatively similar to that of the two-year-old. Language is used more proficiently and three- and four-year-olds are gaining new information to think about. However, the thinking skills of these children are still limited.

The Self-Centered Child

All of us see the world from our own perspective, and this is especially true of preschool children. They interpret events from their own point of view and have a difficult time putting themselves in someone else's shoes. This attitude of the young child has been referred to as *egocentricity*. Young children's egocentric attitudes can be the source of discipline problems during the preschool years. Many children of this age have a difficult time appreciating that other people have wants and needs that are independent from their own, assuming instead that "What's good for me is good for everyone." Problems often occur in play groups because each child believes that the whole show is being run just for him or her.

Sharing

Sharing becomes a major issue. Egocentric three-year-olds just do not understand the need to share. They have difficulty seeing the situation from another point of view. Their toys belong to them;, and so should the toys of other children. Enforcing sharing among three- and four-year-olds takes some effort on the part of the supervising adults, but it's necessary. In the absence of rules, the situation is ripe for the biggest and oldest kids to take what they want when they want it, training them to be playground bullies.

Explanations concerning *why* children should share don't hurt. Three-year-olds may not truly appreciate these explanations, but they serve as the basis for an understanding of social give-and-take that will be valuable several years up the road.

Taking Turns

Related to problems with sharing are problems with taking turns. When children are involved in an interesting game, they want to play it as much as they can. They don't appreciate that other children have the same wants. Fights and disagreements often arise about who goes down the slide in what order, how many times a child gets to throw the ball into the basket, or whose turn it is to move in a game of "Candyland."

As with sharing, these disagreements are inevitable, and, as with sharing, they need to be handled. Just because children's limited intellectual and social skills make it difficult for them to understand the importance of turn taking, it doesn't mean turn taking should not be enforced. What it does mean is that the responsible adults should understand preschool children's self-centered views and deal with the problems as calmly and consistently as possible. Complicated turn-taking games can be adapted for little ones, or play limited to games that several children can play simultaneously or that involve only short waits between well-defined turns. Again, keeping the intellectual skills and shortcomings of young children firmly in mind can help remedy problems, or avoid them altogether.

"Reasoning," as generally understood by adults, will not work. Three- and four-year-olds will listen to you and may even nod in agreement. But it is unlikely that they are actually able to follow your logic. This does not mean that explanations shouldn't be provided; the important thing is to keep them brief and straightforward. Be as concrete as possible. The further one gets from the obvious, the less likely it is that preschool children will understand you. (For further examples, see section on Communication in Chapter 3.)

Kids *learn* to share, to follow rules, and to obey, the way they *learn* to ride a bicycle. Parents need to be patient and understanding. You should not expect perfect performance just

because you've told them once what to do. Parents would
never expect their children to be perfect bike riders after only
one lesson; rather, they hold their children up on the bike and
run along behind them until they are able to do it alone. And
even then, they aren't surprised by a few skinned knees. Disciplined behavior should be taught the same way.

The Early School Years (Five to Seven)

Changes in children are gradual over the next several years.
In many ways the five- to seven-year-old child is much like his
or her younger counterpart, and will continue to display a
generally egocentric perspective of the world. Yet they are also
moving toward a more mature form of thought. How things
look is still important, but these children are not apt to be
fooled into thinking that changing one's clothes alters one's
gender. Similarly, their egocentricity is less extreme. They
play more easily with other children, being more apt to accept
the necessity of taking turns and of sharing.

They also know so much more than the three- or four-year-
old, and use this knowledge to interact with others. These years
are a transition period from the illogical and intuitive thought
of the preschool child to the more logical thinking characteristics of school-age children.

However, in most ways, the problems one is apt to face with
the five- to seven-year-old are not drastically different than the
problems one is apt to face with a three- or four-year-old child.
As in years past, the area that is apt to cause most conflicts will
center around independence. Five- and six-year-olds truly can
master much of their world and are more capable of complex
feats. And they will, as they should, demand more freedom.
How much should parents give and when?

Increasing Freedom

As at any age, parents should let the child lead. One thing
that parents sometimes do is to give children more freedom of
choice than they really want. Let children ask for privileges.
This can only be done, however, in an environment where
there is open discussion and children are not afraid to make

requests of their parents, and parents don't feel threatened or challenged by their children's developing independence.

As with younger children, five- to seven-year-olds often demand more freedom than they can handle. One child, who had occasionally accompanied his father to afternoon hockey games, announced that now that he was six, he was big enough to attend the evening games, too. When told he could do no such thing, he was angry for a week.

Parents feel most comfortable increasing children's freedom when it can be done slowly. For example, we live on a street without much traffic, five or six cars will pass by in the course of an hour. One woman on the street did not permit her five-year-old son to play outside alone or with other young children without the presence of an adult. Yet she could not be outside with him as often as he liked and she finally gave in, starting with warnings about not straying into the street. Then she permitted him outside alone, when she could watch, surreptitiously, through the window. It wasn't long until she was convinced that he knew and would obey her rules. Soon, her son was allowed to skate up and down the sidewalks by himself, and by six, he was bicycling on the sidewalks. Each step, however, was watched carefully by his mother and each was allowed only after he had demonstrated responsibility for less daring ventures.

Increasing Responsibility

With freedom comes responsibility, and this is where many conflicts between five- to seven-year-old children and their parents crop up. If these children are old enough for greater freedoms, they are also old enough for greater responsibilities. For example, five- to seven-year-olds are capable of cleaning their rooms, making their beds, and generally picking up after themselves. However, many find the imposition of such chores true drudgery, and either argue and whine that "it's not fair," or conveniently (and frequently) "forget" assigned tasks. This is particularly true if children had almost no responsibility with regard to their belongings and the messes they made during their first four years.

Some parents recommend weekly check lists as reminders of jobs that need to be done. Most children of this age like constructing such lists themselves (with the help of a parent) and derive pleasure from putting checks or stars in the boxes after completing each chore. A checklist like the one below may be all one needs.

	Mon	Tue	Wed	Thu	Fri	Sat	Sun
Cleaning Room							
Brushing Teeth							
Making Bed							

Some parents and child-rearing experts believe that a reward at the end of the day (or week) should be given. For example, children might receive a nickel per day for each chore completed, or a special treat at the end of the week if a certain number of checks have been accumulated. This isn't a bad idea, but we'd recommend not starting out this way. This changes the chart from a memory aid the parent and child worked on together to a reward system the parent imposes on the child. Many children actually enjoy the responsibility of creating the checklist and completing the job for its own sake. Children may bring their list to a parent at the end of the day and show how many checks or stars they have. Some positive statement from the parent is definitely appropriate at this time, even if all the chores were not done perfectly. But keep the emphasis on the job, not on the chart—it's only an *aid*.

Also, remember, if the job was done by a five-year-old, don't expect an eight-year-old job. You're not looking for perfection here; you're looking for your five-year-old to take responsibility commensurate with his or her abilities.

The Problem of Getting Things Done on Time

One frequent problem parents report with children of this age is getting them to do things promptly. These kids have real deadlines—such as getting to school on time—and parents often find themselves yelling and nagging. Many times, it is the parents who get all bent out of shape when their child dawdles on the way to the school bus. "If you don't hurry up you'll be late and you'll miss story time!" "Don't you care if you get there late? I'd think you'd be embarrassed to come into class after the teacher has already started."

Well, chances are the children *would* hate to miss story time and *would* be embarrassed to disrupt class in the middle of the teacher's first lesson, but few of these dawdlers ever have to worry about it. Their parents worry about it for them, making the threat of late arrival an empty one—"Mom gets so hyper about this every morning, she'd *never* let me be late."

Six-year-old Heidi seemed to have a similar attitude. Her father drove her to first grade on his way to work. To make sure she got to school on time, both father and daughter rose early, giving themselves a little extra time in case some morning mishap should occur. One morning, however, she was particularly slow in getting going. Dad asked the usual set of questions—Have you brushed your teeth yet? ("No"), Do you have homework? ("No"), Where's your other sneaker? ("I don't know")—but Heidi seemed unconcerned.

"You're going to be late today," her dad said.

"I don't care," Heidi responded.

"Well, hurry up," said her dad. "I'm going to read the paper. Get me when you're ready."

Heidi finally did get ready (after a few more calls from her dad), and on the drive in it became clear that she would be at least ten minutes late for school. Contrary to her previous claim, this upset her considerably. When Heidi blamed her dad, he pointed out, "You said you didn't care, and we left as soon as you were ready." After that Heidi seldom dawdled.

One mother, who reported a problem with getting her daughter ready for school, admitted that much of the blame was hers. She wrote that when her daughter was young, "I allowed her to explore freely without restrictions. She seemed to enjoy going from one thing to the next, and I followed her around picking up the pieces! Now she suffers when she has tasks to do for school or someone else."

One particularly difficult task was getting ready for school. Mother would follow her daughter around all morning, making sure she finished her breakfast, went to the bathroom, brushed her teeth, and got dressed properly. One day Mother decided to stop all the nagging and pushing and let the child take the consequences of her own behavior. "If she doesn't do the daily routine without my nagging or taking her by the hand, it doesn't get done and she must go to school 'as is.' Every day I set a timer and I don't say anything except 'that means we are going to leave in ten minutes.' So far, she has made it to school dressed every day, but on occasion has forgotten the new barrettes she wanted to wear or her toy for sharing time. It's still on trial, but so far so good.''

Children *do* change over their first seven years, and the types of problems parents are apt to encounter change as well. Such "problems" are inevitable, but most are resolvable. Knowing what to expect of your child at any age helps parents anticipate problems. Many potential problems can be avoided by parents being ready for changes in their children.

5. Parents as Models of Discipline

When it comes to undisciplined behavior, parents sometimes focus too much on their children and not enough on themselves. For example a friend of ours told us the following story.

"When Benjamin was six, he had an annoying habit of leaving his belongings all over the house. Nothing I said to him seemed to make a difference, and one day, after tripping over his sneakers and stepping on one of his toy trucks, I really lost my temper.

" 'Ben!!' I screamed, 'I could just kill you. I've had it! Pick up this junk on the floor and be ready to spend the rest of your life in your room if you ever leave it out again.'

"I stayed mad for another hour, and he was smart enough to stay out of my way. I saw shoes poking out from under the kitchen table, and was about to let him have it when I recognized them as mine. Next I noticed my address book on the counter and my coffee cup on the bookshelf in the dining room. All at once it hit me—I get the angriest at Benjamin over the things that remind me the most of *me*."

This variant on the old "Do what I say, not what I do" theme is understandable and certainly forgivable. We easily recognize faults in our children that we have trouble seeing in ourselves. The problem begins when we start covering up, making excuses, and otherwise justifying our double standards.

Parenthood gives us a second chance at life. We *know* we're not perfect and haven't always done things the best way, but we somehow expect our children to do better. After all, we have the wisdom of our past experience and if they would just listen to us, we could save them a lot of time and trouble—right?

Wrong. And it was wrong when *our* parents tried to do *us* the same favor, we didn't listen. We made our own decisions and our own mistakes, yet we feel our generation ought somehow to be different.

Wanting your children to have the things you don't have is a big part of the American way of life and a loving part of parenthood. However, wanting your children to have the self-discipline you lack can lead to problems: kids feeling parents are overly demanding and critical, parents feeling kids don't respect their rules and values, and parents feeling defensive when they are "caught" being less than perfect. In child rearing, as in many other aspects of life, honesty is the best policy.

Imperfect Parents Cannot Expect to Raise Perfect Children

Problems are bound to happen when parents expect their children to be more disciplined than the adults in the family. Parents must examine their own behavior to see if they are acting in a way that is consistent with what they are expecting of their children. For example, do parents insist that children always tell the truth, while Mommy cautions the kids not to let Daddy know about the expensive dress she bought? Are children expected to complete all their chores before they're allowed to play, while parents leave supper dishes on the table and watch TV?

One day, when Max was two, I heard him sputtering angrily and turned to see him kicking the cat. I yelled *"Stop it"* and he did, but there was hell to pay for Max. I abhor physical violence, especially to defenseless creatures. After calming down, I realized where Max may have gotten this idea from.

First thing in the morning, a howling cat at my feet makes *me* angry. If a cat persists while I walk into the kitchen (which it sometimes does), I nudge him away with my foot. If the cat causes me to stumble, I get very angry, curse, and kick the cat away. (Oh, nonviolence, where art thou?)

Max was doing what he'd seen me do—one of the most noxious things I can imagine—kicking an animal. Funny thing is, Max has always loved cats. What was I teaching him?

There have been similar incidents since, when his actions made me very angry. It is only afterward that I inevitably realize: he's modeling one of my own worst traits.

The best solution would be to make sure you are perfectly disciplined yourself, but that's not a reality for most of us. Instead, here's a list of second-best alternatives.

1. Don't Be Afraid to Admit to Your Children That You Are Imperfect

It may be tough to confess that you aren't the best at putting your dirty clothes in the hamper or putting away your tools after a job, but it's better than having your children point it out in the middle of one of your lectures criticizing similar behavior on *their* part. "I'm working on it" is a good theme for both generations.

When I got upset with my five-year-old daughter for not keeping her room neat, she pointed out that mine was a mess, too. It made me stop and think. I know I'm not a great housekeeper, but I'm a single parent with a full-time job. I've gone through some rough times lately and, I'm doing all I can. Having a neat room is a little much to ask of me right now. And maybe it's a little too much for me to ask of my daughter, who's been through a lot lately, too. I told her I was doing my best, and that's all I wanted her to do, too.

2. Remember, Imitation Is the Sincerest Form of Flattery—Even of Undisciplined Behavior

None of us are perfect, and the people who know it the best are our family members. Rather than hiding your imperfections from your children, maybe you should throw in the towel and declare some traits a family fault.

My husband leaves his shoes and socks in the living room every night and it's always been a pet peeve of mine. So you can imagine my anger when I found my son's tiny sneakers next to Dad's big shoes. I was ready to blow up at both of them when I realized how cute it looked. I took a picture and put it in his baby book. Then I sent a copy to my sister-in-law who has the same complaint about *her* husband. We all had a good laugh over it.

3. From Each According to His Strengths; to Each According to His Needs

Sometimes a good solution to parents' imperfections is to ask for help from the kids. We don't *all* have to be good at *everything* in a family. If Mommy has trouble remembering to buy milk at the store, maybe her four-year-old son can help remind her. If Dad *never* puts his cereal bowl in the dishwasher after breakfast, maybe the job can be assigned to his three-year-old daughter. Kids have so little chance to "help" parents; they enjoy this, especially if parents are big enough to admit they just aren't very good at this particular task.

4. Remember Your Virtues, Too

When it comes to discipline, we always think of our faults, but for every black mark, we certainly have a hundred gold stars. We go to work each day and get there on time. We do a day's work for a day's pay so we can put a roof over the family's head and food on the family table. We pay our bills on time and budget our money. We remember family birthdays, put out the trash on the right days, and keep the lawn mowed. We go to school at night to get better jobs and work second jobs for extra income. Start a list and post it on the refrigerator door. It will make you feel like a saint.

Being a parent is a tough job, but there are times it seems all worth it. Like when I hear my four-year-old daughter "mothering" her doll by using the same words I use with her and singing the same lullaby I sing, I don't know what else she will be, but I know she will be a terrific mother and I feel proud of myself for that.

5. Last But Not Least—Make Some Changes in Your Undisciplined Behavior

It's not such a radical idea. Parenthood is a good time to change some traits that you've always wanted to get rid of, such as smoking, always being late, and using language some folks might consider objectionable. Doing it for yourself may not have been enough in the past, but maybe now you can do it for your child.

> My twenty-six-year-old daughter has always used coarse language and I have always detested it. The tables were turned one day when her three-year-old son, Toby, began using some of her "bad words." She decided on the spot to clean up her language. She even told Toby that those were "bad words" and that she was going to try not to say them anymore. She's done real well, and when she has a slipup, Toby is usually the one to remind her. I can't imagine admitting anything like that to a child of mine, but I admire her for it. She has shown Toby that she can be wrong and that she can change. That's probably a better lesson than showing him that she is perfect to begin with.

Some of the most common problems parents report with preschool children involve social behavior. However, parents may be guilty of modeling these behaviors themselves. If some of the following child behaviors seem familiar to you, make sure you're not modeling the adult behaviors that are similar.

1. Child: Using tantrums to get what she wants.
   Parents: Yelling at family members or using physical force to get what they want.

2. Child: Jealousy over new baby brother—acts like a baby herself.
   Parents: Wishing for the good old days before they were tied down with children.

3. Child: Using force to get his way with younger children.
   Parents: Making children obey by physical threats.

4. Child: Being bossy with other kids.
   Parents: Being curt and insensitive when dealing with people under their supervision.

5. Child: Being oversensitive—crying whenever he is criticized.
   Parents: Being oversensitive—ranting and raving to family whenever they are not obeyed or appreciated.

6. Child: Not sharing with other children.
   Parents: Not wanting neighbors to borrow their yard tools.

7. Child: Jealousy over older siblings—she wants privileges and freedom of ten-year-old sister.
   Parents: Jealousy of adult sibling who makes more money, drives a better car, or doesn't do his share for Mom and Dad.

8. Child: Being insensitive to parents' feelings.
   Parents: Being insensitive to spouse's feelings.

9. Child: Not taking turns and playing fairly.
   Parents: Being impatient in traffic and using illegal shortcuts.

10. Child: Not listening to instructions or following directions.
    Parents: Being a "know it all" and not taking advice from anyone.

11. Child: Whining to get what he wants.
    Parents: Complaining about a hard day at work to get out of going to a boring party.

12. Child: Conflict with baby-sitter.
    Parents: Conflict with a next-door neighbor over parking spaces.

13. Child: Fighting with siblings in the car constantly over who sits in which seat, who gets which toys, who is the biggest baby, etc.
    Parents: Bickering with your spouse in the car over which way you should have turned at the last intersection, whether the air-conditioning is too high or too low, whose fault it is *this* time that you are late, etc.

I had given up on quitting my heavy smoking habit when my two-year-old daughter, Caroline, put one of my cigarettes in her mouth and pretended to be lighting it and smoking. It was such a horrible sight! I signed up for one of the American Cancer Society's classes and it was tough, but I haven't had a cigarette in five years. Caroline is seven now and one of her favorite stories is "How Daddy quit smoking because he loved me so much." It's true.

Realizing some of our own shortcomings can help us to evaluate our children's less-than-perfect behavior. As no one needs to remind us, we're not perfect, so it's a bit unreasonable to demand perfection of our immature offspring. One step in the right direction is for parents to do a little self-reflection. It's up to us to demonstrate what self-disciplined behavior is.

Parents as Models for Social Relations

Parents can be powerful role models for ways of thinking as well as ways of behaving. Leading a disciplined life concerns how we deal with people. We need to ask ourselves what lessons our children are learning from us about respecting the rights of others and being considerate of others' feelings.

When we speak of a child as being disciplined, what comes to mind? It may be a child whose room is always clean, who never leaves her tricycle on the sidewalk, or one whose socks are arranged neatly in his drawer by color. Yes, that's discipline, but it's not what we believe parents' major goal should be.

Do your children respect the rights of others, or do they take what they want and impose their will on smaller children? Are they considerate of the feelings of others, or do they charge through life like a bull in a china shop, impervious to the consequences their actions might have on other people?

Of course, we cannot expect children to be more social than their mental limits allow them to be. Two-year-olds do play together, but we can only expect minimal cooperation and respect for each other's property or feelings. But as children grow, so do their social abilities, and knowing how to interact with people becomes a critical part of the person the child is becoming.

We can lecture our children until we are blue in the face about being polite, saying "please" and "thank you" at the right times; we can chastise them for sassing adults or for giving flippant answers to our questions; and we can insist that they remain silent while others are talking. But it will do little good if we don't practice what we preach. Children learn the most about their world from listening and watching, especially during the first seven years.

Above all else, parents are children's models for social relationships. What will our children learn from our behavior? What does our behavior teach them about friendship, respecting other people, how to treat members of the opposite sex, and how to behave toward people of authority?

It is very important for parents to model the interpersonal behavior they want their children to show. In fact, parents who control their children's behavior through harsh punishment and criticism often raise children who can't wait until they get bigger and stronger so that they can control someone, too, just like Mom and Dad do. Recent studies of school-yard bullies show that many children who use aggressive means to get what they want, have parents who use physical aggression to get what *they* want.

In contrast, parents who are firm yet considerate of their children's opinions and feelings are apt to have kids who can stand up for themselves with classmates, but who also can use compassion and understanding in dealing with others.

Parents should ask themselves, "How do I get my children to do what I think is right?" Do we threaten, ridicule, shame, or lose our tempers with them? Do we give them messages that they will lose our love if they don't behave the way we dictate? Do we tell them they must obey because we are in charge? Or because we pay their bills? The very same methods parents use on their children can be the ones older children, teachers, coaches, and other authority figures can use to get our children to do what *they* want—and their values and motivations may be *far* different from ours. For example:

• The peers who pressure your child: "If you don't use drugs, we won't be your friends anymore."

- The coach who bullies your son to play when he's injured: "I know your knee hurts, but the team needs you—don't be a baby."
- The high school teacher who imposes his personal beliefs on the students: "Religion is the opiate of the masses—not many intelligent people believe in God."
- The amorous boyfriend who is out with your teenage daughter: "I paid for your prom ticket, I bought you dinner, and I even rented a limo. Don't tell me you're turning into Miss Iceberg now!"

When we discipline preschool children, we are giving them lessons that they will carry with them beyond our home and beyond the preschool years. Although some techniques may produce desirable, short-term results, parents should also consider the long-term consequences. Are our techniques teaching children positive ways of controlling their *own* behavior (and the behavior of others) when Mom and Dad are not around? Or are our children learning to control others (and to be controlled *by* others) via coercion? Quick compliance has its benefits, but there may be drawbacks. Are the methods we use to make our children obey methods we want them to use on the playground? Are they the methods we want other people to use on our children to force them to comply to their wills? If the answer to either of these questions is "no," it's a signal that we should look to the long-term consequences of our disciplinary styles.

Informal Education: Children Sometimes Also Do What You Say

Some parents have the mistaken idea that at some critical time in each child's life, a parent is supposed to deliver a long lecture defining the rules they should follow in order to live as a civilized member of society. Unfortunately few parents are certain *when* that critical time is, *which* parent should deliver the lecture, and *what* precisely those rules are. It's probably just as well. Young children have little patience for long-winded lectures and are not apt to find much of interest in the rules of civilization. Yet there are ample opportunities each day for parents to provide their children with tidbits of wisdom, some of which may take hold.

To paraphrase an old adage, "If you throw enough stuff against the wall, something is bound to stick." The same is true about wisdom and children, but what sticks is more under *their* control that *yours*. The trick is to take every opportunity to tell them your ideas about the world. Facts can be learned everywhere, but parents have the important job of coloring those facts—emphasizing some of them, putting conditions on others, and absolutely rejecting others.

I have two preschool daughters and it's difficult to go anywhere, much less to get there on time. It's probably not such a big deal, but being on time has always been an important thing to me and I start getting uptight a few hours ahead of time. Instead of suffering in silence, I tell the kids about it. As I get them ready, I talk about how much I hate people being late for things. I tell them about a woman I used to work with who was never on time and how much trouble it caused at work. And I tell them how good I feel when I am early for something and have time to relax a little before it starts. They may not understand me totally, but they listen. It helps me release a little steam and it keeps them interested while we're getting dressed. And it helps them know that I'm not mad at them. I don't know how much sinks in, but now the *three* of us are everywhere *on time*.

On my son's third birthday he turned into a monster. He tore open his presents and refused to say "thank you" to anyone. He got upset because one of the other children had a red balloon and he wanted it. A few days later he started pointing out every toy in the store and told me to buy it for his "four birthday,"—not *asked*, he *told* me. I decided he needed to learn some lessons about giving.

My husband and I have sixteen nieces and nephews who live in other states and whom we try to keep in touch with. Up until Todd's third birthday, I did the birthday card shopping and gift selection on my way home from work or on Saturday when Todd stayed home with his father. I decided to start doing it with Todd along.

It was tough at first. He wanted everything we bought for

other kids. But soon he got caught up in the spirit of things and helped select gifts for Cousin Jimmy or Cousin Holly. He helped wrap and signed his own name on the card. He would point out the cousin on the pictures we keep on the front of the refrigerator and tell everyone whose birthday was coming up and what "he" had bought for them. It helped make his faraway cousins seem real to him. Sometimes now he will be watching cartoons and will point out some toy on a commercial and say, "Let's buy that for Mandy!"

Parents, Know Thyselves

Being a parent can be awfully confusing, especially if you are trying to do well, seeking advice, and looking for better ways to do things. We all know parents who spend more time reading books on parenthood than attending to their children. We know parents who can tell you all the latest child-rearing theories, but don't have time to listen to their children's jokes and stories. It's important to keep informed, but you still have to decide how to *act* as a parent.

There are no right and wrong answers to the following questions, but it's important for parents to know how *they* stand before conveying those ideas to their kids.

Meals—

Should everyone eat together as often as possible, or should some dinners be just Mom and Dad, after the kids are in bed? What table manners are important? Are some just for company or restaurants? Are there topics that shouldn't be discussed at the table? Should family members just wash up before a meal, or should they spruce up a little and show that family meals are important occasions?

When I became a non-custodial father of two preschoolers, I thought it would be easy—McDonalds on Friday night, Burger King on Saturday, and back to their mother's house on Sunday. Then I heard my sister tell someone that it's nice the kids have a "real family" at their mother's house. It made me think, and I decided that a father and two children can be a "real family," too. I plan meals for weekends and we eat off

> real dishes. I have introduced the kids to artichokes, aspara-
> gus, and hollandaise sauce. One night we had salad forks and
> laughed about trying to remember which fork to use. I tell
> them about my week and they tell me about theirs. I remember
> family meals with my folks, and I want them to remember
> their weekends with me as more than Happy Meals and shakes.

Bedtime—

Should evenings be family togetherness times or times for
family members to pursue their own interests? Do some family
members need more sleep than others? And how about Mom
and Dad? Does one thrive on evening hours and make a big
production out of bedtime stories, while the other enjoys early
morning walks or pre-breakfast card games? There's no "right
time" for family togetherness or household routines.

> Bedtime is a problem in our family. My husband works all
> day and then attends college classes four nights a week till ten
> o'clock. I work from eleven to six o'clock. Our three-year-old
> has gotten into the habit of staying up until almost midnight,
> and then sleeping until ten o'clock in the morning. He takes a
> two-hour nap at school, and sometimes another nap early in
> the evening. My mother thinks it's terrible for a child to stay
> up that late, but I don't know when he would see his father
> otherwise. He seems to be doing okay. It's just one of those
> compromises parents today have to make.

Possessions—

How do you feel? Do you share willingly with almost everyone, or do you like to keep your belongings to yourself?
Neither is right or wrong, just your way of doing things. Your
family rules should reflect your feelings about your possessions.

One thing you can teach your children about a disciplined
family life is that parents are individuals, with their own foi-
bles. Some moms rage at the sight of dirty socks on the floor,
while others reserve that reaction for sibling bickering. Some
dads expect the day to run around definite mealtimes, while
others see such routines as stifling after a long day of sticking
to schedules.

As parents, we have our own biases, fears, and expectations that we carry with us as we raise our children. What may work for one parent will not work for another. What one mother views as a problem requiring major disciplinary surgery requires nothing more than a Band-Aid for another. The little quirks and idiosyncrasies of a child that drive one father up the wall will be viewed as cute antics by another. How we perceive our children, what we consider to be problem behavior, and what we do that is apt to "work" in terms of discipline, will depend a large part on the people we are. There are no universal rights or wrongs—no rules of discipline that are guaranteed to work for all parents at all times.

Because of these differences, it is necessary for us to understand ourselves. Why is it that certain things our children do drive us up the wall, while other things that make our next-door neighbor crazy don't bother us much at all? Why is it that we seem to have the most problems with our children certain times of the day or certain days of the week? Are the problems our children's or are they partially of our making? And regardless of whose fault it is, are there things we can do to avoid or minimize them?

The Freedom of Parenthood

Few jobs offer as much freedom as that of being a parent. With few exceptions, the way we choose to discipline our children and run our families is left up to us. Some parents see this as permission to do whatever is easiest at the moment, knowing that it's nobody's business to criticize them. Other parents see this freedom as a way to finally get from life what they think they have been missing—respect, control, love, appreciation, admiration, etc. But the majority of us see this freedom as a great responsibility. We consider carefully the decisions we make about our children and our family, and after making the decisions, we often look back and wonder if we did the right thing. Sometimes we realize we were wrong, and we feel sorry. We lose sleep over problems with our kids, and we discuss them with our own parents and our friends. We read books and magazines about being parents, and we listen to all sorts of experts. But then we realize the decisions are up to us, as they should be. Because who knows our children better, and who cares as much about them?

Being a concerned parent starts off a chain reaction of a sort. As children grow, so do their parents. As we think about our own ideals and values, we improve as individuals. Our lives have more meaning, our outlook toward life changes, and our attitudes toward other people change. We understand our own parents better and we strengthen our marriages. All these things circle back and make us even better parents.

> I always thought of my mother as being too strict with me until I had children of my own and realized how difficult it must have been for her to raise three children by herself while keeping a full-time job.
>
> There is not much leeway when you are gone all day and have to *know* your kids are doing what you told them to after school. And since I was the oldest, she had to be the hardest on me.

This brings us back to the title of this chapter, "Parents as Models of Discipline." We have almost free reign with regard to how we treat our children, as *our* parents had with us. One of the most important things our children will learn from us is how to raise *their* children. We are the most influential models our children will ever have, and the lessons we teach today will reach far into the future, influencing generations yet unborn. Our jobs are important indeed, perhaps more so than most of us realize.

6. Know Your Child

A group of mothers was discussing the pros and cons of various disciplinary techniques and the strong and weak points of several books on discipline they had read recently. One mother, who had been quiet throughout the discussion, finally spoke.

"I'm really tired of these 'experts' telling us what to do, because I don't think there is one right answer. I've got three kids. Although I know that spanking is not good, and I really hate doing it, that's the only way I can handle my youngest. But I don't think I've *ever* spanked the other two. In fact, if I say a cross word to the oldest, she falls apart. But what works for the oldest girl isn't worth a hill of beans with her brother. I really don't have too many problems with these kids, but when I do, I've got to remember which one I'm dealing with, because they're all different, and try as I may, the same thing never works with all three of them."

Although this mother is exaggerating some, she is, we believe, speaking basic truth. Children are all different, and what is apt to work well with one child may not be successful with another. One important factor, of course, is a child's developmental level (see Chapter 4), which greatly affects the disciplinary landscape. But even at the same age there are differences among children, and these differences will greatly influence how easy or difficult it is raising disciplined children.

Getting to Know You

"These are our children, bone of our bone and flesh of our flesh. What's to know? We were there when they were born and have been with them ever since. Our children are extensions of us and we are responsible for shaping them into competent adults."

Yes, our children are *of* us, but they are far more than that. They are unique people themselves, with their own thoughts and feelings. It is all too easy to assume that we know our children well; who else could know them better? But it actually takes some work. Since they uttered their first cries, our children have been developing as individuals, and it is our job to get to know them.

Showing Respect

The key to getting to know your child is to have *respect* for the child as an individual. This isn't always easy. Because of our familiarity with our children, we often take them for granted. We are often too quick to dismiss as unimportant some little thing that is of great importance to a child. For example, when six-year-old Monica was distressed about her first pair of glasses, her father grew impatient.

"Look, Mommy wears glasses, Daddy wears glasses, and so does your friend Julie. They look good on you and you only have to wear them when you're reading. Besides, the doctor said you probably won't have to wear them at all in six months. So stop making such a big fuss. You're lucky you're not like your mother, who has to wear them all the time."

All this may be true, but it offers little solace for a six-year-old. Children's unhappiness should be acknowledged. They have a right to be unhappy, even if it's about something that seems foolish to an adult. A better response to Monica's distress about her eye glasses may have been first to acknowledge her unhappiness.

"You sound upset about this. Well, that's okay, but I think

you still look beautiful in them. Your mom wears them all the time, and I think she's beautiful, too.''

This won't eliminate the child's unhappiness, but it does tell her that her feelings aren't way out in left field. What's more, by acknowledging her feelings, the ''glasses episode'' is not apt to escalate into something bigger. When parents fail to respect children's feelings, children often become stubborn.

For example, Monica didn't let the ''glasses episode'' end when her father told her to. Rather, the glasses became a big deal and a major source of irritation for the family for several weeks. Monica whined about wearing her glasses daily, only to be told, ''Hush, we're tired of hearing you complain so much about these stupid glasses.'' She ''forgot'' to take them to school unless reminded and sometimes ''forgot'' to bring them home. Monica's distress spilled into other areas of family life. During the two weeks after Monica first got her glasses, she was sent to bed early three times for misbehavior at supper and engaged her father in several battles over watching TV, going to bed on schedule, and picking up her toys in the living room.

We do not mean to say that a few understanding words would have prevented all the problems that Monica and her parents experienced because of the glasses. But acknowledging Monica's distress and respecting her feelings, both initially and for the weeks that followed, would likely have reduced the magnitude and duration of her displeasure.

We don't mean that Monica's parents should have told her she didn't have to wear glasses. She had eye problems and glasses would help. It's her parents' responsibility to see that Monica gets the best care possible. Monica *does* need to comply with the doctor's instructions to wear the glasses, but she doesn't have to *like* it, and her parents should recognize this and respect her feelings.

When Should Respect Begin?

Many parents believe respect is something that is earned, so an infant, toddler, or even a three-year-old has probably not yet earned it. It's not that children deserve *disrespect*; it's just that the concept of showing respect to a small child seems foreign. What do they need respect for?

Well, as can probably be guessed by now, we disagree with

this argument. Respect is something that all people, including children and infants, deserve as human beings. But important questions remain: How do you show respect for a young child, and will it really make any difference?

Part of the answer to the first question ("How do you show respect to a young child?") is getting to know your child as a person and accepting his or her individuality. This means making certain allowances for some children that you don't make for others. It means anticipating things that may unnecessarily upset a child, even though they don't upset you or your other children. It means being sensitive to a child's feelings and permitting children to express their joys and displeasures without being unduly reprimanded. And it means learning when to insert yourself in your children's business and when to stand back, acknowledging that they do have "personal business" which may be none of yours.

> We have five children—all different. We never expected them to fit into our family. Our family grew to fit *them*. That's important, I think.

The issue of showing respect for children has been repeated throughout this book. When children are respected, when their requests are considered, and when their feelings acknowledged, they learn that parents are people who care about them and who can be depended upon. Children who are respected find it much easier to learn respect for others. When their privacy is respected, they are more apt to respect the privacy of others. When their possessions are respected, they are more apt to respect the possessions of others. And when their emotional ups and downs are respected, they are more apt to respect the feelings of others. All-in-all, it is much easier to instill respect for others in children who are shown respect themselves. And having respect for other people, their privacy, property, and emotions, is an important ingredient of a well-behaved and self-disciplined child.

Showing respect for one's children is not something that parents should "start" at some specified age. Respecting our children's individuality begins early and continues throughout a lifetime. It is the attitude that "the person I'm dealing with is important and has feelings and ideas of his or her own.''

Now, of course, we don't have to give serious consideration to all the ideas of a ten-month-old (even if we could understand them). But we *can* consider that child's feelings. We can recognize his or her frustrations. And we can treat that child differently than we might treat any other ten-month-old based on what we know about him or her. In other words, by recognizing our children's individuality, we develop a special relationship with them, one that is suited to the uniqueness of the parent/child pair (or trio). This signals to children that they are special, that they are loved, and, most important, that they are *known*.

This special relationship begins in infancy and is constantly modified over the course of childhood. What stays constant is the specialness that knowing our children affords us. And this knowledge will help us immensely in predicting what our children will like and dislike, what situations are good ones to avoid, and when to come down hard on a child for a particular misdeed and when to tread lightly.

> At times I found myself "dictating" to my son because I wanted him to make my schedule easier. As soon as I realized that he has a right to his choices, his moods, and his tastes, I was able to cooperate with his growth stages rather than lock horns with him. As the adult, I could foresee possible conflicts and avoid them.

Knowing your children's personalities, being sensitive to their wants and needs, and respecting their individuality, doesn't mean putting up with misbehavior. It's one thing to understand why a child may be behaving a certain way, but another to let it continue because, "That's just the way she is." Children, of course, need to know limits and must be "put in their place" at times. But when behavior problems do occur, parents should be critical of the undesirable behavior, not of the child. As one mother of two told us, "Don't ever condemn your children for any reason. Praise them instead. Treat them with love and care." Children, even misbehaving children, deserve to be treated with respect.

Love and respect are not the same as permissiveness and

lack of structure. Parents can be loving, respectful of their children's rights, and accepting of their personalities, and still expect them to toe the line when it comes to household rules and regulations. Respecting children doesn't mean letting them walk all over you. It *does* mean listening, considering all their points of view and their feelings, and accepting the fact that they may be unhappy about some decisions you make for them. They don't have to like what parents decide, but parents should acknowledge their children's rights to be unhappy. Respect facilitates self-discipline, but only when parents remember that *they* are the mature ones in the relationship, and the burden for raising a disciplined child falls on *them*, not the child.

My advice to other parents can be summed up in three words: patience, love, assertiveness. Talk at the child's level; messages and information must be clear and correct. Despite anger over X, Y, or Z behavior, let them know they are special and loved, even though you won't tolerate certain behaviors.

Accept the child's personality—listen to him. Physical contact (affection, love) is very healing in the middle of a battle for power. Try to see things through the child's eyes—his joy of learning.

Knowing and respecting your child *does* give you more information to use to make your decisions about child rearing and discipline. It gives you the opportunity to view things from your child's perspective. This perspective should be based on their developmental abilities, shared by all children that age, and also based on their individual personalities, unique to each. But this information should not be all you use to make your decisions. You must, of course, weigh them with what you, as an intelligent, caring, and loving parent, think is right. In a way, taking your children's perspective on things when you make decisions results in more work for you. But there are substantial benefits in terms of greater communication, smoother parent/child relations, and the development of self-discipline.

Try to put yourself in his or her place. Make your choices based on your wisdom as an adult and his or her world as a child.

Children may not know textbook psychology, but they are masters of it in practice. Try to see the situation from the child's point of view, and you can usually then understand their behavior and find a constructive way to deal with it.

Individual Children, Individual Solutions

Because children have unique personalities, we can't have one style of parent/child interaction and expect that it will "work" equally well for all children. We can strive to be fair with each of our children, to be loving and supportive, but being "fair," "loving," and "supportive" will have different meanings for different children.

"My son is very sensitive. It is impossible to reprimand him. He seems to feel so much hurt when I discipline him that I sometimes refrain, which means that he gets away with doing things that he should not do. He wants to do everything for himself and many times he has lots of accidents."

This isn't an unusual situation for a preschool child. Her son likes doing things for himself. He likes having control over things and likes to feel useful. But, as any young child, he feels more competent than he really is, and his mother wants to keep him safe and keep the messes he makes to a minimum. These are all common problems, but the solution for this mother may have to be different from that of other parents because of her son's sensitivity. She writes further that, "beating, talking, screaming never work with my son. He gets more resentful and unhappy."

What then, might work with this sensitive child? This mother reports that all is not lost. For example, she *has* had some success stopping his undesired behavior by promising him that he can help with the housework. Remember, children like to feel useful, and the major problem this woman reported with her son was "he wants to do everything by himself." The promise that he can do some "grown-up" work apparently is enough to distract him from whatever else it is that his mother doesn't want him doing at the moment.

Speaking of distractions, another successful solution this mother reported for handling her son's misbehavior was taking him *out* of the house for walks. Basically when the going gets tough, the smart get going. Removing any child from an undesirable activity is a good way of controlling behavior (see our discussion of this in Chapter 3). And for a child whose behavior may be more difficult to deal with as a result of a scolding than the misbehavior itself, removal from the offending situation (in this case, from the entire house) may sometimes be a parent's best bet.

At times, one must just accept the slightly atypical reactions of children to certain situations. For example, a mother told us about her son, "always [reacting to minor changes] by dive-bombing to the floor and screaming. I would just hold him, hug him, and kiss him until he calmed down. I accepted the fact that it takes him longer to adjust, but if given time and space he warms up."

It would likely do little good to punish this child for reaction to change. Chances are this mother and her husband may have tried punishment for such seemingly overreactions and found that it did not work. However, change is inevitable. What the parents can do in this case is keep change for this child to a minimum, anticipate problems that a necessary change will likely bring about, and accept their child's reactions with warmth and love. As his mother said, if given time and space (and we would add love and respect), he adjusts.

Individuality and Siblings

The issue of respect and recognizing children's individuality seems to be especially important when there are two siblings close in age. Sibling rivalry is real, although the extent to which two siblings get along together varies widely from family to family. But one important thought to keep in mind when dealing with two under seven is that this is an age when children are developing their personalities and their sense of self. Recognizing our children's developing personalities can go a long way to soothing conflicts among siblings in a family and, as well, will foster closer parent/child ties.

> I explain to them that I love them both but there will be times when one child will need more attention than the other, and I hope they understand. I tell them that my love grows for them each day so I'll always have enough to go around.

An important issue reflected in the statements of the woman above, is that siblings often need different treatment. They may need expressions of love, different amounts of attention at various times, and appreciation of their individuality. This sometimes conflicts with what parents try to do in order to be "fair" to their children. For many parents, "fair" means "equal."

"If seven-year-old Julie goes to a birthday party for a classmate, four-year-old Benjamin should get something special, too."

"If Marjorie gets a new dress for school, or a present from a friend, or a ride in Uncle Joe's truck, little brother must receive something comparable."

When my daughter was born, I knew very little about being a parent, but I learned fast. By the time my son was born two years later, I felt very confident. But he was altogether different than his sister. I thought it must be because he was a boy, so I learned different ways with him.

When my third child was expected, five years later, I felt confident again—I knew about girls and I knew about boys, how could I miss? Well, my third was a boy all right, but totally different from his brother *and* his sister.

I finally realized that I could have a dozen kids and they would all be different from each other. One method of parenting just doesn't work with more than one kid. You have to learn all over each time.

One thing implicit in what we have been saying so far in this chapter is that, because children are individuals, we should be cautious in comparing them with one another.

I always treat my two children (one is a boy, age seven, and one a girl, age four,) as two separate human beings. I try not to compare them in front of one another. My love for them is different in its own way, but equal amounts go to both of them.

The point we'd like to emphasize again is that from the earliest weeks on, children develop self-discipline best in an atmosphere of love and respect. Two tips from a veteran mother of two for parents still grappling with children under seven were: (1) respect your child's humanity, and (2) remember that "a child loves and trusts before he thinks and acts." This homily, she told us, was posted on her refrigerator door for years, and it serves as a good reminder of where the roots of self-discipline can be found.

Temperamental Differences

Parents often speak of infants of four or five months of age as finally having a "personality." By this, they typically mean that the babies now have distinct likes and dislikes and particular ways of responding to situations and people. In many respects these observations are on target. Beginning sometime between the second and fourth months of life, infants begin to respond to people differently than they respond to inanimate objects, and, in general, begin to behave "socially."

Rather than speaking of "personality" in young infants, a better term may be *temperament*. Basically temperament refers to a characteristic or trait that is apparent very early in development. Researchers have found that temperamental differences often are quite stable. In other words, children who show certain temperamental qualities in their first months of life will manifest the same qualities through childhood. The inference that many psychologists have drawn from this is that children's temperaments likely have their origin in biology.

Temperamental differences have important implications for discipline. Knowing that your children react to certain events in particular ways, and are likely to maintain these patterns through childhood can be of great help in anticipating how children will react in certain situations and what the best course of action should be given a particular problem.

One word of caution before we start discussing temperamental differences in children. It is easy to describe a child as "highly active" or "inactive," or showing "mild intensity of reaction" or "low intensity of reaction." Many children, in fact, do fall into these extreme groups. However, most children are not extreme with respect to any specific treatment. That is, when temperament is viewed as a continuum, with extremes at either end, most children will fall somewhere in the middle, perhaps closer to one extreme than the other. But some children do fall at the extremes, and these children more frequently pose disciplinary problems. Regardless of whether or not this applies to your child, an appreciation for the type and range of potential reactions will help you develop a better appreciation of your child as an individual, which, in turn, can only be helpful.

Differences in Children's Temperaments

Activity Level

Perhaps one of the most common statements parents make about a child whom they have trouble with, is that he or she is "hyperactive." This is usually somewhat of an exaggeration, but many children who keep their parents on their toes do have a high-activity level. They squirm when being dressed, bounce in their cribs, crawl after the family cat, and forget to learn how to walk but move straight to running. Now being "active" in-and-of-itself does not make for a "difficult child" (we will discuss "difficult children" below), but it can make for an exhausting one.

> I should have known Becky would be a handful early on. It seems she was practicing walking two months before she was born. As early as I can remember, she wiggled and twisted when I changed her diapers, and by the time she was crawling she was never happy being in one place for very long. She was a climber as a toddler. I wouldn't say she was *hyperactive*, just a handful. We had to do an extra special job of childproofing the house and had explicit rules about what could be climbed on and what could not. She made us think a bit more about things than we would have otherwise. When she was three, we enrolled her in a kiddy gymnastic course two days a week and saw to it that she got a lot of running around time outside. It sometimes tired her out and slowed her down later in the evening.

We think it's obvious how children with a high-activity level may cause some discipline problems. They need clearly stated rules. They need to be constantly reminded of these rules, and to take the consequences of their actions when they forget the rules. For example, one technique some parents have used with a high-activity preschooler at mealtimes, is that once a child leaves the table, dinner is over; the leftovers are either thrown away, eaten by someone else at the table who is still hungry, or given to the dog. This, of course, is usually agreeable to an antsy four-year-old who wants to get down from the table and play. But when he returns ten minutes later to snatch another bite, his meal is gone and a replacement is not offered. This is the natural consequence of leaving the table to do other things.

It may seem that a more "disciplined" solution would be to insist that the child stay at the table until everyone is finished eating. For a school-age child, we agree. Meals are made for family togetherness, and, if possible, children of all ages should be part of "family dinner." But forcing a highly active preschooler to "stay put" until everyone else is finished may be more trouble than it's worth, changing the pleasant family dinner ritual into a nightly battle that nobody wins. Children should not be allowed to disrupt meals regularly. Sometimes settling for brief times of togetherness, and then letting children roam to their rooms or to the backyard, may be the best alternative, especially when eating rules (such as "once you leave the table, so does your food") are known by all and enforced.

Although we don't think that anyone would be surprised with some of the discipline problems a highly active child may present, we believe that many would not expect problems from a relatively inactive child, yet in fact, a "slow-to-move" child can cause his or her parents problems, too.

A low-active infant is easy to dress, doesn't splash excessively in the bath, and will play quietly in a playpen or crib. But when a low-active child starts school and has to be somewhere at a specified time, parents often complain that it takes forever (or so it seems) to get him to brush his teeth, comb his hair, and get dressed. Selecting which clothes to wear can be time-consuming, and once dressed, low-active children seem to dawdle eating breakfast. When parents are in a rush (which seems to be the plight of many parents these days), a slow-moving child can be as much of a problem as a child who runs full speed ahead.

Low-active children benefit from schedules and preparations. For example, selecting clothes for children the night before can eliminate a time-consuming step in the morning when time is of the essence. If children just can't seem to eat breakfast "fast" without gagging, a quick (but nutritious) meal that can be eaten in the car may be a good option. As with the high-active child, a little planning can go a long way in promoting family harmony.

Rhythmicity

Rhythmicity refers to children's rhythms—the extent to which they "fall" into schedules. Some babies seem to be born with regular habits. During the first couple of months, they are ready to eat every four hours. By five or six months, Mom and Dad can predict when nap time and bedtime will be. And although the specific schedules of these children change over the years, their general predictability does not.

An irregular child is just the opposite. Parents find it difficult to predict when naps will come and how much these babies will eat at each feeding. As toddlers, naps are brief and bowel movements are at different times each day, often making toilet training difficult. As these children approach school age, they may loudly resist scheduled bedtimes, and on some nights find it difficult to fall asleep. They may be ravenous at dinner time one evening and pick at their food the next.

Obviously, these two portraits are somewhat exaggerated. Even the most regular of kids gets off schedule now and then. They get extra hungry or tired from physical exercise, and the excitement of a new toy or a promised trip to the beach can modify what is usually an "on-schedule" bedtime. But, in general, regular children present far fewer discipline problems as a result of their temperament than do irregular children, and this should not be surprising.

One of the things we have written about frequently in this book is the importance of predictability and control. For the most part, we've talked about *children's* perceptions of being in control or being able to predict what will happen to them. However, predictability and control are equally important for parents. How can you structure your home and your schedules to raise a disciplined child if you can't predict when the child will be hungry, tired, grouchy, or happy? How can you organize your lives around activities that "fit" the child's schedule if the child's biological clock seems to have a loose mainspring?

Well, these are all good questions and there are no single answers to them. Having an irregular child may necessitate more flexibility in family schedules, bending the rules a little bit. For example, instead of setting a bedtime at a certain hour every night, you may wish to set a range of times when your child must turn out the light. For instance, if eight o'clock is the time you think five-year-olds should be in bed, you may require that your daughter has her pajamas on and teeth brushed by seven forty-five. Then, there may be story time, followed by a period when the child is allowed to play quietly in her room. However, by nine o'clock it's lights out.

One caution is called for here. We have heard many parents use the excuse that they have an irregular or "difficult child" as a reason for not developing household schedules. Schedules are more difficult to implement with irregular children, but this is no reason to do without them. In fact, a family schedule may be especially important for irregular children. Even if these young children cannot easily establish schedules for themselves, at least they have models for what a scheduled life is like and some structure in which to develop their own less-than-regular schedules. Very regular children will schedule themselves. It is irregular children who need a lot of outside assistance.

Although most parents would love to be blessed with a highly regular child, these children's rigid rhythms can be the source of some conflict, too. For example, parents who wish to be flexible concerning dinnertime ("We don't know how long Daddy will be working tonight, so we'll just wait to eat until he gets home"), may find that their regular children don't share their flexible view of mealtimes. Likewise, parents who are accustomed to running to the grocery store or mall when the need arises, may find their young wards thrown by the interruption.

Such problems, of course, are not difficult to overcome. They merely require some scheduling which takes into consideration the regular disposition of their children. In some cases, a very regular child can be the impetus for parents to develop a disciplined life-style for themselves.

And a Few More

Differences in activity level and rhythmicity can be easily recognized by parents and have some obvious consequences for child rearing and discipline. However, there are other temperaments that also show up early, are relatively stable over time, and affect the parent/child interaction, and thus discipline.

The temperament that reflects children's tendency to seek new experiences is referred to as *approach–withdrawal*. Some children are true adventurers; they love to try new things. New foods, smells, toys, and people fascinate them. Spending the night at Grandma's house for the first time causes no special problems, and they are not shy in approaching other children and joining the playground fun. Although they may sometimes be a little wary, they are curious about the new people and things that surround them.

Other children are just the opposite. They reject anything new, at least initially. They spit out the new cereal, will not sleep in strange beds, avoid unfamiliar children in the neighborhood or playground, and may hide behind their mothers when entering day care or school. They like the familiar and shy away from the novel.

Although there are differences in children's tendencies to approach or withdraw from new experiences, some children are able to adapt to new people, places, and things more readily than others. Some children seem to adjust to anything. These children adjust to baby-sitters and day-care easily, and as infants they adjust to baths and new foods. It's not that they don't sometimes respond unfavorably to change; they don't let change throw them off balance for too long.

At the other extreme are children who seemingly take forever to adjust. As infants, their separation distress when left with a baby-sitter, persists longer, as does their distress as toddlers in the day-care center or nursery school. Changing their diets may become difficult, and they may spend their preschool years requesting peanut butter and jelly sandwiches for lunch every day. Haircuts may be unpleasant experiences well into the preschool years. All other things being equal, highly adaptive children are easier to get along with and to discipline than those who adapt slowly.

Another temperamental difference that we are certain most parents will recognize concerns *intensity of reaction*. Some children howl when they cry and guffaw when they laugh. Others show their emotions with whimpers and smiles. During play with other children, the intense child may laugh loudly, yell at playmates (both in anger and in joy), and cry when a toy is taken away.

Children with mild temperaments, in contrast, are more apt to play quietly. They are not apt to initiate wrestling matches, and if hit by another child, are not apt to strike back. When given a verbal reprimand, they lower their eyes and remain silent.

There is nothing "wrong" with either temperament. However, the child who reacts intensely is certainly more apt to be noticed, and this can have both positive consequences for discipline (you know what the child is up to) and negative (you know what the child is up to and you don't like it).

One final temperamental difference that greatly affects how we interact with our children is their *quality of mood*. Some children are happy most of the time. As infants, they coo at their parents and smack their lips after tasting new food. They laugh when playing peek-a-boo, and generally have smiles for most people they encounter. Other children are generally unhappy, ready to complain at the drop of a hat. As babies, they fuss after nursing, cry when being diapered, removed from the tub, or given food they don't like. During the preschool years, they get upset and often cry at mild frustrations. They may object to being dressed or to having to do anything that they do not want to do.

It is obviously much easier (and more pleasant) interacting with a child who has a generally positive mood than one whose mood is typically negative. However, as parents we really don't have much of a choice. Understanding that our moody, negative child is not attacking us personally, can help us to respond positively.

It is likely that your children do not fall at the extremes of any of these temperaments, but they probably lean strongly toward one or the other for many of the dispositions we've discussed here. By knowing your children's temperaments and understanding their individual differences you can shape the environment to best suit their needs and those of the family. By knowing what to expect of your children, problem situations can be anticipated and avoided, or at least minimized.

The Challenging Child

Many parents quickly label their children "difficult" if they drive them crazy and don't respond to attempts to keep them in line. In truth, most children are not that difficult, although many children have some combination or degree of those "difficult" qualities that make parenting more challenging.

Drs. Stella Chess, Alexander Thomas, and Herbert Birch, who studied temperaments from infancy to adulthood, have estimated that about seven to ten percent of all infants are "difficult." These infants do not differ from the norm in terms of intelligence, health, or physical development. There seems to be nothing that their parents did or didn't do to make them difficult. Their parents didn't love them too little or too much. These babies were just born that way.

"Difficult" children can be tough to deal with and parents may need to be particularly sensitive to their not-so-easy children. Because of their more irregular and nonadaptive ways, these children may need more patient and consistent care. As we mentioned above, children who are irregular may need the imposition of schedules more so than children who are easy to schedule. This, of course, is more easily said than done. It is not easy being loving and positive to a child who howls at the slightest provocation and who "gives back" less in the way of social reinforcements (for example, fewer smiles and coos and eye-to-eye contact) than other, "easier" children. In fact, it is easy for parents to become openly resentful of "difficult" infants, with this resentment affecting the parent/child relationship for many years.

The resentment is understandable. Parents need to be conscious of their feelings toward their difficult children, and when possible, rise above them. Feelings of resentment can often turn into feelings of guilt. The guilt parents sometimes feel over their less-than-positive attitudes about their children can get in the way of being good parents. They begin to blame themselves for their children's apparent unhappiness and often uncontrollable behavior. These feelings are not warranted. Most difficult children were born that way, and if parents are going to bring some discipline to their children's lives—as they must, they can do it best without the additional burden of guilt.

Perhaps labeling children "difficult" does them a disservice. We may feel better about our temperamental children, and they in turn feel better about themselves, if we viewed them instead as presenting us with *challenges*. "Challenge" has a much more positive connotation for us than does "difficult," and viewing our hard-to-control and hard-to-please offspring as "challenging children," may give us a slightly different perspective on child rearing and on our children.

Bringing Discipline to the "Challenging" Child

One way of dealing with challenging children that rarely has positive results involves consistent and harsh punishment; spanking and severely limiting their behavior by restricting them to their rooms for long hours seems not to work. Such constant use of punishment will have only short-term benefits. Resentment on the part of the child and frustration on the part of the adult are bound to ensue, and parents and children are apt to enter an escalating cycle of misbehavior and punishment that will be difficult to escape from.

The other extreme but equally ineffective, is to just give in and let challenging children rule the roost. Since the children won't conform to adult schedules and fuss so loudly and persistently when they don't get their way, why fight it? But the relative peace that this "surrendering" alternative brings is not worth the cost. A child who experiences little discipline early in life is not going to develop it on his or her own at a later time. The problems such a child causes in infancy and early childhood will be minor compared to the problems he or she will face in the years to come.

The alternative is perseverance. It may not be easy, but challenging children can be scheduled and do eventually adapt to most situations. For example, the toddler who squirms and cries while having his hair cut will not behave any better the next time if mother has gotten frustrated and pulled him out of the chair before his bangs are trimmed. It may be an embarrassing chore to hold the child still while the barber cuts his hair, but making the child complete the task once started is, in most cases, the best course for the future.

Letting challenging children take the natural consequences of their behavior can often be effective. If children refuse to eat, why force them? With plenty of food in the refrigerator and a scheduled mealtime, the fussy and complaining eater will eventually learn to eat what is provided. In other words, the same techniques and principles that work for ordinary children will also work for challenging children. But the job is harder. What parents with challenging children need is patience, consistency, perseverance, and an early start. It is much easier to start training children beginning in infancy than to *retrain* them later on. However, even retraining is possible. It just requires even more patience, consistency, and love.

Truth in Labeling

We must add a few words of caution here before leaving the topic of temperaments. Not all temperaments of children reflect permanent personality characteristics that will be with a child throughout his or her lifetime. Many traits do change. In fact, even the previous list reflects traits and temperaments that are only *relatively* stable, meaning that not all high-activity or challenging infants and toddlers will show the same patterns of behavior by the time they enter school.

As we hope we have made clear, knowing that many of these temperaments do have a basis in biology can help in dealing with children, in knowing what situations are apt to be easy or difficult for them, and what ways will be best to handle problem situations. One problem with believing too firmly that all personality or behavioral characteristics have their basis in genetics is that we very early label a child as "hyperactive" or "difficult" or "aggressive," and expect, whether we like the outcome or not, children to live up to these labels.

And adults are not the only ones who expect children to live up to these labels. Children expect it of themselves. Children learn their identities in large part through others' perceptions of them. If significant people in their lives believe them to be intelligent, or considerate, or industrious, children are apt to see themselves that way. Likewise, if people who are important to them view them as stupid, inconsiderate, and lazy, children can easily come to claim these qualities as their own.

This doesn't mean that we can overcome all the effects of

biology simply by "believing" in a child's abilities, or by convincing a child to "believe" certain things about him- or herself. But beliefs we hold about ourselves do affect our behavior and our outlook on life, and this goes for young children, too.

> From the earliest I can remember, my cousin Joy was a "difficult child," very active and always in trouble. In comparison, her brother Dick was well behaved, an "easy child," who never caused his parents any problems. When they were just babies, I remember people saying how "good" Dickie was and how "difficult" Joy was. Maybe it was true, because as teenagers, Joy gave my aunt and uncle ulcers, but things were pretty good with Dick, I guess. But I sometimes wonder, looking back, whether Joy ever had much of a chance. Everybody knew she was going to be trouble, and sure enough, she lived up to it.

No one can say what would have happened to Joy if she hadn't been labeled so early. She was a difficult baby and preschooler, and it is not surprising that she grew up to be a difficult adolescent. Yet being aware of temperamental differences that may be genetic in nature, and giving a child a label that equates with "trouble," are two different things. The first can help you with prediction and control and with raising a self-disciplined child. The second may also help with predictability, but will not likely lead to control and discipline, including the fostering of self-discipline.

Listen to Your Child

As children grow older, they become more complex. Four- or five-year-olds' problems cannot be soothed as simply as when they were four- or five-months old. But as children's lives become more complex, so does their ability to communicate to us. As parents, we must take advantage of our children's increased communicative skills. To do this, we must practice *listening*.

> By the time Nicky was three, I was an expert at translating his baby talk and interpreting what he *meant* to say. One day on the way to nursery school, he said, "Mommy my waffles are coming out!"
>
> My first reaction was to think, "Now what could he mean by *that*?" Before I could reflect for long, he threw up all over the front seat of the car.
>
> This isn't a very pleasant story, but it taught me that I don't always have to look for hidden meanings in my children's messages.

Many parents find it difficult to truly listen to their young children. We are so busy telling them what to do that listening becomes an afterthought. On top of it all, the younger the child, the less he or she is apt to have to say. A parent can go crazy talking only to a two-year-old day in and day out. We can quickly tune out their words, and respond only with grunts and nods as our own thoughts drift to more interesting topics.

But even young children have much to say to us. This is especially true when problems arise. As parents, we are quick to respond to the outward manifestation of a problem and less likely to look for what lies behind it. Perhaps our child is trying to tell us something via his misdeed.

For example, seven-year-old Josh refused to do his homework. His father set him at the kitchen table and told him, "You've been dawdling long enough. You have half an hour to finish that homework. If it's not done by then, you're getting a spanking and going straight to bed."

A half hour later, the homework was barely begun. Dad was in a bit of a quandary, for this was very unlike Josh. But Dad knew the importance of not threatening something that he was not willing to carry out, so Josh got a spanking and went to bed.

As it turned out, this was the end of a horrid day for Josh. He was wrongly punished for throwing chalk in class, and made to stay indoors during recess. He goofed up his reading in front of the whole class. Josh was upset with his teacher, angry that his teacher had made him read such a difficult part of the book. But how does a seven-year-old express his anger at an authority figure? She's the teacher, after all. Surely his parents would take her side.

Josh's petulance about his homework was the sign of a problem his parents could not see directly. But Josh's atypical behavior that evening should have been a signal to his parents. A few kinds words of support for Josh from Mom or Dad may have been all he needed. The point is, Josh was not sophisticated enough to tell his parents his problems, but his behavior was a sign that something out of the ordinary was happening. Listening must sometimes be done by means other than the ears.

Listening to what is bothering my son and trying to find a way for him to do what he wants in a constructive way helps a lot. Sometimes I offer him a choice. My advice to other parents is to try and be patient and to see the issue from the child's point of view. Usually you can find a working solution.

---

7. Independence

What is the goal of parenthood? What, as parents, do we really want to achieve? On many days, most of us would probably settle for getting our children to behave—to do what we tell them to do when we tell them to do it. But on days when we're particularly farsighted, we confess to a more lofty goal: to raise competent, independent adults.

Fostering independence is likely the most important and difficult task of raising a child. As they develop and become increasingly capable, they *demand* greater freedom. Yet, what children want and believe they are capable of, frequently lies far beyond their actual competencies. Our jobs as parents is to monitor our children's development, increasing the number of situations in which we allow them to act independently. We must always be cautious, never letting children venture farther than is safe. Yet we must be careful not to keep them tied too tightly to our apron strings, lest their natural quest for independence be thwarted and we handicap them. Fostering independence in children is a complex balancing act. Parents must gradually let go while still insuring the safety of their children.

Many of the discipline problems parents report are simply battles in the age-old war of independence. How do we deal with a child who protests at the restrictions we place upon him?

What do we do when children insist upon getting into things we explicitly told them to stay out of? How do we loosen the reins without losing control of the horses?

These are legitimate issues, but keep in mind that independence fosters self-discipline. When children are respected and respect others, their independence is often less of a threat to us. When children can control their tempers and delay their gratifications, we are not as hesitant to grant the freedom they ask for. When we have confidence in our children and they in us, the process of independence can go smoothly and can be rewarding. Keep in mind that parents and children are actually on the same side in this "war of independence."

> When problems crop up, I've learned to try to assess what is important, in the long range, and what is not. My attitude has changed from "what I want my child to do now," to "what I want him to understand about himself and his life."

Independence and Self-Discipline

As we've discussed in earlier chapters, being self-disciplined means having control over important parts of one's life. Children who are taken seriously, who are allowed to make some of their own decisions, and who are consulted on issues that directly affect them, are less apt to "lose control." Of course, children should not be consulted for every decision and should not be permitted to make decisions that require more experience and mental prowess than they have. A self-disciplined child is one who is allowed to develop his or her competencies gradually. Give a child too much freedom too soon, and self-discipline is lost. Limit a child too much, and different but equally serious problems arise.

Developing a self-disciplined child involves fostering independence. As we saw in Chapter 4 on developmental differences, children become increasingly skilled as they grow. No surprise here, but what is important is that parents develop along with their children. As children grow, parents need to assess their competencies and "give in" to their demands when they are reasonable and to say "no" when they are not.

I Want to Do It Myself!

Perhaps the most common expression of independence is children professing that they don't need any help, that they can do it themselves. When they are right, this makes a parent's job easier. But when children are wrong, overestimating their abilities, parents sometimes have to undo what their children have done before doing the job right. This can often cause problems.

We discussed some of these problems in Chapter 2, under the heading "Making Children Feel Useful." Children often want to help Mom or Dad, believing that they are capable of making a real contribution. As we mentioned, parents can permit children to help by structuring tasks for them that are, indeed, within their abilities and that have a small chance of disaster (either for the child or for the project) should they fail.

> When Janet was little, she always wanted to help me wash the car. I thought it would be easy, and that I'd just let her hold the hose or something, and she'd do exactly what I told her to. Instead I found out that she had ideas of her own. She wanted to fill the bucket, put soap on the car, spray the car, and wipe it down. It just wasn't what I had expected. After a while, however, we got into a routine. I'd let her "wash" the car first and then it would be my turn. When it was my turn, she could help, but only when I said so. This way, we got the car "doubly clean," she got to help, and I got to have some time with my daughter.

> Julie (age four) liked to help in the yard when I would plant flowers or prune or weed. I really did not want her walking around my precious flower beds, but I did like the way she wanted to plant flowers "just like Mommy." So we made her own flower bed out back. We bought her some plants and let her dig up the ground and plant them herself. Now when I go out to work on my flowers, Julie works on hers. She weeds and I even let her trim them with my supervision. She tends to overwater a bit, and has trampled several pansies, but she enjoys it and feels very proud of her garden.

Many of the things that children want to do for themselves, however, don't involve helping an adult, but rather involve not letting an adult help them. Getting dressed is a good example. Many children, beginning quite early, don't like the "help" that Mom or Dad gives them getting dressed or undressed. They want to pick out their own clothes and they want to put them on themselves. Getting undressed usually isn't much of a problem (although most of us have seen two- or three-year-olds with their shirts covering their faces, but with their heads still stuck in the shirt). Problems often arise over dressing.

The problems are frequently ones of time. Yes, children can dress themselves, but they put their pants on backward, step into the wrong holes in their underwear, and put their shoes on the wrong feet. Moreover, they often take an inordinate amount of time doing it. It's usually easier for parents to dress their young children than to have them dress themselves.

But here again parents can stack the deck in their favor, giving their children some sense of independence without relinquishing all control. One recent boon to children's dressing is Velcro fasteners on shoes. No longer must laces be tied or buckles buckled; all that one needs to know is how to stretch one piece of cloth onto another—a feat well within the competencies of most two-year-olds.

But how do you get children to put shoes on the right feet? One solution one mother passed along to us is to use "kissing fish." Painted on the insides of her daughter's sneakers were two small fish. When the shoes were on the proper feet and placed together, the two fish would be "kissing." How do you make sure kids get their shirts and pants on right? One resourceful grandmother embroidered little flowers inside the front of her granddaughter's blouses and pants. With a little imagination and not much work, resourceful parents can come up with a long list of timesaving techniques that will benefit both their children's developing independence and their own patience.

Compromise is also possible. Some insistent young children really don't have the ability to dress themselves. What parents can do is get the children half dressed, feet into pant legs, shirt over head, and let the children finish the rest themselves.

When children do dress themselves, they sometimes do a

poor job of it, at least from a parent's point of view. One five-year-old we knew showed up at a picnic with his T-shirt on backwards. Someone mentioned this to his mother who replied, "Yes, I know. He likes the design on the back so much he wanted to wear it on the front so he could see it. So I let him."

And why not? It's a small deviance from convention, and it gives the child control over his appearance and a sense of independence and uniqueness. Not bad qualities to foster in a child.

Out of Harm's Way

Most of the time we're happy with our child's progress and can overcome the inconvenience involved. There are other times, however, when children want to do something by themselves that we fear may cause them some harm. How do we protect our children from danger and still give them the room to develop into independent people?

One simple rule of thumb is to start slowly. Let them take the lead, allowing them to do things that are a bit more challenging than you think they're capable of when you can be there to watch and help out.

One example of "independence fostering" we observed recently occurred on a not-too-crowded subway car. A woman pushed a baby carriage onto the train and started to move to one of the seats. Out of the carriage jumped her diapered son, whom we guessed to be about fifteen months old. Without words, he grunted a few times and made his way to the pole in the center of the car where several adults were standing. His mother followed as her son placed two hands on the pole and stood at attention as the train rolled on. His mother first held his waist, but her hands were quickly shooed away by her son, confident that he could "do it himself." Yet, Mother hovered above, keeping her hands right behind him (but not on him) just in case something might go wrong. When the train came to a jerky stop, she quickly placed a hand between the boy and the pole, avoiding a bump on the nose for her son.

All in all it was a good solution. The youngster concentrated intently on holding the pole and keeping his balance, and the mother permitted him this independence, while staying close at hand. And even if she had not been so fast, the consequences of a sudden stop would not have been disastrous, merely a bit uncomfortable for the toddler.

It does not require much imagination to guess what might have ensued had the mother forbidden her toddler to stand at the pole, or, at the other extreme, had she let him wander off and fend for himself. We have witnessed many children in public places at either extreme, and the results are usually unpleasant—not only for the observers but also for the parents. The right combination of freedom and restraint fosters independence in young children, keeps them out of harm's way, and keeps the peace for everyone.

When to step in and when to sit back is a complex issue, but again, such decisions must be based on the developmental level of the child. As we discussed in Chapter 3 on "Tools of Discipline," it's often advisable to stand back, letting children take the natural consequences of their actions. Taking the consequences of what one does is a form of responsibility. Parents must be careful that the consequences are not too severe, and should not let children do things just "to teach them a lesson." A cat who sits on a hot stove once, may never sit on a hot stove again, but she will also never sit on a cold one. Parents must monitor their children's decisions, and, whenever possible, let them experience the natural outcomes of their actions. Children can be warned ahead of time that the course they are taking may not be wise and alternatives may be suggested; but, generally, saying, "I told you so," is neither necessary nor warranted.

Parents must never step back too far from their young children. We must let then take control of their lives, but at a safe distance. And we must be there to comfort them when their plans backfire.

I Want to Be Alone

Being independent means sometimes seeking privacy. This often bothers parents, who see the young child as an extension of themselves and want to be around to watch whatever he or she does. But children during the later preschool years not only want to do things on their own, they frequently want to do things alone, in private. This, too, is a part of the independence process.

Privacy and the Bathroom

Usually the first requests for privacy concern aspects of life that adults conduct in private, most notably toileting. Children, who months before would walk into a living room full of company and request that their pants be pulled down so that they can go potty, may decide that not only can they go to the bathroom themselves, but that they'd like the door closed. Baths similarly are times when children of kindergarten age often request privacy. They want to have the tub filled for them (or perhaps to fill it themselves) and then bathe themselves. This usually means playing games in the tub as well, but this, too, many children want to do in private.

There is nothing remarkable about this transition. Bathroom behavior is something that is done privately in our culture, and children strive to be like adults. Yet, children must develop the hygiene habits that permit them the luxury of this privacy, and this is something parents often worry about.

When children seem too young for such requests to be honored, what can one do? For one thing, bathrooms can be made safe by placing poisons and sharp instruments such as razors out of reach. If a child does prove too young for the privilege of bathroom privacy, at least no physical harm will come of it.

It's also a good idea to have a way of getting into a locked bathroom. Many young children have managed to lock a bathroom door shut but find themselves unable to unlock it, causing panic on the part of a parent, and sometimes on the part of the children.

Privacy and the Bedroom

Preschoolers not only want privacy in the bathroom, but often request it in their bedrooms. Many parents become immediately suspicious when a preschooler's door is closed or a sign is posted on the bedroom door of a seven-year-old stating "KEEP OUT."

Well, much mischief has been hatched behind closed doors, but there can be much innocence behind such doors as well. For instance:

One afternoon our seven-year-old daughter and her six-year-old friend posted a "NO ADULTS" sign on her bedroom door after the two had mysteriously disappeared from the commotion of the living room. When one adult discretely knocked on the door, he was greeted by a yell of "Don't come in! We'll be out in a little while." Having no clue as to what was going on and being suspicious that the girls were up to no good, it was tempting to throw open the door and assert the privileges of the "Man of the House," but instead, he respected the privacy of his daughter and walked back to the living room. Fifteen minutes later the two girls left the room and announced that they had a surprise for us—a puppet show, complete with hand puppets made of socks and a storyline not too distant from Cinderella.

The point of this story is that the adults involved didn't have any clue as to what was going on in that room. The girls usually played with the door open, and had never before refused an adult admittance. Yet, they were given their privacy. The story had a happy ending (Cinderella married the prince), and the adults involved learned to be less suspicious.

A Right to Be Alone

Children, like adults, sometimes just need to be alone. Although the thinking of young children is drastically different from that of adults, their emotions are more like ours. They too get tired, and sad, and mad, and even depressed. They don't have the intellectual skills to deal with these emotions that we do, and many of the things that affect adults will not affect young children. Nevertheless, complicated emotions do spring up in young children and they sometimes experience the need for solitude; and parents need to respect that need without demanding a justification every time a child wants to be alone.

Respecting a child's right to privacy also teaches children something about the rights of others. It is difficult for adults to insist that young children knock on their parents' bedroom door before entering or leave their older siblings alone when asked, if their own requests for privacy are not granted. Respect begets respect, and if we expect our children to respect our privacy, we must start by respecting theirs.

When to Say "Yes" and When to Say "No"

How do we foster independence in our children without letting them run all over us? How much freedom is too much? When do we as parents lay down the rules and expect our kids to comply, no questions asked, and when is negotiation reasonable?

There are no easy answers to these questions. Each child is different, and each parent has something different in mind about what is best. It is important to take our children's requests for increased independence seriously. If they are to become self-disciplined, they must learn respect for other people, and they do this best by being respected themselves. But being self-disciplined does not mean doing anything one wants to do, especially if you're only four years old. It means realizing, among other things, that there are limits on one's behavior. Growing up, however, means testing and pushing those limits. And being a parent means expecting this and knowing when to stick to your guns and when to give in.

An intellectually easy response is to say "no" to children's demands under all but the most extreme conditions. Although simple, this approach often will result in a series of battles that intensify over time. It does not foster independence and self-discipline, nor a comfortable parent/child relationship. Likewise, granting all but the most outrageous of a child's request is also easy, but potentially disastrous. Children who learn no limits to their behavior come to believe that if they want it, they should have it.

It's So Easy to Say "No"

It's little wonder that the word "no" is one of the first words toddlers learn to say; it's probably the word they hear most often. And with good reason. Toddlers have little sense of right or wrong, safe or dangerous, sturdy or fragile. Parents must use the word "no" frequently and consistently so that young children realize that they are venturing into territory they must retreat from or engaging in some action from which they must desist.

But parents often extend their constant use of this little word, using it every time children make a request that isn't expected or is at all out of the ordinary. Such constant use of "no" usually has one of three consequences. The first two occur when parents back up their "no's" with action. Children ask, parents say no, and that's that. So, children quickly learn not to ask for things out of the usual.

Saying "No" and the Dependent Child

For some children, this leads to passivity and dependence. They quietly wait to be told what they can do or have, never complaining, and causing no problems. They initiate very little in the way of independent thinking or acting.

Although such children may be well behaved, they are not disciplined. Being disciplined means having self-control. It means being able to decide for oneself what is proper in a certain situation and behaving accordingly. And it means making such decisions independent of being explicitly told to. Children who hear nothing but "no" and who quietly learn to abide by their parents' decisions do not learn to be independent. Instead, they learn to be dependent upon authority and to undervalue their own decision-making abilities and to depend upon the decisions of others whom they judge to be smarter or stronger. They suffer from low self-esteem and low self-respect, and may grow into people who are potential victims for any authority figure who professes to know what is best.

Saying "No" and the Rebellious Child

Other children who hear "no" constantly and have it enforced consistently learn that it makes little sense asking to do something or to have something that they haven't already received clearance for. But these children don't necessarily take no for an answer. They sometimes avoid the nay-saying parent and run directly to their other parent. They make their requests quietly, out of earshot of Mother, for example, hoping that Dad will say "yes" without consulting Mom. These children will sometimes manipulate their parents, asking one parent a question and phrasing it differently to the other. Or they wait until one parent is out of the house before asking the other. When things blow up and discrepancies are recognized, Mother and Father are often more angry with one another than with the child. Moreover, it works much of the time.

We had a very difficult time with Timmy when he was little. He always came to me when he wanted anything. His father's attitude was that if you had to ask, you probably didn't need it or shouldn't do it. That's how his father was with him. Timmy wasn't really afraid of him or anything, and they would sometimes play together when Mark (his father) suggested it, but generally, Timmy always came running to me. I guess I was too easy with him. He'd ask for a snack an hour before supper and I'd give it to him, or he'd whine until I'd let him do what he wanted. I just got tired after a while and started getting mad at Timmy for bugging me all the time. And then Mark would get upset with me for giving in to him. I just didn't know what to do. Mark is a good father, and I couldn't figure out why Timmy always avoided him.

The family described above has a discipline problem. The problem, however was not only with the son. The parents do not have a mutual policy of discipline. The father does seem to have some clear-cut rules, the most obvious of which is to reject most suggestions his son makes. The mother, on the other hand, never says that she disagrees with her husband, only that because of his persistent use of "no," she is left having to make the real decisions. She seems to realize that some requests are reasonable and should be granted, but it is obvious that she feels uncomfortable about doing so.

This woman likely feels very insecure about her child-rearing abilities. She wants to do what is best for her son, but she's not sure what that is, and she is probably apprehensive about her husband's reactions. The result is an uncomfortable household in which a child is getting mixed messages about what is acceptable behavior and what is not.

However, a united front is no guarantee that saying "no" consistently will have positive effects. Realizing that neither parent is likely to give in, some children circumvent parental authority altogether. They learn that if they want something done, they should do it themselves. After all, sometimes their parents don't seem to care so long as they aren't consulted. "Mom wouldn't have let me run around in the sprinklers if I asked, but when I did it, she only yelled once, and then said I might as well run around some more, since I couldn't get any wetter.''

Such children learn to make their own decisions, which does foster independence; however, they also learn, at an early age, to be deceptive. They want to get their way without having to ask for it and, they hope, without getting found out. They become proficient at rearranging cookies on the plate so that Mom won't know that one has been taken. Children will lie (often not very convincingly), even about things of little consequence, believing that their parents really don't want to hear the truth.

Granted, such situations are the exceptions. But even when children are relatively honest, they learn to dodge the constant "no," and the result is poor parent/child communication. This may seem insignificant in very young children, but it sets the stage for poor communication in the future, when children will have many serious and important matters to talk with their parents about.

Saying "No" and Not Meaning It

Most parents who say "no" reflexively don't really mean it. It's seldom based on a well-thought-out philosophy, such as the opinion that children are too young to know what is good for them (making any request they make automatically "wrong"). Most parents just say "no" because it's easy. Chances are, they believe their children are going to ask to do more things or to receive more goodies than they should, and "no" is going to be right more often than not.

This "say no" strategy usually prompts children to fuss for what they want. If they don't fuss too much, it just goes to show they couldn't have really wanted it that much in the first place and that the "no" was justified. In contrast, if they fuss a lot, it must be important to them, and, in these cases, parents sometimes give in. But they rarely give in easily or willingly. More often than not, they give in only after repeated skirmishes with their children, which leave bad feelings all around. One place where the ill effects of "Saying 'no' and not meaning it" is most frequently seen (and heard) is in grocery stores.

One of my biggest problems with my children has always been in stores, especially grocery stores. When they were little, they'd sit in the basket and ask for things. When they were bigger, they'd walk behind me and pick things off the shelves and put them in the basket. I'd try to be firm with them. I'd tell them no, they couldn't have any candy or whatever, but they'd fuss or just ask for something else. It was more than once they had made a scene in the grocery store, and I had had everyone staring at me. I felt for sure they were thinking what a terrible mother I was and what bratty kids I had. I felt like it was blackmail. Sometimes I'd make deals with them, like if they'd stop fussing, I'd buy them the candy or toy they wanted. But when they started fussing again and I took back the candy, they'd scream (especially my oldest boy, not so much my younger one). Then I was back where I started. It usually wasn't that bad, but every time it would happen, which it did to some extent about half the time I'd go shopping with them, I'd end up mad and they'd end up sobbing. It certainly wasn't worth it to me, and I'm surprised it was worth it to them because I'd be mad at them for hours afterward. I finally stopped taking them to the store whenever I could get someone to watch them for me. I guess that's the coward's way out, but it's made shopping a lot easier for me.

This mom's solution to the problem really wasn't all that bad. Granted, it may not have made her children more disciplined, but it did avoid situations where problems repeatedly occur, and at least minimized the conflict in her life. As we've mentioned repeatedly, avoiding situations where problems are most apt to occur is a perfectly legitimate recourse. There is much more to raising a disciplined child, of course, than merely avoiding problems but steering clear of such circumstances only makes good sense.

Solving the problem is quite another matter. The problem is one with a history, and it won't disappear overnight either. The root of the problems lies in the mother's giving in to her children's demands after having "firmly" told them "no." This isn't to say that once a decision is made it should never be changed. The actual source of the problem here is that this mother said "no" automatically in grocery stores, setting herself up for conflict.

The way to change this behavior in her children is to change her behavior toward them. First of all, she should actually consider each child's request before replying. Sometimes she may decide, for example, that having a pack of gum isn't so bad. Or she may compromise; sugar-free gum would be all right. Or gum is out, but maybe a bag of pretzels would be okay.

When problems have long histories, the parent may wish to anticipate things a bit. Before going to the grocery store, she may have a brief talk with her children. She has about half an hour of shopping to do. She realizes that it isn't a lot of fun, but she also realizes that there may be some things at the store that the children would like. Then, have them suggest some of the things they might like to buy. At this time she can approve or disapprove of the list the children will make, and can remind them of the approved list when they enter the store.

This doesn't mean that all will go well. The younger the child, the more difficult it is to come up with a complete list of wants, and even older children are bound to come up with items that they "just gotta have." Consider these new items. If they seem reasonable, and don't put you over your budget, say "yes." Don't feel obliged to say "yes" to all new requests, of course, and don't change your mind about the things you determined ahead of time they were *not* going to have. Stick to your guns.

The main thing to keep in mind is that you don't want to go on automatic pilot. Consider their requests, try to anticipate problems, and have a strategy for handling them. At first, all this may seem more trouble than bratty kids. But the more you practice, the easier it gets.

Another thing to keep in mind about supermarkets is that children are going to make requests of their parents, and sometimes those requests are reasonable. For example, researchers who followed women in a grocery store with their four-year-olds observed that children made an average of one request every two minutes. And, on the average, their mothers went along with their children's requests about half of the time. This shouldn't be surprising. Children in the United States are raised to be consumers. Consumerism is pushed in magazines, billboards, and especially on television. In fact, in the study mentioned above, the more commercial TV children watched, the more requests they made in the grocery store.

If children's requests are treated seriously, children will learn that their opinions are worth something and that they are being taken seriously. This will lead not only to better behavior in the supermarket, but also to a more independent and self-disciplined child.

Saying "Yes" All the Time

Fewer parents fall into this category. In fact, none of the parents we talked to considered this a problem (or solution). But parents who say "yes" to all but the most ridiculous of their young children's demands do exist, and the consequences for their children's discipline, independence, and development in general are not good.

What type of parent says "yes" all the time? Well, some children may only make reasonable requests such as permission to clean their rooms or to purchase nutritious, low-cost snacks at the grocery store. The probability of this behavior is slightly less than that of finding life on the moon. Young children are just not that mature. Although they become increasingly competent and capable as they get older, the thought of a three- or four-year-old, or even a six- or seven-year-old always making "reasonable" requests of his or her parent is absurd.

It's more likely the case that parents who say "yes" to nearly all of their children's requests are parents who are insecure about their children's love. They are uncertain of themselves, of what is right and wrong for their children, and they don't want to risk their children's affections by spoiling their fun. Often, such parents will do anything to avoid a scene, and granting any nonlife-threatening request may appear to be an easy solution.

Often, such yes-sayers will believe (or at least profess to believe) that saying "no" stifles children's creativity and curiosity. At the extreme they are likely right. But what does saying "yes" unconditionally do? For one thing it results in children who never know how to take "no" for an answer when one is given to them, often by someone other than their parents. Children of "yes-sayers" are often more of a discipline problem to other people than to the parents themselves. Many of these parents have adopted a "laid-back" life-style and have little in their house that their young children cannot play with, eat, jump off of, or climb onto. They are raising their children to be "free," and, as far as they are concerned, they have no discipline problem.

Well, "free" they may be, but they are not developing self-discipline. As we have stressed continually, discipline involves developing an effective way of interacting with the world. The boundaries of children's worlds quickly expand beyond the walls of their homes, and children who learn no self-restraint, who learn no limits to their behavior, and who do not learn to accommodate to the needs and requirements of others, are in for a tough time. Parents who raise "free" children are not doing them any favors.

Another side effect of yes-saying is children who are frequently insecure. They are essentially raising themselves and lack the parental examples and supervision needed to feel confident in their own place in the world. Confidence and security are vital components of independence, and in turn, to developing self-discipline. And feelings of security develop directly as a result of parent/child interaction, beginning in the earliest stages of life. This point brings us to the final section in this chapter on independence, and that is the issue of parent/child attachment and how secure attachment, commencing in infancy, can have positive consequences for independence and self-discipline throughout one's life.

Fostering Independence— The Development of Attachment

When should parents start fostering independence in their children? The answer here is simple: When children start making moves toward greater independence. This then leads us to the question of, "When do children start seeking independence?" This answer is simple also: in infancy.

The quest for independence starts early. It is clearly noticeable when babies begin to crawl, and from that point on, the rate at which children reach out to explore their world, leaving Mom and Dad behind, increases rapidly. How do we begin to develop a positive relationship with our infants that will foster self-discipline, independence, and, it is hoped, peace and harmony in the household?

In Chapter 4 we referred to parent/child *attachment*. Attachment refers to the close, emotional bond between parent and child. The process of attachment begins, of course, in infancy, but continues throughout life. And the reason we are discussing it here, is because how independent and socially competent children are as preschoolers, is related to how securely attached they were as infants.

Recent research has shown that the way parents interact with their babies and toddlers produces differences in the *quality* of attachment. Mothers (and fathers, too) who are sensitive to their infants' social and physical signals and who respond to their infants, have infants who are *securely* attached. These are babies and toddlers who feel sufficiently secure to leave their mothers' sides and explore their environment. Parents who are less sensitive to their infants' signals and who do not respond to their babies are more apt to have babies who are *insecurely* attached. Insecurely attached infants are less apt to leave their parents' sides to explore novel surroundings. Securely attached infants are more independent than insecurely attached infants, and they display greater cognitive and social competence well into the early school years.

Sensitivity to Infant's Signals

Many psychologists believe the attachment process begins in the minutes and hours after birth. But attachment is not so simple a phenomenon as physical contact between mother and child at the time of birth. If it were, adopted children would never be securely attached, nor would most of the people reading this book, whose mothers were almost certainly under general anaesthesia during delivery! What is crucial, however, is the *interaction* between parent and baby that begins shortly after birth and continues throughout infancy and childhood. It is in this early interaction that the foundation for independence can be found.

Parents (mothers *and* fathers) who raise securely attached children are described as being *sensitive to their infants' signals of physical and social needs*. What exactly does this mean, and how does it relate to independence? Sensitivity to signals basically means being able to *read* a child. When parents are in tune with what their children are trying to tell them, it is easier for them to deal with their young wards and makes it easier in turn for their children to deal with them. This is no simple trick, for infants and toddlers are notably inept at making their needs known. Yet many mothers and fathers are able to read their young children easily, and the result is a smoother running relationship with positive implications for the future.

Why is this so? In fact, one could get the picture of a sensitive mother jumping up every thirty seconds, catering to the demands of her ten-month-old son every time he grunts or gestures. This hardly seems the road to a disciplined life-style. In fact, such a mother could more properly be described as *oversensitive*, unable to distinguish those things that demand immediate attention from those that do not and between those things that her child can do for himself and those he cannot. A sensitive parent not only can read his or her infant's signals, but can distinguish between a major crisis and a minor frustration and between a task that is truly beyond the child's capability and one that is not. What such sensitivity provides is a sense of predictability and control, especially for the baby, but also for the mom and dad.

Just as adults, babies have wants, needs, and moods. They've had enough of this carriage and want to get out (maybe to be carried, maybe to sit on the floor). They are hungry and would like the strained carrots now, not the vanilla pudding. They are tired and need (although maybe not want) a nap. They are curious about the new person who entered the room (or possibly wary), or interested in a toy, or frightened by an unfamiliar cat, or excited about the sound of ringing church bells. For each need and emotion, children give signals. How do parents respond to them? Do they comfort a child who is frightened, share the joy of a child who is excited, and put to bed a child who is tired? Or do they misinterpret the signals, sometime getting the messages right and sometimes not? Or worse yet, do they miss or ignore most of the signals, responding to the child only after he causes a commotion?

Attachment and Independence

Common sense would dictate that parents who are attentive, sensitive, and warm have more loving children. But would such children necessarily be more disciplined? And particu-

larly, why should they be more independent? In fact, the opposite might seem logical. Isn't it likely that the child with the
more sensitive mother may develop a *too close* attachment,
resulting in a child who is tied to his mother's apron strings
and, although possibly well behaved, far from independent?

Yes, this is possible, but only likely when the mother is what
has been referred to as *oversensitive*, unable (or unwilling) to
distinguish those things that children can do for themselves
from those things that they cannot.

Oversensitive parents can cause as many problems as under-
sensitive parents. For instance, one mother related to us the
problems she was having with her six-year-old son. "He
clings, is demanding, refuses to stay with a baby-sitter, and is
altogether too dependent on me." A closer look at the mother/
child relationship indicated that the mother is as dependent on
the child as the child is on the mother. At birth the child was
sickly and his mother became protective in nursing him to
health. By eight months, the child was physically well. However, the mother did not cease her constant vigilance, and the
two became inseparable. The child was two years old before he
would stay alone with anyone other than his mother (including
his father), and the mutual mother/son dependence continued
through the preschool years.

There is no easy solution. Sensitivity must be coupled with
discretion, with parents recognizing that it is not reasonable or
beneficial for them to do everything for their children. Part of
being sensitive is knowing what children can (and should) be
able (and allowed) to do for themselves.

As this last scenario indicates, it is possible to be overly
sensitive to a child's wants and needs, although it is not likely
that a sensitive parent will raise a dependent child. The reason
has to do with control. Babies whose parents respond to them
appropriately (that is, who recognize what baby is "talking"
about, and behave accordingly), develop a sense of predictability and control. They learn that "what I do makes a difference." They come to think of themselves as important
people in the world, people whose actions have consequences.
As we've mentioned repeatedly, children who feel they are in
control of important aspects of their lives are less apt to act out
of control.

Infants who have warm, loving parents and who have de-

veloped a sense of control over their own lives, feel secure.
They perceive themselves as competent individuals, but also
have learned that when the going gets tough, Mom or Dad will
recognize their distress and pitch in to help. They feel secure
both with respect to their own influence on the world and with
respect to their mom and dad, who in their all-powerful and
all-knowing ways can be depended upon. These secure infants
and toddlers feel confident enough to leave mother's side, comfortable in the fact that they can always beat a hasty retreat
back to home base.

What about infants whose parents are not so sensitive? Well,
they, too, become attached to Mom and Dad, and they, too,
believe that these adults are all-powerful. But they don't have
the security of the other infants, and as a result, feel less
confident of their own abilities and are less apt to explore their
environment. These children also love Mom and Dad (we're
not talking about abusive or neglectful parents here). Many,
however, are somewhat distrustful, afraid to let Mom or Dad
out of their sight in a new situation, not knowing exactly what
will happen.

Early Attachment, Later Self-discipline

Attachment, as it has been studied by psychologists, is usually measured during infancy and toddlerhood, typically between the ages of twelve and eighteen months. As we mentioned in Chapter 4, the typical way of assessing attachment is
by placing mother and child in a room, and having mother
leave for a brief period of time, which upsets the child. The
quality of attachment is indicated by how the child responds
upon mother's return. Is he easily soothed, returning to explore
his surroundings (possibly even interacting with an unfamiliar
adult who later enters the room), or does he avoid his mother
or, more likely, cling to her, refusing to leave her side to
explore the unfamiliar room? The first pattern, of course, char-
acterizes a securely attached child, whereas the latter describes
an insecurely attached child.

Research by psychologists at the Universities of Minnesota
and Virginia, among others, has indicated that a child who is
classified as securely attached at twelve months is likely to be
securely attached at eighteen months. Similar stability has

been found for insecurely attached toddlers. However, research also indicates that this stability of attachment over time reflects the consistency of parents' behavior. Parents who read their infant's social and physical signals well at twelve months, are likely to be equally sensitive and consistent at eighteen months. Should the behavior of the parents change drastically over a six-month period, it would not be surprising to find a change in children's attachment. In fact, one research study reported considerable change in attachment classification over six months for a group of children from highly stressed families. The instability in the lives of these children (for example, unemployment or parental separation) resulted in unstable attachment over this brief period. Some children who were securely attached at twelve months were insecurely attached at eighteen months, and some who were insecurely attached at twelve months were securely attached six months later.

What is important here is the notion that secure attachment is not something you get once and "keep." It is constantly developing. But parents who are sensitive early in their children's lives are likely to maintain the pattern as their children grow. The demands are different. Parents of a three-year-old no longer need to be sensitive to facial expressions that signal a wet diaper or grunts of hunger. They now need to be sensitive to needs that are more complex—feelings of injustice a child might perceive, or jealousy, or intellectual challenge. Unlike school-age children, preschoolers often do not have the vocabulary to tell parents exactly what they want. Parents must be sensitive to new signals and respond to their children accordingly.

But what's the payoff? How does all this sensitivity make a child independent, and particularly self-disciplined? Well, as we mentioned before, secure children feel comfortable leaving Mom and Dad's side to explore their surroundings, although they frequently look back. These are children who, as they grow, learn to trust both themselves and their parents, and to make their own decisions. These are not children who reject their parents, but rather ones who can leave their parents and make frequent visits back home for consultations.

Researchers have confirmed some of the later benefits of secure attachment by following groups of children from infancy into the preschool years. For example, children who were securely attached at eighteen months tended to be better problem solvers at ages four and five than those who had been classified as insecurely attached. They were more resourceful in facing a problem, more persistent—sticking with a difficult task longer—and more curious. Importantly, they were also described as having more self-control. They were less apt to have temper tantrums and more apt to exert some control over their own behavior.

We believe this greater self-control is a direct result of parents' continuous sensitivity to their children. Parents who give their children some sense of predictability and control have children who become more independent and feel competent to tackle complex problems. They also develop a sense of self-control, a necessary ingredient to self-discipline.

We do not mean to say, however, that how parents treat their children during infancy *causes* them to be more self-disciplined in childhood. Infancy is only a starting place. The sensitivity parents show their infants needs to be continued throughout childhood, modified as the needs and abilities of children change. It is never too late to develop sensitivity and secure parent/child attachment.

8. Discipline in "Nontraditional Families"

We didn't really think anything was unusual about a recent birthday party we attended until we showed the pictures to a friend and started explaining who the guests were. First, there was Nicky, the two-year-old guest of honor, and his parents, Debra and Richard. Then the grandparents—Debra's mother and stepfather, Debra's father, Richard's mother and father, and Richard's grandmother (who had been a widow for fifteen years and recently remarried) and Richard's new stepgrandfather. Then there was Marilyn—who is Richard's ex-wife—and her new husband, Mike. Marilyn and Mike were there because of Lisa, Marilyn's daughter by her first marriage to Richard. Lisa was also half-sister to Nicky, the guest of honor. Standing next to Lisa was Timothy—Mike's son by his first marriage to someone we don't know. Holly was there also, a cute seven-year-old, who is technically Nicky's aunt—his grandmother's daughter by her second marriage—who prefers to be called Nicky's cousin. Everyone had a wonderful time and didn't think anything was strange until Cecilia and Andy, friends of Nicky's mom, arrived and said in all seriousness—"Oh, we feel so out of place, we didn't realize this was a *family* party!"

Traditional Families Are in the Minority

Over the last generation, the structure of the American family has changed considerably. Approximately half of all marriages now end in divorce, and nearly one of every two children will come from what once were called, "broken homes." Nearly as many will be members of stepfamilies. And children who grow up in homes with both parents will likely have mothers who work outside the home. The days of old-fashioned nuclear families, with breadwinner dad and housewife mom, are gone.

Most of the practices we've discussed about raising disciplined children hold true in any type of household. But special discipline problems do arise in many of the "modern-family arrangements," and most of us are rightfully confused concerning what it is we're supposed to do.

What Makes a Stable Family?

We believe that a solid family structure is vital to discipline, but that this is by no means confined to the mother/father-biological children unit. Nor does it require that the family unit remain unchanged. A stable home provides its members a basic sense of security and attachment, a feeling of being valuable and useful to each other, assistance and encouragement to grow intellectually and emotionally, and assurance of shared goals for the future.

This may seem a tall order, especially when a child's mother and father do not live together. But a stable family environment can be instilled even if "family" is defined as just Dad and his weekend daughter, or working Mom and her preschool son.

One of the things that makes a family stable, and makes discipline easier, is predictability. Families who make it a habit to have routines and traditions, such as Sunday dinner with cloth napkins, Saturday afternoon at the park, or Wednesday evening at the local pizza parlor, provide structure for children. As we've emphasized repeatedly, structure in the form of schedules and predictability play a big role in fostering discipline. Both adults and children know what to expect and when. This is important in any household, but it may be especially important in single-parent families, where time, and often energy, is short.

Divorced Parents and Discipline

Raising a disciplined child is difficult enough when two parents are working cooperatively. It becomes even tougher when the bulk of the responsibility falls on the shoulders of a single parent. Ideally there should be no such thing as single parents. Divorce marks the end of the marital relationship, not the parental one. But practicality requires the parents to interact one at a time with the children, so at best, the result of divorce is two parents interacting one at a time with the children. This can be a positive step if the parents were unhappy and distracted before the divorce and now have a chance to become focused, loving people again.

In theory, there should not be a great deal of difference in raising a disciplined child in a one-parent versus a two-parent household. The same rules apply: consistency, fostering independence, establishing and keeping to schedules, showing respect for children. However, theory breaks down when the realities of being responsible for a child (or two or three), a job, and a household are foisted upon one person, usually the mother. There is often just too much work to do, too many things to keep in mind, and too little patience left at the end of the day to deal effectively with discipline problems.

One vital effort that divorced parents can make is to attempt to get along with their ex-spouses. Although this is often easier said then done, when it can be achieved, it will result in a better adjusted child, which, from our view, is a major characteristic of a self-disciplined child.

Divorced and separated parents should try to cooperate with each other for many reasons. First, it is much easier on the children. It's no fun being in the middle of a battleground, and it's no fun listening to the two most important people in the world criticize each other.

Getting along with an ex-spouse benefits the children in an indirect way, also. Until a divorced person gets over the marriage *and* the divorce, and feels happy and loving, he or she will not be the effective parent children need. Many divorced people spend too many years mourning their lost marriages,

and even more spend too many years fighting and refighting the
battles of their divorce.

There are several situations that make family discipline difficult when parents have separate households. Often parents
aren't aware that these situations exist, and children are too
young to analyze the problems and tell them. If you are a
divorced or separated parent, make sure your children aren't
trapped in one of these situations.

Children as Battlefields

The whole point of divorce and separation is to termi-
nate a relationship that is not working. Parents sometimes
dump all their hostility and rage on the other through their
last link—the children. The other parent is left with the
choice of either letting this happen, fighting back, or walking
away.

Children learn respect for other people from their parents.
Self-discipline requires that children have respect for themselves and for the rights and property of others. Parents who
constantly belittle an ex-spouse are providing a model for their
children, one which shapes not only how they perceive the
other parent, but also how they perceive other people in general. Raising a disciplined child means serving as a model for
respectful and disciplined behavior. A parent's behavior toward an ex-spouse is especially salient to children because of
the importance of that person. This should give parents reason
to re-evaluate how they interact with their "ex" for the sake of
their children.

Children as Messengers

Divorced kids hate taking messages back and forth between
parents. On the surface this seems like a handy way to
communicate—after all, the parents are no longer married and
the kids are traveling back and forth. It's easier to send messages and not have to worry about getting in touch with each
other. It's also more pleasant than to call and discuss the information with the other parent. But kids feel like the prover-
bial messenger who gets "shot" when the news is bad.

> Our seven-year-old nephew told us that he hated bringing the child-support check when he came home from his dad's house to his mom's. He said his dad would "make awful faces" when he wrote the check and looked angry when he gave it to him. Then he said his mother would take it from him and "make awful faces" when she looked at it, and then look angry the rest of the evening. Since it was money for *his* support, he always thought it was somehow his fault. And he was always afraid he would lose the check and *really* cause problems.

Children feel secure when they know the grown-ups in the family are making plans and taking care of business for them. Even though parents don't live together and aren't married to each other, they can show their children that there are two adults on their side to provide for their needs, protect them, and help them make their way through the sometimes confusing world.

Mom's Rules Versus Dad's Rules

This is one of the most-discussed problems of two-household children. We think this issue is made into a bigger deal than it deserves to be and often serves as a smoke screen hiding bigger issues that *should* be carefully considered.

In the first place, if two people were married to each other long enough to be parents together, their household rules will probably be similar. Secondly, as most children who have grandparents can tell you, it is very easy to operate with one set of rules at home and another set of rules at Grandma's house. It's called "discrimination training" in the rat lab, and little furry creatures with much less intelligence than your children are taught to perform flawlessly under complex rule systems.

Different rule systems *can* become a problem for kids if parents try to enforce their own rules in the other parent's house. Here are some examples:

You must say a prayer before *every* meal.
You must *always* wash your hair at night before you go to bed, not in the morning.

You must call Grandma Jones every Sunday, no matter where
you are.

Homework is to be done right after school every day before
you play outside.

You must go to bed at eight o'clock on school nights.

You may stay up as late as you want on weekends.

You are not allowed to watch aggressive TV shows.

Sometimes major differences do exist in parents' rules, and
often those are sensitive issues because they were problems in
the marriage also. Many of these revolve around religious and
ethnic differences. The important thing to remember is that
these would be problems even if the parents had never divorced, so don't be surprised about them now.

• Which religion to practice? This requires some creative
thinking. If the religions are closely related, children are perfectly capable of practicing both. The issues that separate many
denominations are of little interest to children, and most devout
people agree that some religion is better than none.

If the religions are more diverse, parents can handle it as
they would in a married family—they agree on one for the
child to "belong" to and to identify with, but the child is able
to attend the other parent's services as a visitor. Or the other
parent attends the child's services as a visitor.

Parents who are seriously concerned about this will probably
find that their clergy has experience counseling with parents in
this very situation.

• What to eat? This may not be a frequent problem, but it is
a big one when it occurs. It seems that some adults accompany
their divorce with a new philosophy of food—like becoming a
vegetarian or eating only organic food. And to some people,
eating a balanced diet with no junk food is a radical idea. Many
a child has been sent to the other parent's home with a food list,
nutrition book, or even a grocery bag filled with strange-looking
items. As you can guess, the results can be very unpleasant.

Parents who want to change their children's diet habits and
are truly concerned about their children's health should be able
to approach their ex-spouse directly in a tactful way, perhaps
asking him or her to read a magazine article, and letting them
know what they think, thus opening the door to a possible
solution.

• What language to speak? This is a new one also, but many parents (divorced or not) are bilingual and disagree when (or if) their child should be exposed to the second language. For that matter, many disagree on which should be the first language and which should be the second. This problem is usually accompanied by a lot of opinions from grandparents and other family members. Sometimes keeping peace in the family and keeping children in touch with their grandparents is more important than the language they speak. Be sure you aren't condemning part of your child's ethnic identity while arguing your viewpoint. If an outside opinion would be helpful, ask around at your child's school for someone who has studied language development in children.

Children Not Knowing What the Rules Are

In a family with married parents, rules are discussed openly and everyone usually knows what is going on. When children live in two households, parents sometimes assume that the other parent is making the rules and setting the schedules for the children, when in fact, they are not. This usually leads to parents who complain that their spouse "spoils" the kids and they are hopelessly undisciplined. Parents need to create and enforce their own rules in their own homes, regardless of those in the other parent's home. Even if you feel that the rules at your spouse's house are fine for your house, too, kids still need to know in no uncertain terms what the rules are.

One child I know, who has lived in two households for quite a few years, told me that he thought his father was angry with him for eating so much at his house. His father always seemed upset with him at mealtime and he had once heard his father complain to someone about how high his child support payments were. The boy made a conscious attempt to eat less and less until the father finally confronted him about his eating habits. What came out was that the father was upset about the boy's poor table manners and was angry at the boy's mother for not teaching him better. When the father realized the problem his "hidden anger" had caused, he began instructing his son in the etiquette he expected at dinner and the boy quickly complied—relieved that it was something so minor.

New Family Members/Old Family Members

When it comes to raising a disciplined child, single parents can use all the help they can get, and children of divorce can use all the loving family members *they* can get, also.

When my husband and I split up, his mother called me and said that even though she was no longer my mother-in-law, she still wanted to be my children's grandmother. She promised to do anything she could to help me through the divorce, except turn against her son. She baby-sat while I went for job interviews and helped me find a good day-care center for the kids. It was extremely awkward at first, but she has really helped me adjust to being a single parent. When my ex-husband and I disagree about something, she talks to both of us and we usually work things out. My friends think it is great—it's the first time they have ever heard of someone getting rid of a husband and keeping the mother-in-law.

When my son was five, his aunt and uncle separated and got a divorce. It was no surprise to anyone, but it really upset my son. He started talking about moving to a new, bigger house where everyone could come and live together, including Aunt Mary and Uncle Ted. Mary (my ex-sister-in-law) had moved into a new apartment, so I called and asked if my son and I could come over and bring a housewarming gift. I don't think she liked the idea, but I insisted. When we got there, I told her that my son missed her and that if it was all right with her, we'd like to visit from time to time. Once she realized I wasn't there to cause problems, she warmed up. I really liked Mary when she was my sister-in-law, and I don't know why my son and I should have to give her up just because she couldn't get along with Ted.

Suggestions for Relatives of Divorced Couples

People who have divorce in the family and still want to keep good relations with their ex-relatives should follow some simple suggestions:

• Don't make your relationship with your ex-relative look, to anyone, like you are taking sides. Avoid commenting on divorce-related issues and avoid listening to complaints about the other party. Just say, "I'm sorry, but it makes me terribly uncomfortable to talk about this."

• Be patient. Don't be surprised if the newly divorced relative puts you off for a while. Keep in touch with phone calls "just to see how you are doing."

• A good approach is to ask if you can help, with the children, with finding a job, with moving to a new apartment, even with money.

• Let your relative know that you are trying to keep a relationship with their ex-spouse, but that you are not taking sides.

• If necessary, let the children be a reason for calling, a reason to visit, and a safe topic of conversation.

• Don't coerce the ex-relative to attend family functions that their ex-spouse would be attending. It's the job of the ex-spouse to make those arrangements.

• Don't become a messenger service or informant between the divorced couple.

Noncustodial Parents

One important thing to keep in mind is that children still have two parents, even after a divorce. Divorce leads to many single-parent *homes*, but it should not lead to single-parent *families*. (The fact that it often does is no excuse.)

What does a noncustodial parent (almost always the father) do about discipline? Often nothing, and this causes problems. Their visitation is limited to Saturday or Sunday afternoons or to a few hours after work a couple days a week. Given such a limited amount of time with their young children, they don't want to "waste" it on discipline. Instead, noncustodial fathers often want to have as much "fun" with their children as possible.

This can result in the "Good-time Dad" syndrome, with trips to the beach, circus, movies, miniature golf, and so forth, carefully planned every weekend. This can also get exhausting. Although special activities need to be planned for a visiting child, the child should be assimilated into his or her noncustodial parent's everyday life. Non-custodial fathers have an obligation to see their children as frequently as possible, regardless of age of the child. (This must be recognized by the divorced mother as well.) This should not be an excuse for watching four hours of football with one's daughter every Sunday, but the child should become engaged in normal daily or weekend routines of the household. To do this means that discipline is necessary.

But how does a father establish a pattern of discipline when he sees his children only several days or less each week? The easy answer is to use the same set of rules that one would use if still married. The family situation may have changed, but the pattern of discipline has not. One thing that makes this difficult is that in many traditional families, it is customary for the mother/wife to orchestrate "family" activities, including household rules and patterns of discipline. Fathers may be very involved with their children and may be called upon to discipline the children when they act up, but the direction for the interaction may come (often quite subtly) from their wives.

When Dad is on his own, he must take more initiative for interaction and establishing rules and schedules for his children. There will be fewer ready-made "family" situations, and he must take more responsibility in determining when, where, and what to do, what the household rules are, and how they are enforced. Dad becomes not only the enforcer but the organizer of a disciplined life.

My wife and I separated when our two boys were three and five. For the first two months I visited them at our old home and tried to fit into my old "Daddy" role. I let my wife make the plans for us and I went along as usual—I drove the car, I paid the bills, I watched as my wife interacted with the boys. Each weekend I felt more distance grow between me and my family, and my wife made it clear that she was less than happy with this arrangement.

Fortunately I opened up and talked about my problem to a coworker who I knew was divorced and had children. He had not remarried, but he had a house with a spare room for his kids. He invited me and my boys for a cookout at his house and I got to see how he and his kids got along.

What an eye-opener! My friend not only cooked on the grill for the kids, he also had planned the meal, bought the food, and assigned cleanup to the kids (even my three-year-old).

I realized my relationship with my boys had always been through my wife, and I didn't know how to be with them unless she was around. Divorce means my wife won't play that role anymore and I have to become a parent—for the first time.

It was slow going at first. I made every mistake in the book. But I asked advice from everyone, even my mother. Four years later I am a proud father of two fine boys. I have a closer relationship with my kids than any married father I know.

I still don't think divorce is good, but good things can come from bad. I'm sure that if I had stayed married, I would still be very uninvolved with my children. The truth is, divorce has made me a better father.

Stepparents

We took our daughter to a children's play some time ago. It featured various Mother Goose tales put to music, and began with Jack and Jill cowering in one corner of the stage with their wicked stepmother and stepfather sitting positioned in another corner. The stepparents were yelling at the children, pointing their crooked fingers at them and pounding their fists on a table to make their points emphatic.

"You're no good! You're not even our children. You eat too much and you're too expensive. You're lazy, rotten children. We don't want you anymore!"

Jack and Jill whimpered to their parents. "But who will take care of us? What are we to do?"

"We don't care," screamed the stepfather. "We don't want you. You're not ours, and you're no good. Go to London-town and become beggars. Maybe the king and queen will take care of you. But we won't. Now get out of here you lazy, no-good children!" And off went Jack and Jill to London-town, hoping to meet the king and queen and maybe find some new parents along the way.

It had a happy ending, of course. Jack and Jill had all sorts of wonderful adventures with Simple Simon, Little Bo Peep, and the like, and eventually were adopted by Mother and Father Goose. But the image of their stepparents stayed with us.

A generation ago, divorce was less common, making stepparents a rarity. Most adults today had no role models for "how to stepparent," yet we are finding ourselves in stepparent roles at alarming rates. Nearly half the adult population currently between the ages of twenty and forty will be stepparents sometime in their adult lives, and most of us won't know what to do. We know that the Hansel and Gretel school of stepparenting is not appropriate, but we don't have an alternative for what is.

One common conception is that being good stepparents is the same as being good parents. This is certainly better than tossing the children out into the forest to fend for themselves, but most stepparents who try to treat their stepchildren exactly as they do their own offspring run into frustration.

Perhaps the question new stepparents ask most often is, "Should I discipline at all?" In other words, aren't discipline problems something that the parent should handle? The answer, of course, depends on a host of factors. Does the child reside with the stepparent most of the week, or is the role one of a noncustodial stepparent? How many children are in the family and how are they related? How old are they? Do they accept their mother's or father's new spouse, or is there substantial resentment? What kind of relationship do they have with their parents?

It is important to keep in mind, however, that discipline is not just something that a parent or stepparent applies to an unruly child. If that were the case, the "real" parent would discipline, with the stepparent only filling in. But discipline is more than dealing with problem behavior. The goal is to raise a disciplined child, and stepparents can have an enormous influence. They can serve as role models as disciplined adults; they can establish schedules, explain household rules and regulations, even if the enforcement of those rules falls to someone else. And they can show respect for their stepchild—for the difficult situation in which divorce and remarriage has placed the child.

With my stepchildren the biggest problem is building trust and respect. Problems with my husband's ex-wife notwithstanding, it has been tough building my relationship to its present level of respect and rapport. Stepparents must give even more emotionally to their step-children than their own in order to make any headway. My advice to other stepparents is to tread carefully but with confidence. You are their example. Be what you would want them to be—honest, respectful, sensitive, and caring. Most of all, love them a whole lot.

People who have never been a stepparent often wonder what all the fuss is about. "I guess it's a lot like being a parent," they say, "except it's only a few days a week." Those who *have* been stepparents say, "Ha! That's what you think!"

In fact, being a stepparent is one of the most difficult *and* most rewarding roles a person can fill.

Nothing determines the stepparent/stepchild relationship as much as the child's biological parent. Those who are sensitive, caring, and diligent can make a stepparent's job more rewarding. Second, the ex-spouse also has a lot of control over how difficult the job can be. And, of course, the children make a difference. Least influential, probably, are the stepparents themselves. Unfortunately most of the advice in books and magazines is directed at the last two groups, the people who have the least control. Here are a few words of wisdom:

The stepparent's spouse must recognize the need to make the second marriage a success—not only for their own sakes, but for that of the children of the first marriage. As much as children would like to have their original parents back together again, the most realistic thing for them is to have their parents happily remarried to another who will help provide a stable home again and help keep the parent/child bond strong.

The stepparent's spouse needs to realize that the stepparent initially fills the role out of love for the spouse, not the child. Hopefully that love will develop with time, but until then, the stepparent needs to have his or her love for the spouse acknowledged, appreciated, and returned.

I have no children of my own, but have been stepmother to my husband's son since he was three years old. It was rough at first—I had never been around children before—but my husband did everything he could think of to make it easier. I remember the first Mother's Day after we were married, he gave me a huge bouquet of roses thanking me for being his son's stepmother. It made it seem so official and important. Five years later I can't remember my life without the two of them. I think we have a stronger marriage because of his son—not because of anything he has done, but because of my husband's attitude. It's given us a tie that other couples don't have. We're a husband/wife team and a stepmother/father team.

The importance of the Child's Other Parent

Although many people whose ex remarries feel that adjustment problems are the stepparent's headache, the truth is that the children may experience problems, too. Parents who care about their children will do all they can to make transitions easier.

The most important thing the parent can do is to avoid competition between parent and stepparent. This is difficult because the comparison is *so* obvious—you are the first wife, she is the second wife; you are the father; he is the stepfather. And to make matters worse, the children make those comparisons, out loud, in your presence, and with big smiles as though you are thrilled to find out what radio station the stepparent listens to in the car, what brand of cologne he wears, or what style of underwear she buys.

Here are a few suggestions from parents who have gone through this gracefully (and not so gracefully):

• Try to come up with the most positive explanation possible for everything your child's new stepparent does. For example, if your daughter's stepmother sent home all your daughter's clothes freshly laundered and ironed after a weekend visit, think that she is trying to do things right and is unsure about her new role—not that she thinks you are a bad mother because you don't iron anything. If your son's new stepfather tells him endless stories about his tour in Vietnam, think how difficult it must be for the poor man to impress a boy who has grown up with such a remarkable father—not that he is an egotistical bag of hot air. It takes some real stretches of the imagination, but it's worthwhile. And usually your farfetched kindly explanations are closer to the truth than the ugly ones.

• Think about how wonderful your children are and how easy it is for the new stepparent to become attached to them— and how difficult it must be for them not to have them for their very own—and how generous you are to share your children a few days a week with this less fortunate person.

• Remember that children have a special place in their hearts for "real" Moms and "real" Dads, not because of anything they do or buy or say, but because they are Mom and Dad. Their stepparents can spend millions of dollars on candy and toys and trips to Disney World and not come close to that special place in your child's heart. They can love your child dearly (and your child can love them dearly) but they will never be able to compete with you. So let your children form strong bonds with their stepparents. Make it easy for them if you can, or at least don't make it difficult. Try and view it as you would their relationship with grandparents, day-care workers, and baby-sitters. Your child can only win and "real" parents can never lose.

The Role of a Stepparent

Those who try to be "just like real parents" to their stepchildren are asking for problems. Even being a real parent on a part-time basis is the wrong approach. A stepparent is a stepparent is a stepparent. Here are some different ways stepparents have adjusted to their roles:

> After my children were grown and off to college, I married a man with a six-year-old son. "This will be easy," I thought. "I've been a mother for many years; I'll just be his mother on weekends." It was the most frustrating time of my life. I may have had all sorts of experience and wisdom, but I had no say whatsoever in Sean's upbringing. His mother decided what clothes he wore, what medical care he got and from whom, and what school he went to (although I am a teacher at one of the best private academies in the area and he could attend tuition-free). She wasn't the least bit interested in my opinions, and when my husband tried to smooth things over, I felt he was taking her side against me.
>
> I was so frustrated that I began going to our minister for family counseling. He told me that there was no way I could ever be Sean's mother, not even on a part-time basis. His mother was his mother seven days a week, whether he was at her house or at our house. However, I could be his stepmother full-time, seven days a week.

When I remarried, I had an eleven-year-old son. My son's father, who had never shown much interest in him, then totally lost interest. Fortunately my new husband enjoyed doing things with my son, and they became good friends.

I had been seeing a psychologist throughout my divorce and remarriage, and one day she gave me some wonderful advice. I was concerned over my son being ignored by his real father while his stepfather was taking him fishing and becoming so important to him. She laughed and told me that there are few enough people in the world willing to do things for kids. I should just be happy someone was willing to spend time with my son and I should not ask for credentials.

Suggestions for a Stepparent's Involvement

A stepparent's job is to find a nice combination of what they are willing and able to do for the child and what the child needs done. Here are some suggestions:

• Listen with interest and patience.

• Treasure handmade gifts, pictures, and letters from the child.

• Be an audience for the child's musical, athletic, or artistic performances.

• Buy them something without resentment. Some children with divorced parents feel that every purchase made by either parent has emotional strings attached. The one who pays child support thinks the other parent should be buying the extras, since the support is too high, and the one who receives child support thinks the other parent should be buying them, since the support they pay is so low. If a stepparent has his or her own income and buys a child something "just because I want to," it can be a breath of fresh air and a real treat.

• Be an advocate for the child. Sometimes divorced parents use their child as a battlefield, unable to see the harm such behavior causes. A stepparent can often be the cooler head that steps in and speaks in the child's best interest.

• Share some talent or interest with them that is uniquely yours. No matter how great parents are, there are only two of them, and they can't teach their child about everything in the world. You can give some knowledge and experience to your stepchildren that they wouldn't have otherwise.

• Be an example of a happy, loving adult with a positive attitude. Parents who have been through a divorce are often bitter and negative. Your interactions with your stepchildren can show them a different adult outlook.

• Be the model of a responsible, mature adult. This is especially important if the child's other parent has abandoned them or shows little interest in them.

• Show them a stable, happy marriage. Often young children who have been through a divorce don't remember ever living with happily married parents. A child's attitude toward marriage and family is influenced by those marriages they grow up with.

• Be someone who can talk to them without criticizing either parent.

• Be someone who can admire and compliment the parent who is your spouse.

Raising disciplined children is not an easy job. It is even more difficult when the family has gone through substantial change. Adjustment to divorce and remarriage is difficult for everyone involved. Getting to know your stepchildren's needs and dispositions can be difficult when you only see them once a week, or after work when all you want to do is flop in front of the television.

What we have emphasized in this chapter are some of the difficulties parents have with divorce, remarriage, and single-living that are often at the core of discipline problems with children. Yet, raising a disciplined child in a nontraditional family involves the same things as it does when Mom, Dad, and kids all live happily together under the same roof.

9. The First Year

It may sound strange to think about disciplining babies, but the first year of a child's life is an important time for laying the groundwork—working with schedules, getting to know your baby's temperament, building warm, secure relationships between the baby and family members, and making decisions together about the baby. It's a big job, especially if this is your first child.

Although babies do cause problems during the first year, parents need to remember that none of this early "misbehavior" is intentional. At this age, babies are totally incapable of doing things out of spite or revenge or because of jealousy. They are not sneaky, dishonest, or devious. Their thinking processes are so simple that they are incapable of *knowing* what is right while *doing* what is wrong.

Parents who label their young child's behavior as "bad" and feel some punishment is needed to "teach him a lesson" need to rethink their decisions. A better way of looking at early problem behavior is to realize that babies want to be close to their family members and they are curious about the world around them. When young children are punished for their misdeeds, unfortunately the lessons they learn are "Don't look to your parents for comfort," and "Don't be curious about the world around you."

By their very nature, babies cause problems. They are new-comers to a world full of structure. They are not easy to com-municate with, and even if they were, they have little ability to comply with our requests. We can deal best with our young children if we understand their limitations and the inevitable problems they will cause. It is from these early problems and solutions that a pattern of family discipline grows.

Feeding and Sleeping Schedules

Babies come into the world with no feeding schedules at all. Before birth, nutrients were delivered directly via the umbilical cord. After birth, their own digestive systems take over. They need a certain amount of nutrients in a twenty-four hour period, and their stomachs can hold only so much. They settle into a schedule that changes as they grow. Some babies are very predictable, others quite unpredictable, and most babies fall somewhere in between.

Just a few generations ago, parents were urged to put their babies on schedules by feeding them every four hours—precisely at ten, two, and six o'clock. If they were asleep at feeding time, parents were told to wake them up. If they were hungry before feeding time, parents were told to make them wait. Today's parents are advised to find out when their child wants to eat and to learn the cues the baby sends out about his or her needs. They are told to be responsive to those cues and to teach their baby that people near to them are trustworthy and can be depended upon to respond promptly and lovingly when summoned. It's quite a change in advice, but an important one.

Here are some scheduling suggestions:

Late Night Feedings

I have a two-year-old boy and a six-month-old girl, and my biggest problem is fatigue. I don't think I've gotten a good night's sleep since the first one was born. It seems that I just get to sleep and the little one starts crying to be fed. My husband works all day, and I breast-feed, so he doesn't help at night. You can't blame a baby for being hungry, but I dread that cry at night.

• Ask yourself, "What message am I sending to my baby at night when I respond to her cries of hunger?" If it is anger and resentment, something must be done. Talk to your husband. Maybe he can give the baby a bottle during the night and let you sleep. Or perhaps he can take over when he gets home from work and let you have a nap. It's not easy running a family that is open twenty-four hours a day, but these long hours won't last long.

• Fathers of breast-fed babies often get the feeling that they are left out. The truth is that fathers can make the critical difference between a child who feels loved and who feels resented. Sometimes mothers need to make a special effort to let them know how important their help is, too.

• Mothers who do not work outside the home often feel they can't ask for help with the kids from their husbands who have full-time jobs. This is how the "supermom syndrome" starts, not to mention communication problems. Bury your pride and ask for help. Fathers who profess willingness to walk over hot coals for their families certainly wouldn't mind missing an hour's sleep each night for a few months.

As a contrast, here's another mother's story:

> My husband and I have a three-month-old baby girl. He is a graduate student and I had to go right back to work, so she's in a university-sponsored day-care center. We don't have much time together as a family, but some of our best times are when she wakes up for her 4:30 A.M. feeding. My husband listens and tries to get her up and changed before I wake up. Then I nurse her and we have a nice, cozy family hour, even though it's before sunrise. I know how important his time is, and it makes me feel good to know he's doing this for me. And I think our daughter knows how special she is to him also.

This mother probably doesn't get more sleep than the mother in the first example, but since the parents are sharing the "down side" of having a new baby, both are happier. It builds good family feelings for everyone.

Eating Too Much?

I feed my baby whenever she wants, but she is six months old and she eats too much. How do I start cutting back? I don't want her to be overweight.

• Are you sure it's too much? Measure exactly what your daughter eats at each meal. Then check with your pediatrician. It may not be too much for her age.

• Is her food intake consistent? Babies are like some adults—hungrier some days than others. A few days' eating spurt is nothing to worry about.

• Is your baby really overweight? Most infant-care books contain charts defining the normal range of heights and weights that are based on those of thousands of infants, as are the "percentiles" provided by many pediatricians. Consult them.

• Is your baby eating a lot because feeding is the most exciting and pleasurable part of her day? For busy parents, feeding or changing time provides much of the interaction with the baby. Make sure your baby gets plenty of other playtime and cuddling. She might just be bored and lonely.

• If your baby seems overweight, try a little fresh air and exercise before meals. Take her out for some rough and tumble play to distract and relax her.

• If your baby is truly eating too much, try substituting water, fruit juice, and if she is old enough, some finger food such as Cheerios that will take her extra time and effort to pick up and eat.

Eating Too Little?

I have just the opposite problem. My son has always been a fussy eater and I worry about him getting enough to eat.

• Check the first three suggestions above. Normal eating habits and weight vary from infant to infant and from week to week with the same child. Make sure you have a problem before you start worrying.

• If your child is not eating enough and there are no medical reasons, ask yourself what goes on at mealtime? Is the TV on?

Are the older children hustling and bustling to get off to school? Are you edgy and anxious to get your day started? Are you trying to feed the baby while talking on the phone or cooking for the rest of the family? Some kids need more peace and quiet than others, and some need food to be the only game in town at mealtime.

Eating on Schedule

> My three-month-old refuses to eat on any sort of schedule. Sometimes it's two hours and sometimes it's four. Sometimes he nurses for a short time, sometimes for longer. Naps are also a big problem.

• Try playing detective. Keep a schedule of when he eats and for how long. Also make note of what's going on at the time to see if any patterns emerge. For example, when he eats for a short time, was there a lot of activity in the room? It could be that your baby is supersensitive to noise and activity, and more interested in what's happening around him than in lunch. Or, are you anxious about getting those particular feedings over with because you are in the middle of some other task or distracted by something? Your baby may be very sensitive to your cues and not feel quite as comfortable nursing when you are distracted and impatient. Adjustment goes two ways, you know; not only are Mom and Dad adjusting to the new baby, the new baby is adjusting to Mom and Dad.

• Talk to other nursing mothers and compare eating schedules.

• Talk to your pediatrician. You may be eating something or taking something that causes the baby to eat irregularly.

• Don't try to change his schedule by making him wait a certain amount of time before you feed him. At this age, it's more important for him to learn that he can depend on his parents to take care of his needs.

• You might try stretching his waking time a little by playing with him or taking him out for a walk and showing him exciting new things.

• Be patient, and remember the words of a retired family

doctor we know: "All kids are on regular schedules by the time they go off to college."

Regular Evening Fussiness

> Every evening around five-thirty our baby starts fussing and there is nothing we can do for him except sit and hold him. That's the worst time of the day because we're both getting home from work, the sitter is leaving and wants to talk, and we're all starving. It's a madhouse! Is he waking up from his nap too soon? What can we do?

• "Fussy times" are part of many babies' daily routines. Sometimes they are so regular you could set your watch by them. If this seems to fit your son, there's not much you can do to change *him*—he will outgrow it. However, you could change your family routine for a while. Why not delay the cooking hassle and have a family "happy hour"? Have something light (and easy) to eat, sit back, and make the baby the center of attention. Or go for a walk, taking a snack with you.

• See if the sitter will stay another hour each day and take care of the baby while you cook (or maybe even cook while *you* take care of the baby).

• See if the sitter will stay *really* late one night a week so the two parents can meet somewhere after work and have dinner out. Fussy times the other four nights a week won't seem so bad.

• If the sitter can't stay, think about taking turns with your spouse. Each of you could have a leisurely ride home one evening a week while the other holds down the fort at home and faces fussy time single-handedly.

• Your baby might be reacting to all the sudden commotion and activity that occurs at six o'clock. Put yourself in his place and imagine what it is like. It's a nice, quiet afternoon and then suddenly the most exciting thing happens! Mommy is home! Then Daddy is home! It could be overwhelming for a little guy, especially if you add in other family members and a barking family dog greeting everyone. Maybe you could reduce the noise and commotion; perhaps the sitter could call one of the parents each afternoon at work to relay messages and exchange information.

Moving Baby Out of Parents' Bed

> At first, it seemed easy to keep our baby in our bed at night. Now he's four months old and doesn't want to sleep in his room. My husband is really getting upset about this and I don't know what to do.

• First of all, you're not alone. Family group sleeping has become quite common in the last few years, and some experts even recommend it. However, if your husband is "really getting upset," it probably isn't the right thing for *your* family.

• Talk this over and decide how you two feel about it, as parents and as husband and wife. When you reluctantly agree to some practice because your husband is "really getting upset," you are initiating a bad pattern. Establishing and maintaining discipline in a family is hard enough when both parents are committed to the same ideas and values, and far more so in the absence of a united front. You can have mixed feelings, but you can also listen to your husband's objections, tell him how you feel, and reach some mutual decision that you can be committed to one hundred percent. Then it would be, "My husband doesn't like the baby sleeping with us, so *we have agreed* to move him to his own crib."

• Try moving him gradually. Put the crib in your room for a while. When he sleeps well in there, move it into his room and leave the doors open.

• Sleep with a baby blanket next to you and put it in his crib the following night so he can have something that smells like you next to him.

• For a while let him fall asleep in your bed and move him while he is asleep.

• Put a baby-proof hot-water bottle in his bed so he will have something warm to snuggle with.

• Stay in the baby's room until he goes to sleep for a few nights.

• Ask other parents for advice. This is one of the most-asked questions we get from parents, many of whom have five- and six-year olds still sleeping with them—sometimes more than one!

Separation—Baby-sitters and Day-care Arrangements

Somewhere along the line all parents find it necessary to leave their baby in the care of another person, and when they do, it is seldom pleasant. If their child cries and makes a traumatic scene, the parents are crushed. If their child smiles and waves "bye-bye," the parents are crushed. There is no easy solution to the problem of separation, but some practices make it easier.

First, the decision has to be made by both parents. Whether it involves an evening out, mother going back to work, or leaving the baby for a two-week vacation trip to Europe, both parents need to be committed to the decision.

Second, parents need to discuss all their options. Who should care for the baby? How much can they afford? What is the best kind of care for an infant at this age? Are any compromises possible, such as Mom or Dad working part-time or changing schedules to minimize time spent with a sitter?

Third, once the child is being cared for regularly by a sitter, parents need to re-evaluate the situation from time to time to make sure this continues to be the best solution.

To Work or Not to Work: A Family Decision

> I think I want to go back to work soon after the baby is born, but I'm not really sure. My husband says we don't need my income, so I can stay home if I want. I liked my job, but I want to do what's best for the baby. How do mothers decide these things? Why do I feel guilty already?

• There is probably not one working parent in the world—father or mother—who doesn't feel guilty about leaving a child in day-care or with a sitter. Fathers feel that if they just made enough money, the mother could stay home with the baby. Or if they were just less concerned about their macho image, they'd *quit* their job and stay home with the baby while the mother worked. Mothers feel that they have somehow failed personally, that other mothers handle this situation successfully without any guilt or second thoughts. This is a good time for parents to be on the same side and give each other some support and understanding.

• *Together*, parents need to decide the following: Can the family get by with only one income? Could one parent work part-time? Could one parent stay home for the next year (or two, or three)? Are there any job options that would allow one parent to work at home? What day-care and baby-sitting possibilities exist? What are the costs? How does each parent feel about his or her job and about working in general? Once these things are discussed, a joint decision should be made and both should support it. From then on it should be said that, "We decided we both should work and put Melanie in the best day-care facility available." Or, "We decided Jane should stay home until Melanie is two, and then she will go back to work."

When Should Mom Go Back to Work?

> I am four months pregnant. When is the best time for a mother to go back to work after the baby is born? My maternity leave is six months, but I only get paid for two. My husband says he will take a weekend job [to make up the difference] if I want to stay home. My mother says I should stay home the first five *years*! My sister says that six months is the worst time because of stranger anxiety. I'd like to go back as soon as possible, as long as I'm doing the right thing.

• The best time for a mother to go back to work is when she and her husband decide she should. This doesn't mean that other opinions are unwelcome, but the final decision should be up to the parents.

• Do you really have to decide right now? If you could take it a week at a time after the baby is born, you'll probably know when the time has come.

• Your husband's offer to work weekends is wonderful; however, babies need fathers, too.

• Your mother's rule about staying home until the baby is five is a nice idea, too. Try to explain to her how you feel about your career and your financial responsibility. It may be a new concept to her for a woman to have those concerns.

• Stranger anxiety is not as simple as your sister makes it sound. Some babies develop a fear of strangers around six or seven months of age, but some never do. And those who do may have it one day and not the next.

• Your wish to go back to work as soon as possible is the most important factor, but you may change your mind once the baby is here. Maybe some options such as working part-time for a while would be best.

> My mother and my mother-in-law both think it's terrible that I'm going back to work and leaving my six-month-old in a day-care center. They both have offered to lend us money, which makes my husband furious. It's not the money. I want to go back to my job. Yet they say that the best care for a baby is mother care.

• The best care for a baby is happy, stress-free, loving parents. If this means mother works, that's what's best for the baby. Resentful, frustrated parents, who are more worried about pleasing *their* parents than about running their family themselves, cannot provide the best care.

• Second best might be grandparents or other close relatives. Are your parents offering to do this? It's easy to offer criticism, or even money. But how about splitting up the day-care responsibility? Three days with one grandma each week and two with the other?

Exploring Options and Making Compromises

Parents have told us of some very creative options they have found using this method of decision-making, such as the ones that follow.

> My biggest problem was day-care for my two-month-old. I started with a neighbor who took care of babies, but that didn't work out. Then I tried two different nurseries that were terrible. I own my own business, so I couldn't take a year or two off. One day out of desperation, I took the crib to work and set up a nursery in the back room of my florist shop. Mornings were slow and Brian slept most of the early afternoon, but around three o'clock, things got busy and Brian needed attention. So I hired a retired woman who only wanted to work a few hours a day. She came in from three to five-thirty and was my "extra pair of hands." She waited on customers, answered the phone, and rocked the baby—whatever needed to be done.

Some days she just took him for a walk in his stroller. Brian started morning preschool when he was three and then spent afternoons with us in the store. Grandma Rose is still working here afternoons and has learned to be a first-rate flower arranger. I think all mothers who have to work should look for options. It cost less for me to hire someone else at the store than to put him in nursery. I had him with me most of the day and knew he was getting loving care. And the customers thought it was very special.

When Jonathan was born, I had planned to take two years off from my job as legal secretary. After three months, my boss called and asked me to reconsider—they had hired two different secretaries and neither had worked out. I told him about our decision not to put Jonathan in day-care until he was two, and he had a suggestion. He would have a word processor installed in our den and have tapes and documents delivered to me by courier. And they'd give me a raise. I couldn't resist, so I gave it a try.

I can't truthfully say it was easy. I never seemed to have more than thirty minutes at a time to work, and the housework never got done. But my husband took over in the evenings when I had work to do and helped with the housework like he had done when we were both working.

I am a registered nurse and I have two preschoolers. When the first was born, I had a three-month leave and then put her in the nursery run by the hospital, which is excellent but expensive. When I was pregnant the second time, I couldn't find anything I liked for less money. My husband and I looked at all the angles, but couldn't find a way to get along without my salary.

Then the hospital started a visiting-nurse service so patients could leave the hospital sooner. I talked to two other nurses I knew, and we asked the director to hire the three of us for two full-time positions.

It's worked very well. We are given two full caseloads and we meet every Friday morning and divide things up. One of the women is taking afternoon courses toward her masters degree, and likes morning hours; the other nurse is single and works afternoons so she can have her evenings free; I take the night calls and the "on call" hours. My husband is home then to baby-sit, and if I'm called on an emergency, I can always nap with the kids the next day. I always liked the excitement of emergency room work, but this way once the patient is at the hospital, I can go home.

Making Day-care Work

If you and your spouse decide on full time day-care, be one hundred percent committed. This means not telling friends that you wish you didn't have to work, or that your spouse was the one who wanted to put your baby in day-care. Find the best quality of care you can possibly afford and check up on the care frequently. Things change quickly in the day-care business—the place you choose may not be the one your child attends three months later.

When day-care is a joint commitment and you are sure you have the best, then you can leave your child without the guilt and doubt many parents feel. It's surprising how children can sense parents' feelings. Perhaps half of separation tears are caused by Mom or Dad feeling sad about leaving the child or resentful of one another for causing the child's "predicament."

Have a good routine in the morning. Wake up early enough to be able to enjoy your time together. There is nothing like a rushed, anxious morning to cause separation trauma at school.

Many parents have found that a nursery near work makes more sense than one near home. The commuting time is spent together and parents can drop in for lunch during the day.

I went back to work when Lisa was three months old. I chose a nursery near to the office so I could nurse her on my lunch hour. It got to be a nice habit. After she was weaned, I still visited and fed her lunch. My husband works in that part of town two days a week, and he also stops by. The nursery director encourages our visits—they're proud of the first-rate care they give and they appreciate the help at mealtimes. It really picks up my day to stop and see Lisa. I don't think I could leave her all day.

The Right Care for the First Year

> This is an unusual problem, but I'm not sure I'm doing the right thing. I am a single mother and had to go back to work when my baby was six weeks old. I found a nursery near my office that I could afford. It is very clean and cheerful, and the staff takes very good care of my baby. The only problem is that it is a Baptist nursery and I am Jewish.
>
> There are pictures of Jesus everywhere, and the staff plays Baptist music for the kids and sings church songs. I know my baby can't understand these things now, but how long can she go to this nursery without getting confused? I want to raise her in my faith.

• At your baby's age, the important considerations in day-care are physical and emotional: does your baby get her physical needs taken care of promptly, is she safe, and does the staff treat her with tender loving care? It sounds like the only problem with the nursery you have chosen is the religious atmosphere. This won't be apparent to your daughter for several years. Keep in touch with the staff and make sure they have a good attitude toward non-Baptists and toward children of unmarried parents. Most church-run nurseries are very loving, open-minded, accepting places.

• You might talk to your rabbi. Maybe a Jewish day-care facility could match the cost for you, or maybe some "guardian angel" in the congregation would like to underwrite the difference for a conscientious Jewish mother who is doing her best for her daughter.

• Talk to some parents of older kids who attend school supported by one religion and practice another at home. Kids readily accept differences and usually follow their families' beliefs.

Baby-sitters—Mom and Dad Go Out

> Our baby is four months old and has never been left with a baby-sitter. We are going out to an office banquet and can't get out of it. Is she old enough to stay with a sitter? What can we do to make it go smoothly? How long should the sitter let her cry before she calls us? We could take a beeper.

- Make sure you have an experienced, competent baby-sitter and leave your beeper number. Also leave the number of the banquet facility. Your four-month-old daughter should have no problems.
- Now, about the parents. Who is making the decision about your family, you or the organizers of the office banquet? Do *you* think that going to the banquet and leaving your four-month-old with a sitter is the best thing to do? If so, do it and enjoy. If not, stay home, or send the parent that is employed by that company and might possibly have an obligation to attend.
- If *you* decide for both to go, here are some ideas that will help the evening run smoothly:
- Have the sitter come to your house, don't take the baby to his or hers.
- If a familiar person will baby-sit, such as Grandpa or Aunt Sarah, it may be easier than if the sitter is a total stranger. Ask—a lot of relatives would love to baby-sit and don't think to offer.
- If the sitter is a total stranger to the baby, have her come for a visit a day or two ahead.
- On the night of the banquet, have the sitter come at least an hour early so she can get acquainted with the baby while you are still around. It can also be a big help to have someone there to tend the baby while you get dressed.
- Try and avoid last-minute anxiety. Have everything prepared and give yourself plenty of time. Babies pick up on your moods, and a last-minute frantic search for Mom's earrings could set the stage for a difficult parting.
- Tell your baby that you are going out for a while and that you'll be back. Tell him that you are going to an exciting grown-up party and that Mrs. Smith is going to take care of him. Give him a kiss *and leave*. He won't understand your words, but he'll come to understand what they signal. After a few times, he will probably start crying at this point, but leave anyway. Ask any baby-sitter—almost all kids stop crying before the car leaves the driveway.
- When you get to the party, tell other parents that this is the first time you have ever left your baby with a sitter. Listen to their reassurances and words of wisdom, and remember to do the same for others when you are a veteran.

Attachment to Sitter Instead of Mom?

> I take my five-month-old daughter to a sitter while I work. She has been going to the same one since she was two months old. They get along very well. In fact, that is my problem. Is it possible for a baby to get attached to their sitter instead of their mother? Sometimes she cries when I come to pick her up. Should I change sitters?

• Absolutely do not change sitters; count your lucky stars instead! Would you feel better if your daughter hated her and had a miserable time all day while you were at work?

• No, it is not possible that a child can become attached to a sitter *instead* of its loving mother. Babies get attached to all the people who are important in their lives—sometimes even the family pets. Attachment is *not* a one-shot, winner-take-all deal; there is nothing mystical about it. It's simply a loving relationship between two people who are important to each other. The more "attaching" she does—to her father, her brother, and her grandparents as well— the better adjusted she will be.

• Play role reversal. If you were a preschool teacher or daycare worker and spent the day "mothering" other people's children, would you become more attached to them than to your own child? Would it be better if the preschool changed the kids in your class every two months so you wouldn't get attached? There is a difference between mother care and the best of sitter care, and your baby knows it.

On the Home Front

Too many parents believe that discipline is something that should be taken out of the closet and put on when the family goes out in public—like a hat or a pair of gloves. They all agree that certain rules are necessary, but not for "around the house" or on an "everyday basis." The bad news for these parents is that a family can only appear as disciplined in public as it does around the house, and that children cannot be depended upon to show public behavior that differs from the "private behavior" of their family's everyday life. This doesn't mean that we have to sit around the house in our party clothes and talk politely about the weather. But it does mean that if children don't respect their parents at home, they won't respect them in the supermarket. And if children are little savages at home, they won't act like little missionaries at the church social.

The family home is the beginning of learning for all life's important lessons, and discipline is no exception. Although it may seem easier to ignore discipline problems in the first year, wise parents realize that instilling positive behavior early on builds a foundation for later lessons. During the first year, children can learn specific lessons about family rules and relationships, positive methods of communication, and respect for the property of others. Here are some of the specific problems parents have related to us about these areas, and some of the suggestions we have for solutions.

Dressing (and Undressing)

> My son is nine months old and he loves being naked. When I take his diaper off to change him or take his clothes off to give him a bath, he tries to get away and crawl around bare. I think it's cute now, but can it become a big problem later?

> I have a ten-month-old son who hates having his diapers changed. He also hates having his clothes taken off for a bath. Is this normal?

• Many parents of children under one year complain that their little ones either hate to have clothes on or hate to have them off. They also report that they either hate their baths or hate getting out of their baths. This, we're afraid, is an example of the individual differences found among normal, healthy children. However, this doesn't mean that your child should wander through life undressed or unbathed. It's just that some compromises might be in order.

• Younger infants who dislike being undressed are probably either very sensitive to temperature changes or feel more secure being swaddled—wrapped up securely. Try making changes more slowly and in a warm room. Some parents find that changing baby on the bathroom vanity works well, since the room is smaller and easier to warm up.

• Distracting your baby while you dress and undress him or her can help. Try naming the clothes or body parts. "This is your shirt. One arms goes in here, one arm goes in there, and in the middle goes your head. One snap, two snaps, three snaps, and we're done!"

Diaper Wars

Is there such a thing as parent abuse? My seven-month-old son gets so wild when I try to change his diapers that I had a black-and-blue cheekbone last week from one of his shoes. He thinks it's funny, and so did I until he got too dangerous.

• Half the battle of diapering can be won by having everything you need close at hand. Some parents buy duplicate supplies for several "diapering stations" around the house. It can save countless trips up and down stairs and from one end of the house to the other.

• Whether your baby hates having his or her diapers removed, hates having them put back on, or just wants to make every diapering session into a major rodeo event, a good solution is distraction. Some parents hang a mobile near the diapering table or put colorful pictures on the wall. One mother we know mounted a door mirror on its side behind the table, giving her son a full length view of himself and the room while he was being diapered. Other possibilities are shelves with music boxes and other interesting objects, or a special toy only to be played with at diapering time.

• As long as your child isn't already rough and tumble while being diapered, a tickle game or a silly song may serve as a good distraction. We know parents who use everything from nursery rhymes to college fight songs with equal success.

• If all else fails and your child insists on making diapering time an occasion for hand-to-hand combat, stop the songs and games, get the diaper on as best you can, and use your most serious tone of voice to tell your child that his behavior is not acceptable. Take him from the diapering table and put him in his crib, playpen, or other area where he will be safe and leave him for a few minutes. It gives a powerful message, and is also the beginning of getting to know your "serious voice." It's not anger or punishment that would cause anxiety or fear, but just a change of tone that can become a signal for years to come.

Bath-time Blues

My seven-month-old cries whenever I give him a bath. I'd think I was doing something wrong, except my two other children never had this problem.

• This can be another indication of individual differences. Making sure the bathing room and water are warm enough is a good idea. Bath water can be scary, especially all alone. Sometimes babies like to bathe with siblings (although not without a parent nearby in case of mishap) or with the parent. If tub baths are too traumatic, try a sponge bath for a while. Babies have very short memories and may love their bath again in a few days or weeks.

• Distraction works well here, too. Try some tub toys or a song while you bathe him. If he is coordinated enough, he may want to try bathing himself. It may not be as thorough as the job you would do, but there's something to be said for independence.

Hair-care Woes

It took me three kids and ten years, but I finally have a daughter. It's taken her eleven months, but she finally has some hair. Now the big problem is that she hates having it combed or brushed. And shampooing is a definite battle. Does this mean three crew cuts in the family?

• This may just be a child with a sensitive scalp, in which case a short, simple haircut may be the best policy. Try some Velcro barrettes for a feminine touch, or a ribbon around a short hairdo.

• Your daughter may be one of those independent children who just wants to do everything herself. Put some shampoo in her hands and let her think she's washing her own hair. If that works, try the same with the comb and brush.

• Babies who hate hair washing often don't like water in their faces. Shampoo on a washcloth will do the trick if hair is short enough, and then rinsed the same way. And regardless of what some think, baby hair doesn't have to be washed as often as adult hair. After a week or so of struggle-free shampooing with the washcloth, try the running water method again. If it still brings terror, wait another few months. Some kids just won't like shampooing until they are old enough to do it themselves. It's much easier to keep their hair short and to clean it the best you can.

What to Wear?

> This sounds weird, but my ten-month-old girl shows a definite preference for one outfit over another. She definitely does not like fancy dresses, but prefers T-shirts and old overalls. What does this mean?

• It might mean that the new fancy dresses are uncomfortable because of the scratchy ruffles and stiff new material. Old clothes are soft. We sometimes forget that babies have sensitive skin.

• Although it is possible your daughter has a precocious sense of personal style, children seldom have definite preferences for certain items at this age. But they may have definite ideas about what they *do not* want to wear. The most common is clothing that is tight around the neck, followed by clothing that is too warm, and clothing that is unpleasantly stiff or prickly. Again, this is no reason for parents to send their infants out in the winter cold without proper clothing, but maybe some compromises are in order.

Family Communication

Shrieking and Other Bad Habits

> My six-month-old has learned to shriek when she wants attention. I think she learned it from another kid at her daycare center. What can I do to break her of it?

• Six months of age is probably too young to be learning bad habits from other kids. Your daughter and her pal are probably going through similar stages of development.

• Children under a year of age communicate a lot; it's just that many adults don't take the time to listen to them and to understand their messages. They have words and phrases, cries and laughs, gestures, and expressions. Nothing pleases a baby more than having his messages understood. Humans are social creatures and all social contact is based on communicating.

• Children learn to communicate on a trial-and-error basis. Some messages work and some don't. The ones that don't are quickly dropped from their repertoire, while the others are used again and again. If you are not receptive to your children's facial expressions and soft sounds, they may resort to whining and screaming. Which of your baby's messages do you receive and respond to?

• Coos, baby talk, short words.
• Serious looks and silly noises.
• Long strings of syllables only a parent could understand.
• Smiles, giggles, funny faces.
• A rattle shaking in your direction or a picture pointed out to you.
• Hands clapped happily or slapped against the table with a smile flashed to you.
• High-pitched, ear-shattering screams.
• Crying, kicking, flailing about.
• Throwing toys against the wall or on the floor angrily.
• Coughing until they are red in the face.
• Kicking or hitting Mom or Dad.
• Sobbing or whining pitifully.

Drop-in Grandmas (with Friends)

I try to keep my baby on a schedule, but at least once a week my mother drops by with one of her friends and wants to show off her grandson. I tell her he is sleeping, but she always promises to be quiet and not wake him up. He is an extremely light sleeper and always wakes up when she is here. I don't want to upset her, especially in front of her friends. What can I do?

• When you are alone, tell her that you really wish she'd come by when he was awake and more playful. He's so cute then, and her friends would really be impressed. Also, you could dress him in that cute outfit she gave him.

• Invite her over at a set time for lunch or brunch or whatever is your baby's awake time. Ask if she would like to bring a friend. Treat her with the love and respect you feel. There's no reason her enjoyment of grandparenthood has to be at the expense of your enjoyment of parenthood.

• If she arrives unannounced, scold her jokingly. "I just got him to sleep, Mom, and now he'll want to come out and see you." Tell her friend, "He just loves his Grandma so much that he seems to sleep with his ears tuned for her voice. I don't know how I'll get him on a decent schedule."

Parents' Resentment Toward Grandparents

My mother was a career woman back when no other moms even had jobs. My sister and I were raised by the housekeeper. The explanation I always gave myself was that she just wasn't interested in children. Now that I have a new baby, Mom is here all the time. She cancels business appointments to baby-sit and refers to herself as "Nana." I can't help but feel left out. It's as though she liked children all along, but just didn't like *me*.

• There is an old saying that being a grandparent gives you a second chance. As grandparents, we are usually more relaxed, more financially secure, and happier in our relationships than when we were parents. We are also wiser. We can "do it better this time." Your mother isn't the same person she was twenty-five years ago, any more than you are. Maybe she has regrets about her earlier relationship with you and wants to make it up by being a first-rate grandparent.

• Be extremely careful with your mother's feelings. There is an important attachment that takes place between babies and grandparents, and it goes both ways. As the parent, you have the power to block that attachment, either by limiting the time they spend together or by planting bitter feelings in your mother. It's often the first time adult children have had the upper hand with their parents, and it's tempting to repay them for past injustices. But with power comes responsibility. You are the parent now and family unity is up to you. You can make the effort to get along, thereby giving your child a strong sense of family; or you can punish your parents and limit the family circle for your child.

• If you continue to feel hurt by your mother's attention to your baby, talk to a family counselor or psychologist. Your mother may be in the wrong, but the pain is yours. You certainly don't want this to turn into negative feelings toward your baby.

Mom and Dad Disagree

> My husband and I got along fine before the baby was born, but now we can't agree on anything. He has never been around babies before, but he won't listen to anything I tell him. Now he seems to enjoy breaking every rule I make—like waking up the baby late at night when his friends come over. I feel like I have two children!

• It's important that decisions about your child be made by both parents. If your husband doesn't know much about babies, maybe the two of you should take a parenting class together. Since a lot of child rearing is based on good common sense, you might be surprised at how much he really knows already.

• Maybe a little tact on your part would be helpful. Fathers today are expected to be active, involved parents even though few of their fathers served as such models. It might feel good to be more knowledgeable about infant care than your husband, but his relationship with his child (and you) is more important than one-upmanship on your part.

• Having a father proud enough of his baby to wake him up at night and show him off to his friends can be more important than establishing a sleep schedule. Think it over.

• Instead of telling your husband about your rules, try asking him what he thinks. The fact that you have made the rules together is often more important than the rules themselves.

Family Comparisons

> I can't help but notice that my son is not developing as fast as my sister-in-law's son. The pediatrician says he is "within the norms," but I still worry. We are a close family and these boys will grow up together **and always** be compared.

• Normal, healthy babies develop at different rates and your baby seems to be doing just fine, which is what your pediatrician means by "within the norms." What he should have added is that the rate of early development has little to do with later development, especially in complex things such as motor ability and intelligence. In other words, your baby's rate of development now doesn't tell you very much one way or another, and isn't anything to worry about.

• Talk to some parents of older children. You'll find **star** athletes who didn't walk until they were fifteen months **old,** and debating champions who couldn't put a sentence together until they were three.

• Think about how lucky your son is to have a cousin so close in age. Do what you can now to make it a cooperative relationship instead of a competitive one. Don't make comparisons yourself and try to dismiss those made by others with a joke.

Grandma's Old-Fashioned Advice

> I am a new mother and my mother-in-law is driving me crazy. She wants to be helpful, but her ideas are so old-fashioned. She lives near us and this is her first grandchild. She is a good friend, but I don't know how long I can take this!

• Ask Grandma to go with you to a class on child care, or send her to one of the new "grandparenting refresher courses" offered by hospitals and community groups. Then *listen* to what she tells you and consider her advice before making decisions.

• Give her a new child-rearing book and tell her you haven't had time to read it. Ask if she will and tell you what she thinks.

If that helps, maybe she can be your "resource person," telling you about TV specials on child rearing or going to lectures you are too busy to attend.

• Even if she doesn't brush up on new parenting ideas, listen to what she tells you. Many of the supposedly "new" child-rearing ideas are old-fashioned ideas under new labels.

• Make a "house-rules" deal with her—the rules depend on whose house you are in. As long as her ideas aren't really harmful, let her have her way when you visit or she baby-sits. Grandparents usually end up doing this anyway and kids get along fine.

Serious Grandparent Problems

> Our baby is six months old and reaches for everything. Last week she broke my mother's necklace and my mother slapped her hand. It surprised me so much I didn't know what to say. I haven't really thought much about spanking because she's so young, but I don't want her to be undisciplined.

• There is a lot of controversy about spanking, but six months is too young for children to understand punishment. All your daughter knows is that someone she loves and trusts did something to hurt her. If this was an isolated occurrence, it won't make a lasting impression, but you still need to take some action. Talk to your mom and tell her that you think your daughter is too young to be physically punished. Ask about her ideas and make it a real heart-to-heart talk. Chances are, your mom reacted without thinking and was embarrassed about it.

• If your mother doesn't agree, then tell her gently that she will just have to go along with it because this is your child. If she continues to physically punish your daughter, don't leave the child with her. There are some differences in child-rearing practices that can't be smoothed over and that children can't be expected to adjust to.

Visits, Outings, and Trips

Lunch with the Girls

> My daughter is four months old and my friends keep asking us to go out for lunch. I'm the only one with a baby. How can I make things go smoothly for everyone involved? I really miss my friends.

• The best way to plan outings when babies are involved is to follow *their* schedule. Is your daughter a morning person who takes long afternoon naps? Maybe a brunch would be the best time to show off her social skills. Or does she have the late morning "grumpies"? Maybe a late lunch would be the best time to catch up with old friends while the baby naps in her infant seat or carrier. Plan accordingly.

• The location is important, also. Select a restaurant that has room for baby paraphernalia and seems open to family clientele. This is probably not the time to be sampling the latest in exotic cuisine or sophisticated atmosphere. If you aren't sure, call ahead.

• Brush up on some non-baby topics for this first post-baby get together. And remember to ask what has been going on in *their* lives. New parents can be very egocentric. Keep in mind, too, that childless friends are likely to underestimate and even resent the extraordinary demands of an infant. If possible, schedule some child-free time, when you *won't* be interrupted or distracted.

• Don't hesitate to cancel if things are not going well. There's nothing wrong with calling and changing plans, with apologies of course. And if the lunch gets difficult, don't hesitate to leave early, with apologies and an offer to try again.

Baby's Jealousy of Mom's Friends?

> Being home with a new baby is lonely enough, but it seems like every time I get on the phone, the baby wants my attention. I try and get her interested in something else, but she just wants *me*. It's like she is jealous of my friends. What can I do to make her understand?

• A baby is not capable of such a complex idea as jealousy of your telephone friends. She's incapable of knowing that there is a person on the other end of the line. And she is certainly not capable of understanding that you need social contact with your friends and that she's interfering.

• Interpreting her behavior as jealousy makes you feel angry and trapped. Try another interpretation. For example, when you talk on the phone, you are probably happy and laughing, and your baby wants to be part of the fun. Think of some ways to include her, such a letting her talk for a few moments or getting her a toy telephone she can use.

• Make life simpler for yourself and plan long telephone visits during your baby's nap time. If friends call earlier, ask if you can call them back later when you have time for a good chat. They should feel honored.

Infants and Air Travel

My parents live in another state and we are planning a visit for the holidays. Our baby will be three months old. I have heard people talk about babies on plane flights, and I am dreading the whole vacation. How can I be sure she will be on her best behavior? You just can't stop a plane and get off.

• Be prepared. Talk to your pediatrician and see what you can do to avoid painful ear pressure. Sometimes a decongestant helps if the baby has a stuffy nose or cough. Also, a pacifier or bottle helps, too.

• Try scheduling the flight at a time baby usually sleeps.

• Call the airlines for suggestions. This is a problem they deal with daily, and they appreciate the chance to make your flight pleasant for everyone.

• Once your baby starts fussing on the flight, don't let it rattle you. Try and stay calm. The new sensations and unfamiliar surroundings are upsetting to the baby, and the best comfort is a calm and controlled parent. Also, passengers are often more disturbed by the parents' anxiety than the baby's fussing.

• In the final analysis, remember that you have paid for your tickets (and sometimes your baby's). Your baby has a right to travel to his grandmother's home for the holidays and is simply behaving like a normal baby. Apologies might be called for in a movie theater or a fancy restaurant, but babies do belong on planes and crying is part of their normal behavior.

The first year of life provides the foundation for patterns of parent/child interaction, for children learning trust, prediction, and control, and for both parents and infants to get to know one another. These are all critical factors in developing a disciplined, family life-style.

Discipline at this age does not involve dealing with misbehavior, since during the first year babies do not have the mental ability to misbehave intentionally. Yet they do make our lives difficult at times. Problems are most easily handled when the developmental abilities of the child are taken into consideration, when parents take the time to get to know their child well, and when both parents are involved in the decision making.

10. The Second Year (Twelve to Twenty-four Months)

During the second year, babies become more of everything —*more* mobile, *more* independent-thinking, awake *more* hours, and *more* able to communicate *more* of their own ideas. Fortunately parents have grown, too, and now have *more* experience and *more* confidence in their abilities. Hopefully they have laid the groundwork for making joint decisions, support each other's viewpoints and solve family problems together.

After the first year, couples with babies have begun to think of themselves as parents. In fact, they may have difficulty remembering what life was like before babies and wonder why they waited so long to have them.

Toddlers at a Glance— The Importance of Communication

The closer children get to their second birthdays, the more their minds come to resemble our own. They are learning that they are separate, thinking beings, who are independent from their beloved parents. They understand the world better and differently from a year before, and this increased understanding leads them to experiment with as much of the world as they can get their hands on.

If we had to choose one aspect of dealing with toddlers' problems and preparing parents for future ones, we would surely select *communication*. Communication with a toddler involves watching carefully, learning their moods and dispositions, and making your own wishes clear. During the second year, children's ability to use language begins to flourish, which makes family communication even more of a two-way process.

Children learn by overhearing speech, but especially by being talked to and listened to. Having the ability to use language has a snowball effect. Each word and expression opens the door to a dozen more words and expressions. When families communicate with each other and with their toddler, the home is full of as much language as the child is able to take in.

Learning also occurs when toddlers see family members communicating with each other. These early lessons are valuable because they shape how the child views gender, adult roles, values and morals, as well as conveying general knowledge about the world. They also establish the patterns that will continue throughout childhood and will have important consequences for discipline. When children are listened to, they are more apt to pay attention. When children have their questions answered, they will continue to ask them, avoiding discipline problems later on down the road.

One of the keys to a disciplined family is effective communication. When both children and parents know what is expected of them, when rules are stated explicitly and understood, and when parents appreciate the limitations of their children's communication skills, many behavior problems can be avoided.

Mealtime and Bedtime Rules and Schedules

During the second year, children become capable of some control over their lives. What's more, they *want* it. You can give control this willingly in situations you feel are appropriate, or you can engage in "battles of will" with your child, which result in the child winning control at times when you are too tired or distracted. The choice is yours.

Another feature of toddler life is curiosity, and not just the passive type when the child sits quietly and watches Mom or Dad turning the pages of a book. Toddler curiosity is the active type. Toddlers want to experience the environment directly, and to know how their own actions affect it. "What happens when I pound the spoon against the high-chair tray? Now what happens when I pound the spoon against the plate? Now what happens when I pound the spoon against the glass?" It helps to remember that Albert Einstein and Madame Curie probably started this way.

Table Manners

Toddlers have all the ingredients for charming dinner companions—they can sit up in a high chair, they can eat "people food," they can drink from a cup, they enjoy family companionship, and their feeding schedule can be juggled to fit the family. What more could you ask?

> How old does my child have to be before he can be taught table manners? He is eighteen months old and eats like a wild boar.

• It depends on what you mean by "table manners." If you mean dipping his soup from the far side of the bowl and using the left hand to hold the fork while the right hand cuts the meat, you can begin in about ten years. But if you mean trying his best to eat like everyone else, you can start now.

• The best way to teach a toddler to eat like a civilized member of his species is to put him at the table at mealtime. Imitation is probably the best teacher, and the family dining room is probably the best place to learn.

• Begin with food he can easily feed himself and a cup he can drink from without accidents. Be patient, praise him, and don't expect perfection.

• Be aware of your child's motor abilities. Eating with utensils takes a lot of skill. Early attempts may indeed resemble those of a wild boar, but may be the best he can do.

• Don't postpone participation in family dinners until he has the proper manners. Kids don't acquire them by themselves. We have heard stories about college students from very proper families having to take etiquette lessons before they interview for jobs. Somehow the parents never felt the kids' manners were good enough to join the family dinner hour.

Mealtime or Playtime?

> My toddler plays with his food and thinks it is funny when I get mad. He finger paints with it on his high-chair tray and then pours his milk in it to make splashing sounds when he slaps it with his hands. Then he smears it in his hair and all over his face. I could go on but I think you've got the picture. Is this a stage of some kind? Does it last long?

• If it's a stage, it's called toddlerhood and it lasts about two years.

• Don't get mad, but do what you can to prevent it from getting out of hand. Serve food and drink separately, serve small portions, and take it away if he starts "playing," telling him he can have it back if he eats like a "big boy." Praise his good manners when he uses them.

• Take the food away once your child has stopped eating. Hungry kids seldom play with food.

• Give your child ample opportunity to play with real finger paint, bath-time body paint, bubbles, and shaving cream. Also sandboxes and wading pools are good sources for making messes.

Tiny Appetites

> My fourteen-month-old eats like a bird. She used to eat like a small horse. She wants to feed herself but can't do it very well. Would she eat more if I let her do it herself?

• Toddlers often eat like birds. It is a time of slow growth and development. Check with your pediatrician and make sure she is getting enough of the right food.

• Let her feed herself the things she can handle reasonably well. That's how she learns—through practice.

• Mealtime is one of the first arenas in which toddlers seek control. If parents decide what control they want their child to have and then happily give it, many problem are avoided. For example, toddlers can feed themselves "chunky" food with their fingers or with a small fork. They can handle some soft food with a spoon, especially if it is sticky like mashed potatoes. And awkward food such as soup, can be repackaged in a cup for easier handling.

Family Meals

> How old should a child be before he can eat with the rest of the family at suppertime?

• The earlier the better, especially if the evening meal is the only time the family is together.

• Moving up supper time to fit the schedule of the youngest one may make things go more smoothly.

• Feeding the toddler first and letting him have his dessert while the rest of the family eats supper is a good transition also.

• Don't expect the toddler to stay at the table for more than five minutes to begin with. Let him leave before he gets fussy.

• Don't let the older children regress to the toddler's level or laugh at his rookie table manners. Imitation teaches both good *and* bad behavior. Tell them how important their good examples are for little brother—and that someday he will probably sit at the head table during their wedding receptions, where everyone they know can see the manners he learned from his older siblings.

Fussy Eaters

> My daughter likes apple juice, strained peas, carrots, hamburger, chicken franks, and vanilla pudding, period. She won't eat anything else. She drinks very little milk. How do I get her to try new things? Can you force a child to eat?

• First make sure she is getting the nutrients she needs. Keep an exact diary of what she eats and drinks during a seven-day period—food and amount. Check with your pediatrician to make sure the diet is healthy. It doesn't sound too bad, but you might want to add a multivitamin preparation of some kind.

• You can also gain some peace of mind by comparing her weight with other kids her age and height and talking to other parents of toddlers. It is a slow growth stage and appetites seem to decrease also.

• Now, about the variety of food. How is the rest of the family? Does Dad eat asparagus and brussels sprouts or is he a corn and peas man? Do you eat pears and tangerines or do you limit yourself to apples and oranges? One strategy to increase your toddler's food preference is to have Mom and Dad model that behavior and try new foods, too.

• Use your imagination and dress up food so it looks like fun. Find a children's cookbook and see how to make pineapple salads look like bunny faces and how to cut sandwiches into cute shapes.

• Make sure you aren't spicing up your toddler's food too much. Parents often add salt, pepper, and spices to fit their own palates. That's usually too much for little ones.

• If your child is getting enough nutrients and seems healthy and happy, don't worry about the lack of variety. Many adults raised on peanut butter and jelly have become gourmet cooks and connoisseurs of fine food.

Nap-time Resistance

My eighteen-month-old went from two naps a day to none. He gets so whiney by supper time that he falls asleep before he finishes eating. How do I get him to nap? He needs the rest and so do I!

• The rare toddler can get by without naps, but this pattern is usually apparent in infancy. Many toddlers actively fight going to bed, both at night and at nap time, which has nothing to do with needing or not needing sleep. It has to do with being so interested in exploring his exciting world that he hates to miss anything. Yours sounds like he resists in the afternoon but is too tired to struggle at night.

• Try separating nap time from bedtime. Let him sleep in a different bed or on the family-room sofa. Have a small blanket or afgan just for naps. Make a different ritual for nap time than you have for bedtime. For example, if you read stories at bedtime, play a game at nap time or listen to a record or tape.

• Take a nap with him. Tell him it is nap time and you'll

both lie down, cover up, and read one story. Then you will close your eyes and go to sleep. Let him pick the story. Once he is asleep, you can get up quietly and enjoy the solitude, or you can take a nap, too.

• If he doesn't want to sleep, tell him he can just lie there with his eyes closed. A tired toddler in a quiet room with his eyes closed for two or three minutes will very likely fall asleep.

• Don't expect it to be easy to establish a nap-time habit. It's worth the effort. And don't be surprised if his bedtime behavior becomes more troublesome for a while. It seems he has been going to bed easily because he was so tired from not napping. Now he may have the energy to fight bedtime. If you haven't yet, establish a bedtime routine and stick to it, just like the one at nap time.

Wide Awake Baby, Wide Awake Toddler

My son is thirteen months old and he doesn't sleep. I put him in his crib at 9:00 P.M. and he plays and talks to himself until ten at least. Then he is awake at 6:00 A.M.. He has never taken morning naps and now skips his afternoon nap almost every day. He will go in his crib for an hour, but he doesn't sleep. None of my baby books prepared me for this!

• If your toddler gets by with eight hours of sleep per night and no naps, *and* seems good-natured while he is awake, *and* has always gotten by with little sleep, you have one of those rare babies who doesn't need much sleep.

• Don't give up the early bedtime or the afternoon crib time. It's a good way to divide up the day, to get him to rest a little, and to spend some quiet time alone. It's also a nice break for Mom and Dad.

• Another reason for establishing a "rest-time" schedule is that when your son goes to nursery school or kindergarten, the other kids will probably take afternoon naps and it won't be a new concept for him.

• Thomas Edison started this way.

Escape Artist

> My twenty-month-old daughter climbs out of her crib in the morning and plays with toys in her room until we wake up. She seems very proud of herself and I hate to discourage her independence, but I worry about what comes next.

• Next she'll probably climb out of her crib at night, and go downstairs in the mornings and fix herself breakfast. You are right to worry. But you are also right not to punish her independence and her pride. Toddlers do not understand your concern for their safety.

• Make sure your daughter's room is completely childproof. Put a gate across the door. Teach your daughter to call you when she wakes up. Make sure potential hazards such as stairs and swimming pools are completely inaccessible. Putting a mattress on the floor or buying a low bed avoids accidents when crawling over the side of the crib.

• Wise parents worry more about their child's safety and self-esteem than their own sleep. They go to bed earlier, take naps, or take turns getting up with the little one.

Separation: Day-care, Nursery School, and Baby-sitters

Many of the ideas from the previous chapter will apply here. The decision about who takes care of the baby is an important one and needs to be discussed at length by the baby's parents. Opinions by grandparents, friends, and child-development experts need to be considered, but the final decision should be made by the parents, based on what is best for all members of their family.

Once a decision is made, and whatever it is, both parents need to be committed to it. This rules out *any* of the following:

"I really miss work, but my husband insists I stay home with the baby. You know what a male chauvinist he is."

"My wife wanted to stay some with the baby, but I sent her back to work. The way she spends money, we need her income. And when she's at work, she's not shopping. Ha-ha."

"I'd love to quit work and stay home with the baby, but my

husband won't let me. He's trying to start up his own business and these next few years are critical ones.''

"My husband said if I wanted a baby, I'd have to quit my job and stay home until she started kindergarten. So here I am, with three years left to go.''

To summarize, whatever the arrangement, both parents should feel certain it's good for the children, it's good for the marriage, and it's for the relationship with grandparents. In many ways the actual decisions parents make are not as important as the way those decisions are made and supported.

Sitter Spoils Child

I am a divorced mother with a sixteen-month-old baby. I have an older woman who comes to our house each day and takes care of the baby. Everything went fine until recently, but I think she is spoiling him. She picks him up out of his crib as soon as he makes a sound and feeds him as soon as he seems the least bit hungry. Then, when I am home, he expects the same attention. I am busy. I have all the housework to do plus the paperwork I bring home from our shop. My sister has three whiney brats and I certainly don't want my son to end up like that.

This sitter is very dependable and I hate to let her go because she needs the money. But I want to do what's right for my child.

• Responding to a child's need promptly is not spoiling. The only time it can be a problem is if it is so extreme that the child doesn't learn to communicate because everything is provided before he has a chance to ask, but it doesn't sound as if that is the problem here.

• On the other hand, there is a difference between prompt responding to a baby's needs and overreacting. Talk with your sitter and be sure she is reading your baby's signals correctly. She should be able to tell the difference between sounds that say, "I'm ready for lunch," and others that say, "I'm awake and enjoying a quiet conversation with my teddy bear."

• It seems like you have two very different forms of child care: the sitter, who only cares for the baby, and the mother, who not only works at the shop but does housework and shop work at the house. That's enough to keep several people busy. When you add baby care to the list of jobs, it's almost impossible. Explore your options.

• Hire more help at work so you don't have to take the book work home. How about a part-time bookkeeper, perhaps a young mother who left her bookkeeping job to stay home with her baby?

• Expand the sitter's duties. If she needs the extra money, she may welcome a chance to add some light housework to her sitting duties. Then you will have a more relaxed time when you are home with your baby.

• Maybe the sitter can stay later each day, or come in on alternate Saturday mornings to take care of the baby while you get the book work done. You can probably do more in an uninterrupted hour than in several hours being distracted by household demands.

• Have you asked the sitter about her ideas of spoiling and responding promptly? She might know more than all of us.

• We doubt if your sister's children became brats from getting prompt attention. If you watch closely, they are probably ignored until they whine and cry. Then when it gets really annoying, the parents give in angrily and resentfully to whatever they are whining and crying about. This is not a very successful child-rearing method.

Clinging to Mom at Day-care

My son is eighteen months old and has been in day-care since he was six months old. Lately we have been having problems with him clinging to me and crying when I drop him off in the morning. Is this just a stage he is going through, or is it something I should be worried about?

• If your child has been going to day-care cheerfully since he was six months old and now cries and clings every morning, the most likely explanation is that something has changed in his life—either at day-care or at home—and he needs a little extra security right now.

• Does he have a new teacher or care giver during the day?

This is a major change for a toddler, even if he likes the new person immensely.

• How about a new room, or a change in the daily routine? Some children are very sensitive to changes and become upset for a while when something in their world has altered.

• Has there been a change at home? Do you have a new car? Have you moved your child from his crib to a conventional bed? Have you painted his room and rearranged his furniture? Have you gotten a new pet or lost an old one? Has your brother left his wife and moved in with your family? Whether positive or negative changes are involved, it takes time for some children to adjust.

• Children also react sometimes to tension in their parents. Are you under unusual pressure at work recently, or are you concerned about some other aspect of your life? Parents are often surprised when small children react to events such as work deadlines, corporate mergers, and annual-employee evaluations. Actually they are reacting to the parent's stress instead.

• Some children go through a type of stranger anxiety in the late teen months, and that should be considered. But since your child hasn't yet shown it, if the day-care personnel are all familiar, this is a long shot.

• Be sympathetic about your child's feelings, but be firm about going to work. Suggest that he take a favorite toy to school, or a blanket to use at nap time. Some parents give their toddler a family picture to carry with them or put in their lunch box. Photo shops sell key rings with plastic picture holders attached that can be fastened to belt loops or buttonholes.

• Ask the teacher or care giver for some suggestions. When they know you are concerned, they will make a special effort with your child.

• Try having Dad drive your son to day-care for a while.

Adult Vacations

My husband travels a lot with his job and I often have opportunities to go along with him. We usually go in the middle of the week so he can work three days, and then spend the weekend vacationing.

Our baby is twenty-two months old and my parents are

willing, competent sitters. The only problem is the baby—she screamed and cried so much that we ended up taking her with us on the last two trips.

What can we do to get her to stay? Are we wrong to leave a baby so young for five days?

• Such decisions as these need to be made by the parents, after consulting the grandparents, friends with babies this age, a book on child care, and maybe the pediatrician. They should not be made by the twenty-two-month-old baby. You missed out on two adult vacations, Grandma and Grandpa missed out on time with their granddaughter, and your daughter missed out on a fun time with her grandparents—not to mention the benefit of happy, well-rested parents.

• The next time you decide to take a trip without your daughter, tell her what is happening. If she complains, be sympathetic, but tell her it is a trip for grown-ups and she is staying with Grandma and Grandpa. You probably won't convince her that she doesn't want to go, but that isn't necessary.

• Call Grandma and Grandpa from the airport and hear the news that she's already having a great time. Then leave and enjoy yourself.

• Make arrangements to phone your daughter at specified times. It will let her know that you haven't disappeared off the face of the earth and let you know how well she's adjusting.

The Right Stuff in Day-care

My daughter has been in day-care since she was six months old. Now she is eighteen months old and I am beginning to wonder if she needs a different type of care. The two women who run the nursery are very kind and loving, but they don't seem to interact with the kids very much or offer much stimulation. I know my daughter is well fed, clean, and safe, and maybe I should be thankful for that.

• It depends on what you mean by "stimulation." Toddlers do need social interaction with adults and need to be treated as intelligent little individuals. If you feel your daughter is being fed, washed, and then left to stare into space until the next diaper change, you should find another day-care arrangement. But if you mean that she isn't being given "academics"—pages of workbooks to color featuring letters of the alphabet and counting exercises—it really doesn't matter. Toddlers are too young to benefit from such "stimulation," and schools that offer it do so to compete for the "day-care dollar."

• Talk to the director of your day-care center or the teacher and express your concerns. The atmosphere you see when you pick up your daughter may be misleading. Some teachers like the kids to relax and unwind at the end of the day and may plan some mellow, low-key activity around closing time.

• One benefit of your present day-care is familiarity. Maybe you could do something to add a little stimulation during the day, such as donating some age-appropriate toys and games.

On the Home Front

Potty Training

My son is twenty months old and shows no interest in using the potty. My sister's kids were all trained by this time. We have a play group at our church that he can go to twice a week if he is out of diapers. What should I do?

• Don't worry about it. Most experts believe that potty training before two is a wasted effort unless kids show some inclination to use the potty on their own.

• "Potty training" is a little misleading. Kids learn to use the potty, of course, but the real trick is being able to predict the need for the potty and then wait long enough to get there. If you think about it, it involves quite a few mental and physical skills. Unless all those systems are mature enough to be functioning together, it is a hopeless task, despite the best intentions from everyone.

• A backlash problem can occur if too much training is done too early. Depending on their dispositions, children can learn that they are unsuccessful, a disappointment to their parents, or not as accomplished as their cousins. The resulting frustration and anger can come out as tantrums or angry outbursts anytime during the day. They can decide not to cooperate anymore and not to go anywhere near the potty for months to come. So besides it not working, it can cause more problems than you had to begin with.

• Find out what the deal is with the play group that requires potty training. If it is only half a day, there's no reason your child can't attend in diapers and be changed afterward.

Childproofing II

> My son never walked—he started running at thirteen months and hasn't stopped. I feel like I'm living with a small tornado. When I read about childproofing, I laugh. He childproofed our home himself—he has already destroyed everything valuable we have. But what do I do when we visit other people?

• Childproofing is more than just protecting your valuables. It's protecting your child as well. Many parents do a thorough job of it when the baby is born, but slack off after the first year, when it's even more important. Toddlers are actively exploring everything and learning to open cabinets, twist-off tops, and push buttons. They also reach higher, climb, and go from room to room quickly. To complicate things further, they learn new tricks almost overnight. Examine your house with a fine tooth comb and with this question in mind: "What's the *last* thing I would expect my toddler to get into in this room?" Then fix it, because he will.

• Your son sounds like a high-energy kid—the turbo model. And you sound like a parent with a sense of humor, which can be a good survival skill. Make your first priority your child's safety. Your second priority should be enforcing a few good family rules to ensure some structure and security for everyone. Bedtime, nap time, mealtime should all be routinized as much a possible. Important rules need to be stated simply and patiently, over and over.

• At this stage and with this child, visiting in other peoples' houses is looking for trouble. If possible, ask friends and relatives to visit you for a few months, or meet friends at the park, where your child can run and play.

Disciplining Other People's Children

> I can handle my toddler just fine, but when other people visit with their kids, I have a problem enforcing my rules. One of my friends spends our time together following her child around and punishing him for every move he makes—even things I let my own child do. The other sits and visits and lets her son do anything he wants. Is there a middle ground somewhere?

• There is no simple answer. Generally visiting parents should impose the same rules on their children that the resident children live with. For example, if the kids of the house are *never* allowed to play in the sprinklers, visiting kids should not either, even if it is allowed at home. Even toddlers can understand that there may be two rules here, (1) We can play in the sprinklers at home, and (2) We can't play in the sprinklers at Jennifer's house.

• There are rules that visitors follow at home and the host family does not—for example, eating everything on one's plate before getting dessert. Most of these rules can be left at home during occasional visits.

• Then there are important rules that both host and visitor may find necessary to impose on each other's family. For example, if your child regularly takes an after-lunch nap and is cranky without one, it would be a good idea to make that clear to friends and plan visits accordingly, regardless of the other child's nap habits. And if your toddler regularly strips down to the buff to play in the backyard wading pool, you might want to put a bathing suit on him if your guest has strong feelings about toddler nudity.

Reprimanding or punishing children works best if each mother supervises her own. However, when rules vary extremely, you should address your concerns to the parent, not the child. "I really don't mind if he plays with the sofa pillows—I bought washable ones intentionally," or, "I think you should tell Megan to stop pulling on the dog's ears—he's never bitten anyone yet, but I'd hate for anything like that to happen."

Doing It Himself

> My twenty-two-month-old has decided to dress himself now. He insists on it and we have real power struggles every morning. He is much too young to be able to do it, but he won't listen to me. How do I convince him to let me dress him right?

• It is very difficult to convince twenty-two-month-olds of anything, especially on matters of their own limitations. Instead, be happy that he is showing such independence. It takes a good parent/child bond for children to be so sure of themselves and their abilities.

• It is also difficult to convince a toddler that the results of their efforts are not perfect. This is also something to be happy about—if young children had any idea of how poorly they did things, they'd get discouraged and never try again.

• Are there parts of dressing he *can* do well, such as pulling down his T-shirt once it's over his head or pulling up his socks once the toes are in place? Let him do that and make a big deal of it.

• Don't think in terms of "power struggles." All he wants is to feel good about himself. A real power struggle would be if he told *you* what to wear and when to get dressed. He just wants a little control over his own life, which is the goal of parenting anyhow.

Doing It Himself, Part 2

> I have a problem with my toddler. He is seventeen months old and keeps taking his clothes off. I just get him dressed in the morning and start loading up the car for work and there he is, stark-naked, happy as a lark. The worst was at my mother-in-law's after Easter dinner. The kids went in the playroom and the adults sat at the table talking, and suddenly Eric appeared in the doorway without a stitch on. His grandmother was shocked, and my husband and his brothers thought it was hysterical. Am I raising a little exhibitionist?

• Two rules about toddlers: (1) they like to do things themselves, and (2) there isn't much they can do. When these are combined, you get behavior such as Eric's Easter surprise. Eric would probably like nothing more than to dress himself, feed himself, and drive himself to Grandma's house, but he can't. However, he has learned recently that he *can* undress himself. Instead of being happy as a lark that he was naked, he probably was happy as a lark that he had managed to take his clothes off. That's quite a feat for a seventeen-month old.

• Adults often read things into children's behavior that isn't there, as illustrated by the differing reactions of Grandma and Eric's male relatives. It's always nice if a parent can quickly run interference so Eric doesn't feel rotten about his accomplishment. Next time (and there is sure to be one), swoop him up and say something in mock desperation like, "Oh Eric, I know you are proud to be able to take your clothes off, but Easter is not the place for a demonstration!" His pride and happiness will set a far better foundation for appropriate behavior in the future than anger or confusion.

• Give him lots of opportunity to undress at appropriate times, such as before baths. With a little practice, he should be able to dress himself soon.

• Write down the story of "Eric's Easter Surprise" in his baby book and tell him about it when he gets older.

Problems with Dressing

> My son wants to make dressing time into playtime and I often don't have time to fool with that in the mornings. The madder I get, the wilder he becomes. I just get his shirt on and turn to reach for his pants when he bolts away and runs down the hallway. Any suggestions?

• Toddlers have limited thinking space, so if they are busy with one line of thought, they won't have room for another. That's why distraction works so well. Try giving him a small toy he can hold and work with his fingers while you dress him—maybe something with movable parts. Or give him his shoes to untie while you are putting on his clothes.

• Keep a box of objects nearby that are fun to touch. Examples would be elastic (it stretches), bells (they jingle), Scotch tape (it's sticky), cotton balls (fuzzy), and aluminum foil (crinkly). Plastic paperweights filled with water and "snow" that falls on scenes inside are fascinating, too. Reserve these things for special times and they'll serve to distract.

• Keep dressing simple. For example, if you manage to get all his clothes on him, don't worry about his T-shirt matching his shorts or his socks not quite matching each other. He certainly won't care, and it doesn't sound as if he'll hold still long enough for anyone else to notice either.

• Keep him entertained with a nursery rhyme or song, or talk to him about where you are going once he is dressed. For example, "Do you know where we are going this morning? We're going to the grocery store. And do you know what we are going to buy? Some milk for Daddy and some apple juice for Mommy, and what do you want?" Asking questions of toddlers, especially when it involves something interesting like the kind of cookies you are going to buy, takes their mind off horsing around long enough for a swift-handed parent to dress them.

Baby Jeckyl/Baby Hyde

At fifteen months, my wonderful, even-tempered baby turned into Oscar the Grouch. We finally saved enough money to move into a house with a nice yard and a big family room so Sean can have all his toys out to play with. There are kids around his age, but he has been in such a rotten mood I hate to invite them over. I know the two's are supposed to be stormy, but isn't this a little early?

• Toddlers don't know that a house with a yard and a family room is more desirable, only that home is more secure and familiar. Sean may be reacting to the changes—the addition of the new things, the loss of the old things, and the stress parents are experiencing with new mortgage payments and commuting schedules. Be patient with him and bring out some old familiar toys and belongings.

• Extreme changes in a child's temperament could signal health problems, so a call to your pediatrician is recommended (the old one who has all Sean's records).

• Sean won't suffer too much if you don't feel you can invite the other neighborhood kids over to play. At this age, they aren't very interested in their peer group anyhow.

• One benefit from meeting the new kids, though, is meeting their parents. Other parents are great sources of suggestions when you have problems with your kids. There's usually one parent you know who has had a similar problem, and if nothing else, they can give you a little sympathy or support.

Tub-Drain Terrors

> Until recently my twenty-one-month-old loved his bath. Now he seems terrified of it. We have been trying to remember if something happened recently to scare him, but my husband and I are really at a loss. What could make a kid change so quickly? What can we do?

• At this age some kids develop a fear of things that disappear quickly, such as draining the tub and flushing the toilet. Psychologists believe it has something to do with children developing the thinking skills to realize that things don't just disappear magically, they go somewhere else. Even though they can't see them anymore, they are *somewhere*. Fortunately it's a transitory stage and if parents handle it calmly, there should be no lasting problems.

• Try filling the tub before he gets in and taking him out of the bathroom before the water is drained.

• If that doesn't help, give him sponge baths for a while and try to distract him from the "tub-drain" issue until he outgrows it.

• Don't try to explain the mechanics of drains to him and expect him to reason his way out of this fear. He needs to mature a little, and then he can figure it out for himself.

• Think about this situation and file it away for future reference. Who knows how many of these transitory fears are possible? Psychologists don't know about everything, especially short-lived problems that only affect a few children. The next time your child is showing some strange behavior or irrational fear, give him or her the benefit of the doubt. Comfort them, respect their wishes, and avoid the frightening situation for a while. Toddlers' minds are little works of art, but we sometimes forget that they have a way to go before they see the world like we do.

Forgets Rules

My son is twenty months old and I have a problem with him forgetting the rules. For example, he is not allowed to open the desk drawers in the den and he will do just fine at that for a few days, then there he is, opening the desk drawers. I tell him no, slap his hand, and put him in his room, but none of this helps. What can I do?

• The only thing that works at this age is to childproof your house. This means either closing off the den, moving things out of the drawers, or putting locks on the drawers so he can't get in.

• Slapping his hands and putting him in his room are a waste of energy for you and can cause your bright, adventurous, curious little boy to become confused and afraid of his surroundings. He is too young to understand your message, no matter how carefully or how often you tell him.

• Check out a child-care class in your area or join a parents' group to find out more about what to expect from your son at various ages.

Visits, Outings, and Trips

During the first year, the most important aspect of planning a visit or outing is the baby's sleeping and feeding schedule. Now that a little more flexibility is available, many parents feel that they can fit their toddler into their adult schedules. The irony of it is that it works to a point. A toddler *can* wait to have lunch later than usual when a friend is delayed or the waiter is slow, and a toddler *can* skip a nap while running through the mall on an afternoon shopping trip. But the result is often whining, fussing, out-of-control behavior.

Much behavior parents consider "discipline problems" are caused by children who are hungry or tired. This "bratty" behavior is further complicated when parents realize that their child is capable of better behavior and for some reason isn't displaying it. We hear accusations of "defiant" toddlers engaged in a battle of wills with their parents, of "revengeful" preschoolers punishing their parents with obnoxious behavior displays in front of important clients, and of "controlling" children misbehaving on purpose as part of a power struggle with their parents.

Preschool children are not capable of the kind of thinking required for such sophisticated plans, plots, and schemes. It is not until a child is at least five or six years old that he can consider the consequences of the right behavior and then compare it with the wrong behavior.

Toddlers get tired and hungry. They don't have much patience. They feel discomfort and insecurity when they're not fed. They have short fuses when they are sleepy. They don't want control or revenge, they want lunch and a nap. The best solution for many discipline problems out in public is to plan shopping trips and other outings for times your child is in the best mood and to keep them short and sweet.

Visits with Other Children

> My wife and I agreed that she would stay home with the baby the first year. Now our daughter is fourteen months old and I think she should be in a nursery school or somewhere that she's around other kids her age. My wife doesn't agree and thinks I just want her to go back to work. I don't care about that. I've just seen other kids her age that seem more advanced, and they all go to nursery school or to a baby-sitter who has other kids around.

• Kids don't seem to need social interaction with other kids their age until they are older. At your daughter's age, she would probably ignore another fourteen-month-old, or at best, play side by side with her. Right now she is still learning about things in her environment and interaction with family members.

• As your daughter gets older, she may enjoy being with other children. There are some compromise situations, such as forming play groups in the neighborhood, having a baby-sitting co-op, and having kids in day-care for only two or three mornings a week. This would give your wife a little time off and a little interaction with other mothers.

• Whether or not your wife works seems to be a side issue and should be discussed separately.

Toddlers Won't Share

> My sixteen-month-old is very selfish with her toys. We talk to her about sharing, but when my friend's toddler comes over to play, Erica won't let her touch anything. It's really embarrassing.

• Teaching a child to share takes more than talking, it takes maturation. Erica is not capable of understanding the concept of ownership, nonownership, and social graces.

• Keep talking to her about sharing in a very positive way. She won't understand for a few years, but at least she will know the words and the situations.

• Don't be embarrassed by your daughter's "childish" behavior. She's just acting like a sixteen-month-old.

Toddler Aggression

> Whenever my nineteen-month-old plays with other kids, he gets real aggressive. He hits and kicks and throws things at his friends. I don't know what to do. I plan to put him in day-care soon and I want him to be able to get along with other kids.

• Nineteen-month-old babies don't have friends. They have very little idea of other people and really can't be "taught" social niceties such as sharing and getting along with others. If your son is hitting and kicking, it's probably not directed at anyone in particular; he's just angry and frustrated about something.

• The best thing to do is make playtime short and at a time when he is well-rested and fed. If he starts aggressive behavior, remove him immediately from the other children and take him home. This is more prevention than punishment. Tell him, "It looks like you aren't having a very good time with the other kids, so I think we should go home."

Grocery Store Mania

> Timothy is nineteen months old and I dread taking him
> grocery shopping. He starts out fine, but then he gets bored
> and starts taking things off shelves, throwing things out of the
> basket, and grabbing things out of my purse. I keep thinking
> he will outgrow this, but it just seems he is getting worse. I
> have even thought about getting a sitter while I go shopping!

• The key to young Timothy's behavior may be the word
"bored." Parents often fall into the trap of thinking that the
only fun children have are with name-brand toys or at theme
parks. The truth is that kids have fun in the darndest places,
like the grocery store. Young Tim starts out having fun, but
then as you say, he gets "bored." If you had to ride around in
a cart for forty-five minutes, you might throw boxes of cookies
around, too.

• Start involving Timothy in the shopping. He belongs in the
family and he eats—good prerequisites. Talk to him about
what you are buying. For example, "Now we need cereal for
Daddy—he likes this kind. Where is Timothy's cereal? What
do you think your bother would like?"

• Name things for him. Show him apples and bananas. Remind him that he had pears at Grandma's house last week. Let
him repeat things after you, or ask him to name familiar products.

• Give him your list and let him cross things off with a
crayon. He won't know that he's not doing it right. Hand him
nonbreakable items and let him put them in the basket. Let him
hold things.

• One more comment—what's so funny about hiring a sitter
so you can go grocery shopping? It might be worth every cent
to both you and Timothy.

Car Travel

> We have planned a trip this summer to visit relatives and it
> will take two days by car. Our baby will be twenty-three
> months old. Any suggestions?

• Consider driving at night. Give your child a bath, put him in pajamas, go through your nighttime ritual, and put him in the car. Hopefully, he will sleep through the night and you will make good progress. It's probably a good idea for one parent to sleep also, or to take turns.

• During the daytime, it's important to stop often so your child can get out of his car seat and move around—also to have a different view to look at.

• Bring toys and perhaps a tape recorder with favorite songs. Keep items in reach in a storage compartment that fits on the back of the front seats

• Also consider taking an older child along for the trip if you have relatives or close friends that are familiar to your child. A ten- or twelve-year-old can be a big help on a trip to entertain the baby during the long ride and to be an extra pair of hands at rest stops.

Toddlers can cause problems, primarily because of their increased abilities. Perhaps their greater mobility is the most direct cause of problems that children in the second year present us, but a close second is related to their increased mental abilities. Their intellectual blossoming is a marvelous thing to watch, and it will continue. And many of the problems children present to us in the twelve- to twenty-four-month period will be magnified during the "terrible twos." Thus, the "Year of the Toddler" can be thought of as preparation for the "Year of the Two-Year-Old." One way to get through the next few years in good shape is to get off to a good start with the less complicated toddler.

11. Twos: Terrible and Otherwise

The remarkable aspect of the period from twenty-four to thirty-six months is that toddlers begin having their own ideas and wishes. If parents have viewed their roles as molding little lumps of clay into wonderful works of art, they'll be very frustrated. On the other hand, most parents are fascinated to see this little individual emerging.

Two-year-olds are quite accomplished. Not only can they walk, climb, and hop—they *know* they can and are proud of their new abilities. Not only do they have possessions, they *know* they do and are quick to point out what is "mine." Not only can they do an adequate job of feeding themselves, they *know* they can and often insist on "doing it myself."

The second half of the two-year-old's year is affectionately called the "terrible twos," although that time period is approximate. Some parents report that their children began the day of their second birthdays and others report that their children were little angels the entire twelve months.

One of the things that makes two-year-olds terrible is their frustration. Children at this age *know* a good deal more than they can *do*. This can be said of children at most ages, but this is the first time in a child's life when he or she can envision so many possibilities. Yet skills are very limited, which understandably leads to frustration. The discrepancy between their awareness and their abilities means that much of the time children will not be able to have or do what they want. This frustration sometimes causes anger, which almost always causes trouble. But remember, the trouble is a sign of a developing intellect—of a child coming to grips with the difference between thinking and doing.

Mealtime, Bedtime, and Other Schedules

Most two-year-olds sleep about thirteen hours per night and take a two- to three-hour nap in the afternoon. By this time parents should be able to predict their child's sleep needs and schedule the family routine accordingly. For example, staying up late for a special Saturday night celebration should be a signal to plan a quiet afternoon on Sunday and perhaps an earlier-than-usual bedtime Sunday night.

Still Sleeps with Mom and Dad

> My son is two-and-a-half and I wish he would sleep in his own bed at night. It seems like everytime we try and change this arrangement, he gets sick, or the weather turns cold, or my husband goes on a trip and I like the company. How can we get him to sleep in his own bed?

• Communal sleeping arrangements are encouraged by some experts while others consider it harmful to the child. The important thing is what you and your husband believe. Think of the message you are giving your child. You let him sleep there, but you don't like it—unless your husband is out of town and then you "like his company." Those certainly are mixed messages. Discuss this issue and then take some steps to put your beliefs into action.

• If you decide to move him, make a big deal of it being "his own bed." Two-year-olds are big on ownership. Tell him that no one can sleep there unless he says so. Ask him if his teddy bear can sleep in his bed or if Raggedy Ann is allowed. Take his permission seriously. Try a new set of sheets with cartoon characters on them. Then you have to be tough. Stay with him in his room for a while at night so you aren't depriving him of your presence. Be consistent, regardless of whether he is sick, the weather is cold, or your husband is out of town.

• Having your husband out of town might be a nice time to start enforcing "everyone in their *own* beds" rules. That way it won't be interpreted as parents' rejection of the child.

• If you decide to let him sleep with you, give him permission and make it one hundred percent okay.

Won't Take Naps

> Nicholas is thirty months old and won't take naps at home, although he does at school. Could it be that he needs the sleep more the days he is at school? He sleeps eleven hours at night and on weekends he sometimes falls asleep before supper.

• Instead of counting the hours slept, consider his mood and behavior on the days he doesn't nap. Does he enjoy his toys, his shopping trips with Mommy, his baby brother? Or does he get upset easily, whine, have angry outbursts when things don't go his way? Although there are other reasons for this kind of behavior, lack of sleep is a prime suspect.

• How does he go to sleep at school? Does the teacher read a story, play music, turn the lights down low? Start your own nap-time ritual. One mother we know lets her preschooler take his nap in his older brother's room, as long as he acts like a big boy and goes to sleep nicely. Another grandmother we know keeps a Mickey Mouse sleeping bag in her closet that belonged to the kids' uncle. They can pick any room in the house for a nap and use the sleeping bag to "camp out" *if* they go right to sleep. (These kids never nap at home, but always take two- or three-hour naps at Grandma's.)

• This is not a silly suggestion—take a nap with your toddler! The only folks who need naps more than two-year-olds are their parents.

Breakfast Blues

> Breakfast time is our biggest problem. We are all in a hurry to get off to work and our various car pools when our two-year-old starts causing trouble. He dawdles, but refuses to let anyone feed him to hurry him up. If I pour his milk, he cries because he wanted Daddy to pour it. If I give him his Care Bears cereal bowl, he wants his Mickey Mouse bowl. Nothing we do makes him happy, and quite frankly, I am very glad to drop him off at nursery school after a morning like that. Is this a stage he will get over or a real problem?

• Parents often need to play detective when these problem situations set in. Your child could be just going through a "terrible-two" stage, practicing oppositional behavior simply because he can do it. Clues would be that he is closer to three than to two, and that he approaches this negative behavior without much negative emotion such as whining and crying. If this seems to fit, be as patient as possible and use your sense of humor. He's just learned some new tricks and is trying them out. Give in to the demands you can tolerate and be firm on the others.

• On the other hand, your son could be reacting to an overload of stress in the morning—at least an overload for him. Kids don't like feeling out of control, and if the whirlwind of family activity pushes him in the corner, he might feel a need to take some action himself. Clues would be if he has always been rattled by fast changes and confusion, and if he seems to improve on weekends and when things are less hectic. If this seems to be the case, do what you can to make mornings more tranquil.

• A third possibility is that your son may not be getting enough sleep. Clues would be negative emotion accompanying his demands, such as whining and crying. Move his bedtime up gradually and see if this helps. Also, make sure he is napping at nursery school.

Miss Independence

My twenty-seven-month-old daughter wants to pour her own milk and juice. I really don't feel like cleaning up the table and floor several times a day. Sometimes she even refuses to drink unless she pours it herself. At what age can children pour carefully? What do I do until then?

• Wanting to pour her own milk and juice is something that should be encouraged. It is an important skill to have and not just some silly privilege she's demanding. However, no one likes cleaning up after the "learning process."

• Think creatively and look for some options or compromises. For example, how about letting her pour it, with your help, over the sink? Or, how about letting her pour water, which is not expensive and easier to clean up. She also could assist in the cleanup if necessary. Or why not put the juice or milk in a small container that is easier to pour?

• These are good problem-solving skills for parents to develop. In just fourteen years or so, she will want to drive your car.

Wants Weird Food

Jason is two-and-a-half and has very definite tastes, such as crackers and peanut butter with a slice of pickle on top. My mother-in-law thinks he might have some kind of mineral deficiency or something, but I think his older brother and sister have something to do with it. They think it is hysterical. Is he too young to be influenced by peer pressure?

• What a deadly combination—a two-year-old and an adoring audience of older siblings. You are lucky peanut butter and pickles is the worst combination they could think of!

• As long as Jason is getting balanced meals, you shouldn't worry about his weird tastes.

• Do what you can to make Jason's relationship with his brother and sister strong and positive.

• Complain (when your children can hear you) about how much Jason loves his brother and sister and how he will do anything to make them laugh—even eat peanut butter and pickles! Also point out more positive things that Jason does to entertain the older kids or to imitate them.

• Take a picture and write this in Jason's baby book.

Separation: Day-care and Sitters

Security Blankets

> Stephanie is thirty-three months old and still takes her "banky" to school. It's getting old and gray, and I have to wash it several times a week. Also, it's a little embarrassing to have such a big kid carrying this blanket around. How do I get her to stop?

• It is not unusual for children Stephanie's age to still be carrying their "bankies" with them to nursery school. It provides a little help during the day, and with all the things kids have to deal with these days, parents shouldn't worry about such behavior.

• Ask Stephanie if she would like two blankets; then cut it in half (maybe when she isn't around to watch). This way the one she takes to school will be smaller and less conspicuous, and you'll have one to wash. If that is successful, try halving the blankets again into fourths a few weeks later.

• One child we know had handkerchief-sized "bankies" all over town—one at school, one at his mom's store, one at his grandma's house, and one in the car. He was so secure that he went away to college at seventeen and left all his bankies behind, at least as far as we know.

Won't Play Alone

> My two-year-old spends half his time telling me to let him do everything himself and the other half of his time not wanting to let me out of his sight. It's perplexing to me, and sometimes quite frustrating.

• Two-year-olds can only be independent if they are securely attached to their parents. You can see a good example of this at the playground. He will stay by you for a while and then wander away to play. After some fun, he'll return to "touch base." The older he gets, the farther he'll go and the longer he'll stay away. If he has a slight accident on the swing, or if a new kid appears, he may run back quickly and climb into your lap for a while. Then, when he feels safe, he will go back and explore again, sometimes with a new friend.

• Two-year-olds also venture out emotionally and intellectually. They want to "read" the book themselves; they turn and reply *"No!"* to your requests. That's as courageous a step as climbing on a new seesaw at the park. But then they have to touch base again, sometimes by climbing in your lap to be held like a baby or staying close to you and "not letting you out of their sight."

• Let him venture as much as possible and be there when he needs to touch base.

On the Home Front

Sibling Rivalry?

> Our kids are eight, six, and two. We never had a problem with the older kids being jealous of the baby, but it looks like the baby is getting jealous of the older two. For example, they do homework after supper at the dining room table. My wife is a former teacher and she helps them with their lessons. We always make sure the little one has toys to play with so he won't be a nuisance, but he wants to get in between my wife and the other kids. He has her at home all day to himself, but it seems like he's still jealous that she is spending evening time with our other two children. Should we send him to a nursery so he won't be so clingy?

• Absolutely not. Try looking at the situation from a more positive angle. Your two-year-old seems to be part of a warm, loving family, and he has recently realized that he is one of the group. When your wife helps the older kids with their homework, the toddler senses that something special is going on around the table and he wants to be part of it. After all, he is one of the family now. Putting himself between your wife and the other kids is probably his way of getting right in the middle of all that warmth and happiness and family togetherness. What toys can compete with that? And wouldn't you feel terrible sending him away from his family during the day to keep him from being so family oriented?

• An alternative would be for you and the little brother to join the family at the dining room table and do something quietly, such as coloring or looking at picture books. Or you could involve him in some other family activity, such as walking the dog, drying the supper dishes, or going to the store for a surprise dessert to eat after homework is finished.

Resistance: In the Car Seat, In the Bathroom, At the Table, etc.

> My two-year-old absolutely refuses to have a seat belt on in the car. It is a law in this state for two-year-olds to be in a car seat and wear a seat belt. He will sit in the car seat, but not wear the seat belt.

> Erin is twenty-eight months old and refuses to use a spoon or fork. She wants to eat everything with her hands. If I try to force-feed her, she clamps her mouth shut. If I insist that she use a spoon, she pushes the plate off the high-chair tray.

> I have a two-year-old son who refuses to let me put his shoes on him. The problem is that he can't put them on himself and he gets very frustrated and goes outdoors in his socks. When I try and help him, he hits me.

> My daughter was toilet trained completely six months ago and now she refuses to use the potty. She wants to use the big toilet, but she can't reach it. If I don't remember to help her, she will remove her pants and make a puddle on the bathroom floor. Then she puts her pants on again, cleans up the puddle with toilet paper, and flushes it away.

• One of the big problems with being two is that kids have bigger ideas than abilities. Parents hate to squelch this budding self-confidence, but sometimes it is necessary.

• Words of wisdom: Some things are worth fighting for and some things aren't. Parents should make that decision and then act accordingly—especially with two-year-olds whose behavior is bound to get better.

• For example, wearing seat belts is clearly worth fighting for. The shoe issue is debatable, depending on the weather and the child's destination. (It might be a good idea to buy some shoes the child *can* put on, such as those with Velcro fasteners or some sort of sandals.) Table manners are not worth fighting for at this age for most parents. (The resistant kid should be given finger food until her silverware skills improve. A small fork is sometimes easier to handle than a spoon.) The problem with the little child and the big toilet is probably worth fighting for, but it may depend on how many other issues the parents have to fight for that week. (A small step stool could solve a lot of problems.)

• Generally speaking, issues that involve independence should be handled with care. Toddlers aren't trying to take control of their parents, they just want control over parts of their own lives. Wanting to dress, feed, and toilet oneself are healthy goals, and parents shouldn't get upset if the child does it according to his or her own schedule and style.

Family Communication

The two-year-old who wants to imitate his older siblings but can't make his limbs obey, or who can't find the words to express his important ideas, is bound to get frustrated. Parents need to appreciate these intentions and respect their children's dignity—even at two. They need to help their toddlers express themselves and assist them in their quest for independence, even though it may seem at times like aiding and abetting the other side.

Whining Instead of Talking

> My daughter learned to talk early, but now that she is almost
> three, she whines constantly. I have a new baby to take care of
> and suddenly Carey is more trouble than she was six months
> ago. Are there stages where kids go backward?

• Technically, no; all stages go forward. Sometimes it appears as though kids backslide in one area of development or another, but it usually shows that new learning has taken place that leads to a new fear or more cautious behavior. For example, kids around the age of twenty-two months sometimes become afraid of taking a bath. It's not a backward step in development, it's just that they realize the possibility of being "disappeared" down the drain like the water. Younger kids aren't any more courageous; they just never realized the possibility.

• Your child seems to be going through that age-old stage called "regression due to new baby in the family." Instead of seeing it as jealousy, think about it as something positive— loving her new brother so much that she wants to be like him.

• Be patient. Tell her how much you enjoy having a big girl who can talk and do things for herself. Find something mature that she has done everyday and tell Daddy when he comes home from work, or tell Grandma when she calls, making sure Carey overhears. This is especially important if your conversation is usually about the new baby.

• Help establish her "big-sister" relationship with her new sibling. A child who feels that there is a role for her in the family won't be jealous when a new child is added. Let her help with the diapering and feeding. Tell her that she has to help teach the new baby nursery rhymes and songs. Let her help select between two outfits the baby will wear for some special outing.

• Remember that at this point your two-year-old needs more individualized attention than your new baby.

• Use "natural consequences" for your daughter's refusal to speak clearly. If you know that she is capable of asking for a certain toy on the high shelf and she points and whines, ask for clarification. "What do you want? I can't understand you."

Use a normal tone of voice and don't add any lectures about talking like a baby. The purpose of speaking clearly is to communicate our ideas, and the natural consequences for people who refuse to speak clearly (when they are capable of it) is that they are not understood.

Interruptions

> Everytime I talk to another adult, my son thinks of something earth-shattering to tell me and has to interrupt our conversation. He is two-and-a-half years old, and his idea of earth-shattering is that he saw a car go by that looked like Uncle Allen's. I know it's rude behavior for adults, but when do you start teaching etiquette to kids?

What you're noticing is a combination of excitement about the world and a very short attention span. This results in behavior that would be considered extremely rude in an adult, but is perfectly normal for a two-and-a-half-year-old.

• Interrupting your adult conversations is not a sign of jealousy, nor a premeditated plot to lure your attention away from your adult friend.

• Parents who punish children for interruptions are actually punishing their excitement about the world and desire to share it.

• Lecturing to children about interruptions and complaining to your adult friends about how frustrating the situation is, causes more disruption in the conversation than the child's interruption did to begin with.

• There are several good ways to handle interruptions from toddlers. First, you can say to your adult friend, "Excuse me a minute," and then listen with interest to your child and comment briefly. If you feel uncomfortable, you can apologize to your adult friend and add, "He's just so interested in the world these days. You know how two-and-a-half-year-olds are."

• Second, you can teach your child to include your adult friend in the conversation. "Why don't you tell Auntie Sarah and me all about the bug you saw on the swing."

• If your conversation is truly at a critical point, tell your child, "wait," and then hold his hand or pull him onto your lap while you finish the thought, then welcome his news with interest.

Threats

> When he doesn't get his way, my son tells me "I hate you." I expected this in the teenage years, but he's not quite three!

• Look behind the words. He is telling you that he is angry, that's all. He has no idea what the concept of hate is, nor respect for parents, etc. It's a phrase he heard somewhere and thought he'd give it a try. Evidently it worked very well.

• A friend of ours tells her kids that they can't hate her, since she is their mother and people aren't allowed to hate their mother in the state of Florida. That usually works pretty well with a defiant toddler who is years away from law school. It also says that you know that they don't mean what they say and you aren't going to take it seriously.

Defiance

> My daughter's favorite word is *"No!"* She will even use it when I ask if she wants an ice-cream cone. She's thirty-two months old. Do the terrible two's end at three?

• Although there are many individual differences and no distinct age boundaries, most parents find three-year-olds to be pleasant, happy, and agreeable.

• Think of your daughter as wanting to be competent and capable, just like her mom and dad. Mistakes are made when parents begin interpreting toddlers' behavior as directed *at* them. Two-year-olds are not capable of such sophisticated mental processes.

• Avoid asking your daughter any questions that can be answered by "yes" or "no." Try saying, "I know you want an ice-cream cone, do you want vanilla or chocolate?"

• Allow her to change her mind—a lot. If you fix her an ice-cream cone and she decides she doesn't want it, say, "I'll put it here in this bowl in the refrigerator in case you change your mind." This way, you have given her an option.

• Compliment her on how well she says, "no." Ask her if she would like to learn the German word for no—"nein." Then there is Russian—"nyet." It may liven things up for you, but it also gives her the message that you aren't taking her opposition at face value, but as some kind of learning experience (which it is).

• Above all, don't take her seriously and cause the situation to escalate into big problems. Strategies parents should avoid at all costs are telling the child not to say "no," trying to reason with them about the fact that they shouldn't say no for something they really want, trying to explain to them that it makes Mommy and Daddy angry if they say no all the time, and thinking that the child is doing it on purpose to "get back" at the parents for something.

Aggression Toward Mom

> My son is thirty-four months old and ever since he started nursery school, he hits me when I tell him he can't have something. It's silly, but I sometimes think he is mad at me for going back to work.

• Ask the nursery school teacher about hitting among the kids. Your son probably either observed it in other kids or else tried it by accident and found that it is very effective for getting what he wants from other children.

• Make it clear to him that hitting *anyone* is not tolerated in your family. When he hits, you, look him in the eye and tell him in a very serious, calm voice that we do not hit in this family. Then put him in his room or somewhere where he will be safe for a few minutes alone and tell him to think about it. Don't leave him for more than three minutes—he'll forget what he's in there for.

• Remind him at bedtime that he is a good boy who loves his mommy and doesn't hit her (or his daddy or his sister or the dog).

• Make sure he isn't learning bullying behavior at home from you, your spouse, or his siblings.

• Above all, don't hit him for hitting you. Think about it.

Aggression Toward New Baby

> My daughter is two-and-a-half and has started hitting her new baby brother when he cries. Other than that, she seems very loving toward him.

• It sounds like it might be misguided attempts to make him stop crying. She is old enough to know that crying is a sign of distress in someone else and to want to do something to help. Teach her some more successful techniques, such as winding up his music box or patting him gently.

• If that doesn't seem to help and if her hitting seems more hostile in nature, keep them out of situations where she could cause harm to the baby. Don't leave them alone together, and sister-proof the nursery.

• Next, find out what is going on. Has she learned to hit from other kids and needs to know it's not allowed in your family? Read the suggestions above.

• Has she learned from her parents that hitting is one of the ways big people control little people? Then you and your spouse need to examine your ideas about being parents and perhaps enroll in a class to learn some new skills.

• Was your daughter the "baby" of the family until the new baby arrived? If so, she may very well feel threatened and replaced. Let her know that she is the two-and-a-half-year-old of the family and a very valuable part of the household. Furthermore, your children should feel that they are individuals and not interchangeable—and that she is the only Jennifer you have and to compare her to the new baby would be like comparing apples and bananas.

Emotions Out of Control

> My two-year-old has tantrums and I don't know how to deal
> with them. I have tried ignoring him and threatening him and
> even bribing him, but nothing helps. And he always does it at
> the worst possible time. The most recent was at the beautiful
> new home of my husband's business partner, who doesn't like
> kids to begin with.

• Tantrums seem to be the main reason that age two has such
a terrible reputation. Although tantrums are fairly rare, this
isn't much comfort for parents of kids who have them.

• The worst effect of tantrums is the embarrassment it causes
parents. A little assertiveness training is helpful: Tell yourself
that tantrums are part of childhood learning experiences and if
a business establishment (such as a grocery store or a shopping
mall) is open to parents and their children, tantrums are going
to occur there.

• Try to handle your embarrassment with humor. Look at the
people around you and say something like, ''I understand a hot
temper is a sign of intelligence—I think I have a little genius
here.'' Or laugh and say, ''My mother said I did the same thing
at that age—I guess I'm getting paid back.'' You might be
surprised that the sympathy you receive; certainly more than if
you lost *your* temper and resorted to yelling or hitting.

• Once you can deal with your own embarrassment, you can
help your child cope with his or her emotions. Most, if not all,
temper tantrums are simply a child losing control. If a two-
year-old has ever intentionally had a tantrum to manipulate his
or her parents, it would be quite an intellectual feat.

• The best cure is prevention. Don't take kids out when they
are tired or hungry. Don't put them into situations where they
get bored for long stretches of time. Don't take them to new
situations (such as the new home of your husband's child-
hating business associate) where you will be tense and so will
they. If you can avoid it, don't take them anywhere when *you*
are in a bad mood. Emotions have a way of building up to a
boiling point and then exploding.

• Tantrums are ten times worse for the child than the parent.
Losing control of one's emotions and becoming a public spec-

tacle is not pleasant. Children gradually develop the self-knowledge to reroute their emotions and to express themselves in a more positive way before they lose control. Parents can help them by doing all they can to prevent tantrums, and by letting the child know that the parent will still stay in control and will help the child to do so.

• Learn the early warning signs of your child's tantrums. If you can't prevent them from happening at all, at least try to catch them before they get out of hand. Identify the situation to the child, ''It looks like your anger (or your emotions, or your temper) is getting out of control.'' Then offer to do something to help. ''Would you like to go out to the car with me for a few moments to cool off?'' Ask these questions kindly and helpfully, not as a threat or punishment. Make the child's feelings your major concern, even if you have to leave a party or abandon your grocery cart in the store.

• Let your child feel you are on his or her side, that you have confidence and want to help.

• Above all, don't lose control yourself. The scariest thing for a child at times like that is to find out that parents aren't in control either.

"Foreign" Grandparents

> My daughter is two-and-a-half and speaks English very well. My parents, who live nearby, speak Spanish most of the time, although they know some English. The problem is that my husband (who is Anglo) and I have asked them not to speak Spanish to our daughter now that she is learning to talk. They just laugh at us and insist that she can learn both languages together. We don't want her to have problems at school because of confusion. How do we get them to take us seriously?

• This is really two problems—grandparent/grandchild communications, and how to get your parents to take you seriously.

• Getting your parents to take you seriously is a tough one, especially in a two-culture family. Your parents probably feel that they are the heads of your extended family. To further complicate matters, they may not understand why your husband is taking an interest in the minor details of parenthood.

This is a much more common attitude than you would think, especially in Hispanic families. Find out if there are any groups for young people in your community with similar problems. If not, try to find other young parents in your situation to talk to. You need more than advice—you need support and understanding to find that perfect balance between being effective parents yourself and still keeping ties strong between your children and your parents.

• Talk to your mother about these things. Sometimes when family ties are at risk, the mothers can work out compromises.

• As far as the second language is concerned, your parents are right. First and most important, the grandparent/grandchild relationship is very significant in a family and it's wrong to impose a language barrier between them. Obviously your parents don't feel that they can communicate well enough in English to pass down all their knowledge and wisdom to their grandchildren, and this should be respected.

• Secondly, being bilingual is a very valuable skill, and the easiest time to learn a second language is as a toddler. It doesn't interfere with their first language if steps are taken to keep the processes separate. You have an ideal situation. Have your grandparents speak Spanish to your daughter; you and your husband speak English. Or have everyone speak Spanish at Grandma's house and English at your house. Your daughter will have an advantage over her one-language peers throughout her school years, and also will be able to learn a third language much easier. Don't deprive her.

Visits, Outings, and Trips

This is the age at which children truly begin to enjoy trips to the zoo or shopping trips for a special birthday gift. But they also can be quite insistent about wanting to go home, wanting to get ice cream, and wanting to have their own way. It is also an age at which children enjoy playmates, but can suddenly decide to solve differences through aggression. It's as though they have enough maturity to start activities, but not enough to follow them through.

Embarrassing Comments

I was very proud of my son's ability to speak clearly until he began making comments about the other people in the mall, on the bus, and at the park. He points out fat ladies, bald men, and anyone in a wheelchair. There's no doubt about what he is saying, and I don't know what to do.

• There is no way a two-year-old can be taught not to say embarrassing things in public because he can't understand what is embarrassing and what is not. Again even if he could, he couldn't appreciate how it makes the other person feel. Furthermore, it is beyond his understanding to separate what he says in public from what he says to you privately. You might have some luck advising him on one particular problem, like telling him not to mention how fat people are or not to talk about people in wheelchairs, but it probably won't work.

• Identify particular problem situations. They probably involve being with a group of strangers for a period of time and not being able to disappear into the crowd—such as being on a bus or in the dentist's waiting room. When these situations are expected, bring along some toys or books to occupy your son so he won't have time to study the people around him. In short-term situations, such as elevators, find a way to distract him. Show him the numbers flashing over the door, or ask him if he feels the elevator stop. If you notice someone coming your way who might provoke comment, point out something in another direction or ask him a question. A good one is, "What is that toy you told me you wanted for your birthday?"

• If your attempts fail, remember that it is normal behavior for a child that age and it is normal for a child to be riding on the bus (or whatever). Don't punish him or get angry; he's too young to understand. Don't start a lecture about hurting other people's feelings; the additional emphasis will just make the situation worse. If you must do something, give him a big hug and say to the other person, "I certainly hope you were two once and understand." Or just, "I'm very sorry. He's only two."

Runs Wild in Parking Lot

> I have a two-and-a-half-year-old daughter and a three-month-old son. When we go out shopping, it's a major production to get in and out of the car with two car seats, a stroller, and packages; my hands are always full. That's always when my older one takes off running through the parking lot, laughing like it's the most fun she has ever had. I have yelled, spanked, and threatened everything I can think of, but she seems to think it is a big joke. How do I get her to understand the seriousness of it?

• You can't. She is too young to understand the possible dangers involved. You need to establish a safe routine for getting everyone and everything in and out of the car, with your children's safety as the main priority.

• Car seats with restraining belts are great safety devices. Make sure the kids are the last things you take out of the car and the first ones you put in. And since your younger child is less mobile, put the older child out last and in first.

• Two-year-olds like routines. Tell her the steps involved in getting into and out of the car and make it a drill of some kind. "How do we get out of the car? First the stroller, then the baby, then the big girl, then we lock the doors. Did we forget anything?"

• If you need to distract her on the way out to the car, give her the keys and ask if she would like to *try* to unlock the door. Tell her to be very careful not to lose the keys. This should keep her thinking serious thoughts until you get to the car.

Refuses to Sit in Grocery Basket

> My daughter is in the terrible twos and the latest problem is that she has decided she is too old to sit in the grocery basket seat. If I force her to sit there, she screams like she is being tortured. I dread grocery shopping.

• Your daughter isn't making outlandish demands, just premature ones. Someday she *will* be too old to ride in the grocery cart, just not today. Here are some suggestions that might work:

• Tell her that she really is getting to be a big girl, but she has to be four before she stops riding in the grocery cart. However, she *is* old enough to pick out what kind of oatmeal she wants for breakfast, and as soon as she gets into the cart, you will go right over to the cereal aisle and let her choose.

• Tell her that she can walk with you on short shopping trips, but she has to ride in the cart on long trips. Ask if she will hold the list and put a check by the items as you buy them. (It doesn't really matter what she checks.) Then tell Daddy or Grandma how she helped you at the store today.

• Tell her if she cries in the store like a baby, you will have to leave and *take her right home.* Then do it, even if it means another trip for you, or take-out chicken for supper. Shopping with a screaming two-year-old is cruel and unusual punishment. Give her another chance the next day to sit in the cart and act like a big girl, but if she cries again, take her home and make arrangements to shop when she can be left at home with someone else. Try again in a few months. It's worth the baby-sitting fee not to go through the emotional turmoil (for you, your child, and the other shoppers).

• If you absolutely must shop with your child, find a friend with a toddler and shop together. We have neighbors who get together weekly for a shopping trip. One mom drops the other mom off at the park with all three kids and she shops for half an hour. Then the other mom gets half an hour while the first mom stays at the park. In thirty minutes they get the shopping done that used to take an hour, and they all end up in a good mood.

Fights with Friends

> My two-year-old always wants his friend Jimmy to come over and play, but once he's here, Todd treats him terribly. He won't share his toys and if Jimmy won't do what he wants, Todd hits or bites him.

• This might make it easier for you: Two-year-olds don't have friends. They may have kids they ask to play with, but friendship as we know it does not exist. So don't expect Todd to follow any sort of civilized rules of friendship. He is too young to understand that Jimmy is an individual with feelings and needs of his own which Todd, as his friend, should consider.

• Don't tell Jimmy's mother, but it might help if you thought of Jimmy as a toy Todd asks to play with instead of a friend. That's probably closer to Todd's view of the situation.

• This doesn't mean that Todd should be allowed to hit and bite Jimmy. It just means that at this age you shouldn't expect Todd to understand that such behavior is wrong. By all means tell both boys that they should play nicely and not bite and not hit. But think of it as instructions for the future, don't expect them to understand right away. Think of it as a learning experience.

• Watch the kids when they play together, and do what you can to prevent aggressive acts on either part. If situations heat up, distract them with other toys or move them apart.

• Don't feel bad if Todd doesn't have anyone to play with on a daily basis. It's not necessary at this age, and probably easier on Mom and Dad.

• Let Todd play with a slightly older child every now and then who knows about sharing and compromising and is big enough to handle Todd's aggression.

Everything Is "Mine"

> Tracey is thirty months old and the biggest trait she's developing is selfishness. She puts all her toys in the toy box and tells her five-year-old sister that they are "mine." We have taught Lindsey to share, but it is all falling apart now.

• Tracey has just learned the concept of possession and she is really enjoying it. Don't argue. Take her statement at face value only and don't read things into it. She is telling you that the toys are hers, not that she won't share with her sister or that she has chosen to be selfish. She isn't mature enough to think that far down the line yet. Agree with her. "Yes, they are yours, and there are a lot of them, aren't there?" That may be all she wants to hear.

• Play games with her. "Who's bear is that? It's yours? What a nice bear you have, Tracey. May I please hold it for a minute? Thank you. Now I will give it back because it's yours."

• Tell Lindsey that Tracey is a baby and doesn't understand how to share yet. (It's true.) When Lindsey shares something, tell her how glad you are to have a big girl who is old enough to share, and that you know Tracey will someday learn how.

• Tell Lindsey that she is Tracey's best teacher for sharing. (It's true.) When Lindsey shares something with Tracey, comment on it. "Tracey, I hope you notice that Lindsey is sharing with you even though you don't know how to share with her yet. I hope you'll learn to be like her someday." When Tracey refuses to share with Lindsey, comment on that, too. "Lindsey, I hope you realize that Tracey is just a baby and is too young to understand about sharing. She loves you a lot and I'm sure that someday she will learn that you share with people you love."

Two-year-olds can be some of the most interesting people on earth. Their enthusiasm for life can be so refreshing. As they become increasingly acquainted with the world, they can appreciate it in new ways. Their growing abilities give them a totally new perspective on things, and they are excited about their new knowledge and ability to communicate what they know.

Of course, with these newfound abilities and discoveries come problems. Parents put barriers up to prevent exploration, don't understand what they are trying to say, and toddlers' own little bodies refuse to do what their little minds insist upon. This too will pass, but the terrible two's are children's introduction to a thinking world, and many of the discipline problems these children present us are easier to solve if we keep this in mind.

12. Discipline with Three- and Four-Year-Olds

If two-year-olds cause problems because they are more independent physically, three- and four-year-olds cause problems because they are more independent mentally. They can think about things before they do them and they can have things going on in their heads that parents know nothing about. One mother tells the story of her little child picking up a crayon and saying, "Don't write on the walls, don't write on the walls," while heading toward the hallway with its long expanse of newly painted, blank wall. The mom can't remember the child's age, but we are willing to bet it was under three. Three- and four-year-olds may not be able to tell parents to look the other way while they write on the walls, but they're smart enough to keep their plans to themselves before they execute them.

Three and four are the first ages that children truly can be "bad." However, their misbehaviors are seldom the premeditated, malicious deeds parents sometimes think they are. Three- and four-year-olds probably forget ten times as many rules as they break on purpose. And when they break rules on purpose, they are most likely overcome by the temptation of the moment, or just curious if yesterday's rules also apply today (or if this morning's rules carry over to this afternoon).

Sleeping, Eating, and Other Schedules

Sleep Problems

> About once a week, my three-year-old wakes up in the middle of the night with nightmares. It's usually when we go out. We use three different sitters, and it doesn't seem to matter who the baby-sitter is. Now my wife is beginning to think that we go out too much and he feels insecurely attached.

• Signs of insecure attachment would be apparent during your child's waking hours. He would be clingy, afraid of his environment, afraid of strangers, and maybe even somewhat hostile toward you and your wife. He would be hard to comfort, even if you held him every minute. In other words, securely attached children of this age like their parents, but don't necessarily want to live in their laps. They are curious about the world and other people, and their parents give them confidence to venture out. Insecurely attached children don't seem to feel safe or happy anywhere. They may whine and cling to their parents, but their presence isn't much of a consolation. They don't seem curious about the world, and everything and everyone is frightening. Children who act this way are mistakenly considered to be overly attached and spoiled and ''mommy's babies,'' but a closer look indicates otherwise.

• Some sleep disturbances are known to be related to immature nervous systems. Many three-year-olds have immature nervous systems (immature everythings, actually), so sleep problems are quite common in the preschool years. Most children outgrow them.

• Sleep disturbances also are known to be related to stress and fatigue. If your child has nightmares on particular nights (like weekends when you go out), the cause may be related to something about the weekend day rather than the baby-sitter— like not taking a nap, getting overly tired, or just having too much fun. See if making the days a little more mellow helps.

• If you want a scientific approach, try getting a sitter during the week and staying home on the weekend. If he still has nightmares on the weekend, you can be fairly certain the catalyst is something about the weekends, not your departure.

• Talk to some other parents and see how often they go out and leave their kids with sitters. Unless it's really excessive, a good night out for parents can be in the best interest of the child.

Bedtime

> This is an unusual problem, but I don't know how to put my four-year-old son to bed. Up until now, he would just get sleepy around seven-thirty or eight o'clock and I'd sit in the rocking chair with him for five or ten minutes and he'd be asleep. Now he can keep going until *my* bedtime, and I don't know what to do.

• Set a time and tell him that it's bedtime. Show him on the clock and tell him an hour ahead and again a half hour ahead. Make a ritual out of it. If he doesn't seem sleepy, give him a nice quiet bath and a glass of milk and a cookie.

• Sit in the rocker with him and talk quietly about the day. He is old enough to understand when you talk about yesterday and tomorrow, although he may get a little confused.

• Read him stories. This is the greatest bedtime activity for any age (we've even read to teenagers). Choose some subdued stories and nursery rhymes. Save the silly stories and the rough-and-tumble tales for daytime.

• After the agreed-upon number of stories, put him in his bed and turn off the light. Tell him good night and help him say his prayers or whatever you like to do, then leave. If he cries, go in periodically and tell him you are there, but he has to go to sleep. This is really tough for a few nights, but it gets better quickly.

• Night-lights are fine, but as dim as possible. When there is nothing interesting to see or hear, sleep is a good alternative.

Security Blanket

> My three-year-old still sleeps with her "banky." My husband thinks she's too old for it, but she refuses to give it up. She whines nonstop at bedtime whenever we take it away. I always give in and give the blanket back to her. When should kids give them up?

• Some kids hang on to security objects longer than others, and three is not a time parents should worry. The need for security objects seems to have less to do with stress or upset or lack of security than with individual personalities.

• Parents shouldn't make kids "give them up." If children feel a need for their "bankies," understanding parents will respect that and allow their children to satisfy that need. After all, we have our own security objects—lucky coins we hold onto during an important presentation, a special piece of jewelry or tie we wear when starting a new project, a favorite restaurant we go to when celebrating anniversaries.

> My grandson takes his blanket to school and gets real upset if we forget it. He is four and I think this may be a problem. He stays at my house in the afternoon and seems anxious about letting it out of his sight, and gets very irritable whenever I try to take it away from him. When he leaves it, his mother actually has to drive back to get it (eight miles across town). What is the new thinking about security blankets?

• Quite a few four-year-olds take their security objects (blankets, pillows, stuffed animals, etc.) to school. Most nursery school teachers are very understanding about this and feel that some kids just need to bring a little touch of home with them.

• One grandma we knew told her four-year-old that he "probably wouldn't want to take his blanket to school when he was five." Evidently he respected her wisdom, and the day of his fifth birthday, proudly left his blanket at home.

Thumb Sucking

> I put my three-year-old to bed at eight o'clock and he sleeps until seven o'clock the next morning. He takes an hour-and-a-half nap every afternoon. But starting about five in the afternoon, he starts sucking his thumb. Telling him not to does no good. He complies for a while, but as soon as I turn my back, the thumb goes right back in his mouth. I then yell at him, which makes him mad, and it sometimes just gets out of hand. It's too early to put him to bed and too late for a nap. I

> don't know what to do. Then I'm afraid he will push his teeth
> out of place. Is twelve-and-a-half hours enough sleep for a
> three-year-old?

• Thumb sucking is quite common at this age and doesn't
necessarily mean your child is tired or needs sleep. It's com-
forting, and for some reason he needs a little comfort that time
of day. Maybe he senses your tension, maybe his own biological clock is run down, maybe he needs a high protein snack,
or maybe he is bored and wants to get out of the house for a
while. If his thumb sucking really bothers you that much, try
some alternative afternoon activities.

• Realize that your child is going to have some needs that
you can't interpret and be glad that he is able to comfort himself. If his behavior the rest of the day is happy and secure,
don't worry about the afternoon thumb sucking.

• If you are really concerned about his teeth, talk to your
dentist.

"Do-It-Yourself" Lunch

> I have a four-year-old daughter who insists on doing every-
> thing possible for herself. I think her first words were "Me do
> it!" The biggest problem lately is lunch. She not only wants to
> feed herself, she also wants to pour her own drink and make
> her own sandwich. When I tried to be tough about it, she just
> wouldn't eat. I know independence is nice, but aren't there
> some limits? What if she wants to drive herself to nursery
> school?

• Keep control of the lunch situation by deciding what things
your daughter can reasonably do for herself and what things
she can't. Distract her with the things she *can* do. If she wants
to pour her own milk, try putting it in a smaller container. Or
tell her you'll pour and she can stir it. Maybe she can manage
parts of the sandwich-making routine, such as unwrapping the
cheese slice and putting it on the sandwich while you do the
rest. Or maybe she could manage squeeze bottles of jelly or
mayonnaise. If you can't find them in the store, you can buy
your own squeeze bottles and fill them yourself.

• As you have learned, it's not a good idea with independent children to get into showdowns and ultimatums. Saying "do what I say or no lunch," can often result in no lunch and a terribly guilty parent.

• Choices work well with four-year-olds. "Do you want to make yourself a bologna and cheese sandwich or do you want me to make you soup and crackers?" A parent who asks a toddler "what do you want for lunch?" is asking for trouble.

• Don't joke about driving. We have a five-year-old in our family who thinks he is ready. So far he is content with telling his mother which way to turn and what color the traffic lights are.

On the Home Front

Following Instructions

> How do you get a three-year-old to listen to his parents and do what he is told? I know he is old enough to understand me and I know he is able to do the things I tell him (like pick up his toys, close the closet door, and brush his teeth). He starts on things, but when I look in on him later, he's playing.

• Three is old enough, as you say, to understand simple instructions and to do simple tasks. Make sure the instructions you are giving him are direct and complete, such as "Pick up your blocks and put them in the box. Then put the box on the shelf where it belongs." Remember, little kids are extremely literal-minded.

• Make sure you aren't giving a long string of instructions that your child can't remember completely. A good rule of thumb is one task for each year of age. The instructions above contain three tasks (pick up blocks, put them in the box, put the box on the shelf). That's about the limit at three.

• Three-year-olds are usually easily motivated by praise. They like to think of themselves as being "good" and "helpful." If you have been using threats and ultimatums, your child may not "hear" them anymore. Try some compliments and affection.

• Three-year-olds also like the idea of their own possessions. They like having things lined up in rows and nicely displayed. To put away toys, an open shelf works well with three-year-olds. They like having a designated spot for each toy. You can also label boxes or drawers with a picture of the items that belong inside.

• It's a good idea to limit toys to a manageable number if you expect your child to be responsible for cleanup. A few favorite books, a coloring book and crayons, a set of blocks, and about five other toys is all a three-year-old can manage (and enjoy). Parents do children no favors by providing them with a roomful of toys. It's overwhelming and it makes it difficult for them to enjoy any of them.

Too Many Toys

My daughter turned four in November. She is an only child and an only grandchild. This means that she has lots of adult relatives who are nuts about her and who buy her tons of toys for every occasion. We are a young couple on a limited budget. I clip coupons and my husband works overtime to make ends meet. However, we have a daughter with a wardrobe and toy collection like a crown princess. And she doesn't really enjoy them that much. On her birthday, she got tired of opening presents and actually threw a tantrum of sorts when I insisted that she open all her gifts. At home she flits from one toy to another, often making a mess of the house (and her mother) as she plays. This is probably too many questions at once, but what can we do about the toys, the relatives, and most of all, our daughter?

• Read the earlier comments about toddlers being overwhelmed by too many toys.

• If friends and relatives have given your child a great number of toys, put them away and out of sight. Bring out a few at a time if your child seems tired of her current toys.

• What to do with the rest of the toys? Buy some cardboard storage boxes and keep a box of toys wherever your child is likely to spend a lot of time, such as Grandma's house, the sitter's house, your childless friend's apartment, and Dad's office. Keep another box in the trunk of the car in case you have to spend unexpected time somewhere. If there are still more toys, donate them to an appropriate charity.

• Tell your closest relatives or friends that on the next gift-giving occasion, you would appreciate it if they would start a savings account for your daughter and if they'd tactfully recommend it to some of the others. They could keep an album of birthday and Christmas cards from the folks who contributed, and call it "Kimberley's College Fund." In a few years she'd enjoy looking at the cards and especially when she is ready for college. It will be wonderful to appreciate all the friends and relatives who contributed over the years.

• The fund could also be for a wedding, a sweet-sixteen party (or fifteen), a bas mitzvah, a graduation trip, or whatever traditions your family observes.

• Whatever you do, do it carefully. Having so many friends and relatives who are "nuts about her" is a highly valuable gift for your daughter, and sometimes short-term solutions aren't worth the long-term losses.

Playing Alone

When my daughter was a little over three, my wife went back to her teaching job and I began staying at home to write a book. It has been two months now, and I haven't been able to get much done. My daughter wants me to play with her all the time, and if I don't, she whines or gets very angry.

When my wife was home with her, she was able to accomplish a lot, but I spend all my time trying to type with one hand and play tea party with the other.

Not only is this upsetting to my parental ego, it has become a major stumbling block in our plans to combine careers and parenthood without putting our daughter in day-care.

• Three-year-olds can enjoy solitary, independent play, so your plan was basically a good one. What you didn't consider was the drastic shift in your daughter's life: not only did Mom go back to work, but Dad began to stay home. In her scheme of things, it's not a simple matter of substituting Dad for Mom. She has to adjust to a new relationship with Mom *and* with Dad. Her need for attention could be due to normal adjustment problems.

• You do need to establish a pattern of daily interaction with her. Even if she were able to substitute Dad for Mom, you aren't doing the same things Mom did. It may be possible to make a grocery list or write a friendly letter while attending to a child, but writing a book demands more concentration. Instead of trying to fit into Mom's routine, start from scratch and make your own.

• Writing at home with a three-year-old demands a lot of discipline, but so does writing at home *without* a three-year-old. Buy a professional weekly appointment book—the kind that goes from 8:00 A.M. to 9:00 P.M.—and schedule your week. Begin with the unchangeables—Mom leaves for work, Mom comes home, mealtime, nap time, and bedtime. Then divide up your work by levels of concentration and match up the heavy work with your daughter's nap times, or perhaps evening hours when your wife is home. That schedule should provide fifteen to twenty hours a week of concentrated writing time.

• Do less demanding work during designated "work times" during the day while your child is awake. Balance these with designated "playtimes," and make sure she knows the difference. Use time signals such as, "When 'Sesame Street' starts, it's Daddy's work time. You can watch 'Sesame Street' or you can do something quietly by yourself. When 'Sesame Street' is over, it's playtime and we'll go for a walk to the park."

• Collect games and activities your daughter can do alone, such as puzzles, coloring books, and matching games. Put them in a special box in your workroom so she can play with them only while you work.

• Don't ever think that you will be able to easily fit in household chores and errands because you are home all day. Consider yourself employed forty hours a week (or more) and split up the housework and shopping with your spouse. If you do plan errands and housework, do them in a designated time slot. If you put off work until the chores are done, you'll never write a book.

• Be aware of strange types of writer's block that make you feel guilty about not watching "Sesame Street" with your daughter "just this once."

• Seriously consider enrolling your daughter in a nursery school several days a week or just mornings. She is at an age that she would enjoy other kids and it might do wonders for your writing career, your relationship with your daughter, and your marriage. It's not the same as "day-care," you know.

Family Communication

"Foul-Mouthed" Fours

> My four-year-old attends a nursery school that we thought was very nice. Recently he has been coming home with a vocabulary of filthy words. My husband and I don't talk that way and don't tolerate such language in our home, so he must be learning it at school. We know that other families don't share our values and we don't want to dictate what goes on in their homes, but when their language comes into our home, we feel we have to take action. Should we talk to the teacher (who must know this is going on and so far has let it happen) or should we take it up with the other children's parents? We have asked our son who uses such language and he has given us several names. Or should we just change schools?

• The only way to protect your child from hearing filthy language is to lock him in the linen closet with earplugs. And the only way to keep him from using it is to tape his mouth shut. Foul language and four-year-olds seem to find each other, no matter how careful parents are. And blaming other kids and their parents is futile—they are probably blaming your son and your family.

• Four-year-olds are on a roll, linguistically, and delight in learning new words. That may be part of the attraction to dinosaurs with their polysyllabic names. They also take to foreign languages quickly at this age. So when they are exposed, however briefly, to a new set of sounds and meanings (such as filthy words), they can't resist trying them out. And when parents fly up in the air and turn all shades of red each time one of the new words is used, there is quite an attraction.

• This doesn't mean that you have to tolerate it. Fortunately four-year-olds are also very sensitive to their parents' approval and disapproval. Instead of getting upset and blaming other kids, each time an offensive word is used, tell your child that you don't like that word at all and don't want to hear it again, period. Say it in your most serious tone of voice, saved for times like this, and change the subject.

• Sometimes four-year-olds seem to be using a lot of impolite language because of the topics that interest them—differences in male and female bodies, excrement, and other bodily functions and sounds. Often kids have no appropriate vocabulary for these concepts because parents and early picture books don't teach them. So when they do hear a word, such as "puke," it's fascinating. Substituting a more acceptable word, such as "vomit" or "throw up" gives them a chance to talk about it without using the offensive word—a slight consolation to parents.

• One of our favorite responses is to tell children that we don't like to hear such talk and that if they want to use those words, they can go in their room (or bathroom), close the door, and say them all they want. Then we pretend we can't hear them. After about ten minutes of blue language, sometimes shouted at the top of their lungs, they emerge with some other activity in mind and the word is seldom heard again.

• Another parent we know tells her four-year-old that only babies use language like that. Does he want everyone to think he is a baby?

• It helps a lot if other family members are modeling the behavior they expect from the four-year-old. And it also helps a lot if the adults and older children around don't laugh when the four-year-old shows off his newly acquired words, although this is very difficult, especially with teenagers in the house.

Annoying Habits

> My three-year-old has started chewing her clothes and it drives me nuts. If there is a collar on her shirt or a bow on her dress, she chews on it until it's ruined. She used to be a thumb sucker and I thought she would never outgrow that. What can I do to make her stop?

• Habits such as thumb sucking, clothes chewing, nail biting, and nose picking are typical self-soothing behaviors in children. If they are coping well with the rest of their lives, you don't need to worry about it. Sometimes we all need a little comfort.

• If your child is also whiney and cranky, or is extremely uncomfortable with new situations and shy, other problems may exist which you could discuss with your pediatrician.

• If you can't ignore the behavior for a while, and it's truly driving you "nuts," by all means bring it to the child's attention. You could compromise by telling her you don't like to watch such behavior and that if it makes her feel better, to please do it privately. Or give her something more acceptable to chew on, such as gum.

• Is your daughter cutting teeth? Some molars come in during this age and she might be experiencing some discomfort.

Imaginary Friends

> My niece is four and she has an imaginary friend named "Bosco." She talks to him while she colors, and she likes to take him with her when she goes anywhere fun because Bosco likes fun. Her parents think it is cute, but I am a little worried. None of my children have ever done that, and I've raised three. Should I say something to my sister?

• Imaginary friends such as Bosco are quite common with children this age. They haven't quite learned to do all their thinking and imagining "inside their heads," and talking to an imaginary friend seems to be an intermediate stage in their thinking abilities. If your niece is doing fine in other aspects of her life, we wouldn't worry about an imaginary friend.

• A cause for concern would be if she ever seemed to be afraid of Bosco or didn't seem to be in control of the "relationship." In that situation, parents should discuss the situation with a child psychologist.

• You might advise your sister not to get too involved in her daughter's relationship with Bosco. It's one thing if the child imagines the friend, but it gets confusing if the parents seem to join in. Children look to adults for reality, so they should make it very clear that they are pretending when they interact with the child's imaginary friend.

Lying

> I have three children, ages twelve, eight, and three-and-a-half. The problem I have with my little one is lying, believe it or not. She seems to enjoy telling lies, and even lies when she has been caught red-handed doing something wrong. It's like she doesn't know the difference between truth and fiction. My mother says it's because we don't take the children to Sunday school, but the older ones are honest.

• It's not a surprise that your little one is the one with the truth problem. That's quite common with three- and four-year-olds, and if your older children didn't, you were extremely lucky.

• When you say that she doesn't seem to know the difference between truth and fiction, you answered your own question. Toddlers have trouble with that distinction, and even when they do grasp it, they don't quite realize that telling fiction is wrong.

• Your daughter is new at describing ideas and events. She has just learned to describe thoughts to you in words—things she only imagined and that didn't really happen. Be patient.

• Help your daughter recognize her lies and her truths. You probably know which is which. If she tells the truth about something, tell her it is the truth and that you're happy when she tells the truth. Tell her that Mommy and Daddy and her sister and brother all tell the truth (and make sure you do), and that when she gets a little older, she will always tell the truth, too. When she tells some farfetched story, say to her, "That's quite a story. Maybe you can remember that and tell Daddy at bedtime. But the truth is that you got your shoes wet in the puddle in front of the house."

• Point out to your daughter when your older children tell the truth or behave in an honest way. Tell her about your own honesty and that of your spouse.,

• Being truthful is not the sole property of Sunday school and organized religion. It's a universal value that's recognized by the religious and nonreligious alike. All parents need to teach their children to value honesty, regardless of religious background. The best way is to demonstrate it.

Outings, Visits, and Trips

Kids Fight While Moms Try to Talk

> I am a stay-at-home mother with two kids in school and a three-year-old home with me. A month ago a new family moved into our apartment complex with another three-year-old and a stay-at-home mother. The mother and I hit it off very well and I really enjoy having another person to talk to, but our kids aren't doing so well. It seems like every time we start talking, the kids fight with each other just to get our attention. What can we do?

• Three-year-olds are just learning to play with each other and really need a lot of practice, with help from watchful parents. You and your friend have years of practice relating to others of your own age, and it's easy to fall into a comfortable relationship. Your kids need more time.

• Both children seem to be accustomed to having Mom "on call." Although they aren't actually trying to sabotage your new relationship, it may look that way at times. What is probably going on is that they are using old strategies that worked before—such as calling for Mom immediately when they need something.

• Look at playtime as training sessions for a while. Keep them short and plan them at a time when both children are in their best moods, such as after nap time or in the morning. Tell them how well they are playing and how proud you are that they are sharing and taking turns so well.

• Buy some special toys for use only when they're playing together. If they start fighting, separate them for a few minutes and take away the special toy. Give them a second chance. If that isn't successful, everyone goes home until the next day.

• Once the kids get to know each other and see how much fun they can have together, they'll probably give you hours to visit with your new friend.

Motor-mouth Syndrome

> I can't believe that my husband and I were ever worried about our son learning to talk. He is now four and the only time he stops talking is when he is asleep. I am home with him all day and he tells me stories, talks about everything we did yesterday, and tells me about what he wants to do tomorrow. Then he calls his grandmother on the phone and goes over everything with her. The big problem is when I have friends over and he wants to talk to them during the entire visit. He constantly interrupts, so we taught him that it was rude to do that. Now he interrupts, saying, "Excuse me for interrupting, but . . ." My sister says he is hyperactive and should take tranquilizers. Any advice?

- The first advice would be to disregard your sister's advice. You aren't describing the symptoms of an attention-deficit disorder, which is the problem sometimes helped by medication. Your son seems to be able to concentrate, stay on one subject for a while, and remember such rules as saying "excuse me" before interrupting.
- From the sound of it, you have a bright, enthusiastic kid who loves the world and wants to share his fun with everyone who will listen.
- It also sounds like you could use a break. Have you considered a nursery school several mornings a week, or maybe a day with Grandma each week?
- Exercise is also great for using up energy. Make sure your son gets outside for vigorous exercise several times a day.
- When you listen, really listen. Sometimes parents half listen to kids like this, who then feel they have to keep talking to get their point across. If you've had enough, tell him, "Mommy's ears are tired, so let's have a quiet time for fifteen minutes until the timer goes off (or until the TV show is over). You can color in this book or put together this puzzle."
- Your son will soon have friends to talk to and be able to keep some of his thoughts to himself as he gets older. There's hope.

Social Behavior and Birth Order

When my daughter was a preschooler, she was bossy and pushy with other kids and the nursery teacher said it was because she was our firstborn and was used to being the big sister. Now our secondborn is a preschooler and is bossy and pushy too. This nursery school teacher tells us that it is because she is the little sister and is used to being bossed around by everyone in the family. Who is right?

• Birth order has always been a popular theory for children's behavior, but as you can see, it doesn't always work. Birth order may predict the behavior of the "average" child, but often isn't very helpful in understanding the behavior of any particular child.

• Secondly, it's difficult to change one's birth order. About all it provides is a topic for nursery school teachers and parents—describing behavior and telling us little about how to change it.

• The fact is that four-year-olds have the ability to play nicely with each other. If they are unable to, parents or teachers need to intervene and try to solve the problem. Blaming it on birth order is not productive.

• Four-year-olds should be supervised, and none should be allowed to push around others. Leadership is one thing, but bossiness is something else. The main difference is that the other children don't complain about leadership—it's given. Bossiness is taken.

• The best reward for four-year-olds is to be allowed to play with the other four-year-olds. The best punishment is to be denied this playtime. Kids who can't play nicely should be reminded about the rules and given a short time out (three to five minutes) to consider them. Then they can return to the play group. If the same behavior returns, they should be separated from the group for the rest of the play period and given something to do alone.

• Lectures do little good, but once the peace is restored, parents or teachers might talk to the child who is having the problems and tell them patiently what is expected of them.

• Parents should not punish children at home for things that happen at school.

Preschoolers and Violence

My four-year-old son is very active and bright. He doesn't sleep much, eats like a horse, and is thin and wiry. He is very well coordinated for his age. My husband thinks he will be a natural athlete and wants to get him involved in sports. My reservation is that he is also extremely attracted to violence. He can be playing on the floor, ignoring the TV, but when fighting or shooting is shown, he'll stop to watch in fascination.

I have never let him play with guns, but he makes them out of his Tinkertoys. He even bit off part of his sandwich last week to make the shape of a gun to shoot at his sister.

Even though I don't let him watch violent cartoons, the others boys at his day-care do and he is quick to join in their violent imaginary play. Is this just a stage boys go through? Is it okay for him to start sports? Do I have a serious problem?

• Yes, this is something many boys go through, as can be seen by the popularity of violent cartoons and toys. Often this is fired by parents who have strange ideas about masculinity, but it often persists in homes where parents like you have made it a point to ban the violent TV and toys. There is just something about violence and weapons and fighting that appeals to many young boys, and the more they watch it, the more aggressive and violent they can get in their play.

• You are right to ban violent TV and imaginary play for your son. You should ask that his nursery school substitute more low-key TV and more pro-social games. It has never occurred to some nursery school workers that a lot of their problems are caused by this type of entertainment, and with the wide variety of videotapes available, there is no excuse. And children can easily be taught to play highly active, imaginary games that are not violent, such as pretending to be firemen rescuing people, or Olympic athletes running relay races. Adults could provide firemen hats, raincoats, and garden hoses for the crew—or gold medals and running shirts with numbers. If your nursery doesn't agree, you might find one that does.

• One explanation is that boys are biologically more active than girls. The activity rather than the violence may be the appeal of such shows and games. Since your son is very active, you should encourage physical activity, such as sports, though, you may want to avoid highly competitive ones, and also those that involve rough physical contact and hitting things with sticks and bats. One solution we've seen used with a similar kid was gymnastics.

• Don't automatically rule out karate and other martial arts. A good instructor can instill concentration and self-discipline in active kids.

• Don't make the mistake of using physical punishment on children like this. You will be a far more potent model for violence and intimidation than any TV show. Model kindness, patience, and maturity. Show him that strong people look out for weaker ones, and that power is strongest if it arises out of respect instead of out of fear.

Three- and four-year-olds are the favorite topic for people who write humorous stories or draw funny cartoons about children. They are quite verbal and can express many complex ideas. But they have so much to learn about the world that they often make silly assumptions about how planes fly, how clouds are formed, or what makes up the important differences between men and women, for example. Like the two-year-old, they are active thinkers, but their increased abilities and greater social skills permit them to sample more of the wonderful world that surrounds them. This, of course, is not only the source of adventure and discoveries, but also of trouble. Keeping in mind that much of the trouble three- and four-year-olds get into is a direct (and often necessary) result of their explorations, helps us understand and respond to misbehavior more effectively.

13. The Early School Years

A generation ago, discipline problems faced by parents of five-, six-, and seven-year-olds were apt to be quite different from those presented by three- and four-year-olds. This was because beginning about age five, children started kindergarten. A home-based life, with parents as the center of a child's universe, shifted to a school-based life with other children as the focal group. Going to school meant increasing influence from other children and adults, experiencing new schedules and routines, and learning to adjust to increased separation from their parents.

Although school is as important in children's lives today as it was thirty years ago, school or its equivalent begins earlier for many children of this generation. For this reason, much of our advice about children during the early school years may also apply to younger children who find themselves in day-care or nursery school on a regular basis.

Of course, there is a difference between the preschool and early school-age child, mainly in terms of intellectual abilities. It is not a coincidence that most modern societies begin formal education during this period. Sometime between ages five and seven, children's thinking goes through some impressive changes, making it more like that of an adult than that of a

249

four-year-old. Yet children this age still have much to learn and need our love and protection while they begin to see the world as we do. They truly deserve greater independence but still require careful supervision.

The early school years can be difficult for both parents and children, especially if this is a child's first time away from the family. But, in more cases than not today, the school years will be a smooth extension of the preschool years. Children will be changing schools, schedules, and friends, but most will be familiar with the demands of the system, making the process easier than it was a generation ago.

Bedtime, Mealtime, and Other Schedules

Morning Routines

My daughter is five and I drive her to preschool on my way to work in the morning. My husband has been gone an hour by the time she gets up, so it's just the two of us. How can I get her to brush her teeth, get dressed, brush her hair, and so forth while I am getting myself ready? I tell her to get dressed while I am in the shower, but when I get out, she's found something to play with and is still in her pajamas. Mornings are our biggest problem.

• It seems like your daughter has a problem remembering all your instructions. Try making her morning tasks into a routine that is the same every morning.

• Maybe some visual cues will help. Make her a picture list of her morning routine. Draw stick figures, cut them out of magazines, or take pictures of your daughter actually doing each task.

• Make sure you are modeling positive morning behavior for her. Do you stay in bed after the alarm goes off and complain about having to get up? Do you skip breakfast frequently because the time just got away from you? Do you make several trips back into the house to get forgotten keys, briefcase, lunch boxes? It's hard to expect your daughter to have her act together if you don't.

• If you're not a great morning person, are you doing all you can the night before to cut down on morning decisions? Clothes can be chosen the night before, lists and reminders can be made and taped on the inside of the front door. Breakfast dishes can be set on the table along with cereal boxes and spoons and fresh fruit. Pour your daughter a small pitcher of milk and she can fix her own breakfast.

• Can your husband help in the morning? Some nurseries have early hours for working parents, and some fathers do much better with morning routines.

Bedtime Fears

> My five-year-old is worried about monsters in the closet at night. He loves to read scary stories, but when the lights go off at night, he's not so brave. I have told him that they're only pretend, but he still worries.

• When it comes to maturity, children often have one foot in and one out. They go to school and act like big brave kids, but sometimes at night they become babies again and need a little reassurance.

• The most important thing is to allow him to be afraid. Listen to him and tell him that you understand how scary things can sometimes be. Don't tell him he is being foolish or immature. Don't get angry. Tell him that you remember being his age and being afraid. Tell him a story about your fears, or one of your siblings' fears. A story of big Uncle Bob being afraid of the dark gives an important message.

• Do what you can to make it better. If he wants you to look in the closet, then look. If he wants you to leave a night light on, then do so. Sometimes a radio helps or having the door propped open.

• Draw the line about things that are not permitted, such as sleeping with his parents or staying up to watch TV.

• Make sure there aren't any daytime situations that he is having trouble dealing with. Sometimes anxiety over waiting alone for the school bus gets translated into fear of monsters at night.

• Listen to him and ask nonthreatening questions. Sometimes big fears can grow out of little misunderstandings. Dad's statement to Mom that he would "be dead" if he didn't get a particular contract at work may be long forgotten by Mom and Dad, but can be the source of a growing fear when overheard by a five-year-old.

• Don't read him scary stories at night.

Bed-wetting

> My son is five and still wets the bed. I have asked the pediatrician about it every time he has a checkup, and he always says it is too soon to worry. Now my son has started making up stories and telling lies about the wet bed. Like last night he said he didn't wet his bed, but that his little brother climbed out of his crib, got into bed with him, and wet the bed. Last week the cat did it. Now I have two problems—bed-wetting and lying. Is it time to worry yet?

• About seventy-five percent of kids stay dry at night by age five, and about ninety-four percent by age eight, so that is why your pediatrician says not to worry. However, if the bed-wetting is upsetting your son to the point that he tries to solve it by making up stories, or if the bed-wetting is causing a family uproar, yes, it's time to worry.

• Start with your pediatrician, especially if he or she has taken care of your son for years. There may be physical problems to rule out. There is no one solution for ending bed-wetting, but whatever is done, make sure your son is treated with respect and dignity. If medical personnel ridicule your son or make him feel embarrassed by the examination and testing procedures, find another specialist who is capable of working respectfully with children.

• Label his bed-wetting excuses as "stories," and tell him that they are very imaginative. Make it clear to him that they are not true and you know it. If he goes along with it, ask him to tell you more. It could be fun to have a different story each morning about why his bed is wet, and might lighten the mood a little around the breakfast table.

• If other family members had problems with bed-wetting, it might help your son to know about it.

School, Day-care, and Separation

Separate Bathrooms at Nursery School?

My daughter is five and started nursery school this year. It is her first experience being away from home and with other children during the day. We picked a very nice school near our home, which is in a nice section of town. The teachers are all certified and we heard many good reports about the school. The one thing that troubles us is that the girls and boys use one big bathroom without doors on the stalls. When I asked about it, the director said that all nursery schools were that way. When our daughter complained about it, the director said that she was shy because she'd been isolated and had never been with other children. Are we being unreasonable?

• There is nothing wrong with a five-year-old wanting to have a little privacy in the bathroom, regardless of her experiences up until now. Her wishes should be respected.

• Although many child-care facilities have only one bathroom, measures are taken to give the children some privacy. For example, some have stalls with doors; others are used by one child at a time. Most nursery schools divide girls and boys for group toileting and send kids separately as needed during the day.

• Most educators who deal with preschool children are very concerned about teaching children to ask for privacy when they feel uncomfortable and to feel they have some rights to privacy and personal parts of their bodies. This is an important part of preventing sexual abuse. The treatment your family received from the school director is in direct opposition to this.

• Find another school. It takes more than certified teachers and good references to make the right place for your child.

• Trust your own judgment more. If you have spent five years home with your daughter, you are an expert.

Separation Problems

My son just began kindergarten and he has become a big problem. We just had another baby also, which might add to it. He gets stomachaches and cries when I leave him. He says he hates school and he hates the new baby. His teacher says to give it time, but she doesn't have to live with it.

• It is not unusual for kids this age to have little lapses in maturity when big changes occur. Your son has had two of these together—starting school and having a new sibling. This behavior is telling you that he is having trouble coping with it all. You might seriously consider keeping him out of kindergarten this year and starting again next year.

• If you do this, tell him that if he would like to, he could go to a play school just for fun. Find a nursery or preschool that will take him one or two mornings a week and let him go as he wishes. He will probably enjoy it a lot once he feels he's not being pushed out of the house.

• Do what you can to make your son feel that he's not being replaced by the new baby. Center activity around your son whenever possible. When you go for a walk to the park, tell him that you and the baby are going to watch him play at the park. Let him show his new sibling how high he can swing.

• Spend some time with your son while the baby sleeps and make sure he gets time with both Mom and Dad without the baby. Get a sitter, and the three of you go out and talk about changes the baby has made on your lives—good and bad.

• Emphasize how nice it is to have a big child that doesn't need to be fed and that can play cards with you.

• Remind yourself that children are delights at every age— not just when they are babies.

On the Home Front

Mr. Independence

My son was fine until he turned six and started school, all in the same month. Now he is Mr. Independent. He wants to cut his own meat, pour his own milk, and decide what to wear each morning. He also wants to decide whether he needs to wear his coat or not—usually the opposite of what I decide. Some things just cause a mess, like pouring, but others are just plain dangerous, like using knives and going out without a coat. How do I convince him to do what I say?

• Ask yourself why he wants to do these things. It's not because he wants to make a mess in your kitchen or catch pneumonia. It's not even that he wants to override your rules. He just wants to make his own decisions and have some control over his life. You should be proud instead of angry. You certainly don't want a thirty-year-old son calling to ask you whether he needs a coat or asking you to cut his meat for him, right? It starts here.

• How can you help him with this independence? You can make tasks easier for him to accomplish alone. For example, cut his meat in the kitchen, but allow him to cut his potato. Six is certainly old enough to use a steak knife under parental supervision. Hang matching shorts and pants together on hangers and put school clothes in a separate section of the closet. Then let him choose any school outfit he wants. And the jacket vs. no jacket question? In our family, we have a thermometer outside the window that decides, and by four years of age, all our kids could read it and tell *us* whether or not they should wear a jacket, proud of their position as family meteorologist.

Helpful Kids

How old should kids be before they can be responsible for cleaning their rooms?

• Depends on how complicated your idea of room cleaning is. A two-year-old can help put toys back in a toy box or put stuffed animals back on a low shelf.

• It depends on how independently you expect the children to act. Remembering to clean one's room each Saturday without being prompted, and to know that it involves vacuuming under the bed and dusting the lamp shades is tough even for adults.

• Children seven and under usually need pretty careful supervision and reminders while room cleaning. Many parents choose to work with the child rather than send them to do the job on their own.

• Some children are so resistant to cleaning their rooms that it becomes a Big Deal, with kids spending Saturdays in their rooms "until it's clean" and parents in a foul mood all weekend. Ask yourself if it's worth it. There are alternatives.

• Tell your children that you have decided to clean their rooms for them as long as they are "little kids." Remind them that little kids go to bed early, don't ride their bikes out of the driveway without an adult, and don't get to choose their own meals when they go out with the family. How do they get to become big kids? They are responsible for their own clothes and toys around the house, they help others in the family, and they sometimes even clean their rooms without being told.

Family Communication

Endless Arguments

I'm sure my son has a brilliant career ahead as a lawyer, but until then, how do I get him to do something without endless arguments? If I tell him to wash his hands before supper, he says they aren't dirty. Then I tell him that he can't always see dirt on them and he tells me he has Superman eyes and there's no dirt. I tell him to wash them anyway because he was playing with the dog, and he tells me he will wash one hand because that's all that touched the dog. This goes on and on until I get mad and chase him into the bathroom. I really don't know why he turns every request into a big fight. He's only six, but he keeps me on my toes.

• Sometimes kids feel that they don't have enough control over their own lives and they settle for little games such as "see how long I can stall hand washing." It's not the angry ending he is after, just postponing the unpleasant deed.

• This doesn't mean that he should be allowed to skip washing his hands between dog grooming and supper. However, try to think of some ways to give him some more control. One suggestion is to tell him that you think he is old enough to know what to do before supper and you are only going to tell him when it's time; the rest is up to him. At some time earlier in the day, you might talk about what is involved. He needs to wash his hands (both of them) and comb his hair (all of them). Then he has to make sure the towels are hung up. You can add whatever you want to this. When the time comes, tell him to "get ready for supper." If his hands are clean and his hair is combed, compliment him on how grown-up he is. If not, send him back with specific reminders.

• It might help also if your son is given more control over little things during the day. It may not be a big deal to you whether he has grape jelly or strawberry jam on his peanut butter sandwich, but these things are important ways of helping him feel responsible for his own life and making him feel like an important individual.

• After six years, parents sometimes feel they have a good handle on child rearing and forget that the rules change as their child matures. How to tell when change is needed? Usually your child will tell you by whining about rules, arguing, flagrantly disobeying you, or doing other rebellious things. Loosening up the control isn't giving in if *you* decide to do it.

Tantrums

My six-year-old has tantrums in public and it embarrasses me terribly. It seems to me that she is old enough to behave better. The last one was at a friend's birthday party. I went to pick her up and while she was gathering up her belongings, her friend's mom started talking to me about joining a social group that some women in town have started. We have recently moved here and I was pleased to be asked, but as we talked, my daughter pulled on my skirt and whined about leaving. I smiled and told her to please stop, we would be leaving in a minute. Finally she said, "I want to go, *now!*" I told her to go to the car and she started screaming and hitting me. When I tried to carry her away, she kicked me. I did manage to get her to the car and get her home. I called her friend's mother to apologize, but she acted very cool toward me. What can I do next time this happens, before she ruins both of our social lives?

Moving causes major stress for both adults and children. Parents are busy coping with their own stress and often are unable to summon up the skills necessary to help their children. During the year following a move, families typically report increased "discipline problems," from bed-wetting to tantrums.

• There is no way to avoid stress when moving, especially when it involves new jobs, new locales, and a loss of the familiar. But there are better and worse ways of handling it. Planning ahead is wise, and after the move, it's a good idea to appreciate the adjustments the whole family is making.

• If you were embarrassed by your daughter's behavior, think a minute about how she felt. Maybe infants feel better after tantrums, but by the time a child is six, she knows about making a fool of herself and is embarrassed by her loss of control.

• Do what you can to keep your daughter from getting out of control. When you tell her to gather up her things to leave and then you stand and chat for a while, she gets anxious. It's a new situation for her and after a birthday party with new friends, she may be at the end of her coping skills. Her whining was a good clue.

• Being impervious to your children's signals and standing tough when they try to influence your behavior does not make you look like a "good" parent. Good parents are always on the same side as their children. At that point, you could have saved the day by saying to the other mother, "I'm sorry, but I'd better cut this short for now. Stephanie's had a big day and it seems she's anxious to get home. Can I call you tomorrow? I'd like to hear more about your women's group."

• Tantrums in public are episodes of being out of control and are very upsetting to a child. Learn your child's signals and head off tantrums whenever possible. Let your child know that you are in control, even if they aren't. Don't get angry. Take your child out of the public eye as quickly and quietly as possible. Leave the groceries in the grocery cart, leave the uneaten meal on the restaurant table, leave the conversation with other adults unfinished. Be calm and firm. "I think we need to go somewhere that's quiet for a while."

• Don't see this as "giving in." Don't think that your children are using tantrums to get what they want, and if you back down or let them get away with it this time, it will happen again. When children have full-blown tantrums in public, they become even more afraid of losing control again. More anxiety causes more problem behavior.

• Children are learning about emotions and control. They need sympathetic parents who are strong enough to take care of situations and to stay in control.

• Out-of-control children don't need out-of-control parents, or parents who walk away and ignore them at such times.

"I Hate You, Daddy!"

> When my seven-year-old son gets mad at me, he yells that he hates me. I don't think I am overly strict, but my wife gets very upset when our son does this. My father was not very involved in my life when I was a kid, and I want to do better than that. I've never spanked my son or hit him, and I try to spend time with him every evening and talk about his day. I've taken two half days off work to go to conferences with his kindergarten teacher. I don't know what I am doing wrong.

• Some kids tell their parents they hate them and others don't, and it has little to do with how well the parent is doing the job. In fact, kids who are scared of their parents are probably less likely to do it than kids who feel secure and loved.

• Kids who tell their parents they hate them do it on various occasions, and they also might tell their parents they wish they would die. Other kids (even in the same family) never say such a thing in their whole lives. Three of our children never said it, one said it a lot, and one especially creative one said, "I know you hate me. I know you wish I would die."

• Defuse the situation by listening and saying something disgustingly mature like, "I know you may feel that way sometimes, but you really don't hate me." Or, "It's quite normal for children your age to think that they hate their parents, but when you get older, you'll know better."

• If it really bothers you, you can ask later for more information. Someday when things are going well and you have time, tell your child, "Last week you told me that you hated me, and I've been thinking about it a lot. Can you explain more about what you meant?"

• If you feel uncertain about your skills as a parent, take a class or join a parenting group. There are many fathers today in your same situation. They want to be involved fathers but have no role models. The same is true of working mothers who themselves had housewife mothers.

• Parenthood has a real "Catch-22." If you are worried that you are doing a lousy job, you're probably doing things right. If you think you are an expert, you should start to worry.

Visits, Outings, and Trips

Grocery Requests

My six-year-old watches Saturday morning TV and grocery shops with me Saturday afternoon. Need I say more? Our shopping trips are battles. She wants everything she saw on TV, and they never advertise anything nutritious or inexpensive. I try to stick to a budget, but try explaining that to a six-year-old. Also, I want her to learn that the TV commercials are often exaggerated and that we shouldn't buy everything they tell us to.

• First, don't take each request as a command. When she says she wants Super-sugar cereal, say something like, "You do? What do you think they taste like? Are they as good as Toasty-O's?" (or whatever she had that morning). Give her a chance to tell you what she knows about that product. She may just want to tell you something you don't know. Kids like having information parents don't have, and Saturday morning cartoons are good sources. Since you are grocery shopping in the cereal aisle, it's a good topic of conversation.

• Make a list before you go and let her help you. When she makes requests that aren't on the list, tell her "that's not on the list this week, but maybe we should remember it for next week."

• Let her choose from two or three alternatives for this week's cereal.

• Let her choose one item each week that can be anything she wants.

• Capitalize on her interest in family spending and let her clip coupons, lick stamps, or check items off the grocery list. Let her find items that are "regulars"—things that you buy every week—and let her put them in the cart.

• Check your own impulse-buying habits. Are you modeling good-shopping behavior?

• Are there other things she can do Saturday mornings besides watch TV? There is indeed a connection between how much commercial television children watch and the number of requests they make of their parents in the grocery store. Although children may insist that they don't want to miss their Saturday morning TV, they often forget all about it when other fun activities are available.

House Rules

My daughter is six-and-a-half and is in the first grade. She attends a private school near my office, which is about ten miles from our home, so none of her classmates live nearby. Our neighborhood had no girls her age and we were seriously considering a change in schools until Rebecca and her family moved in two blocks from us. Katy and Rebecca hit it off immediately and spend every spare moment together. The problem is that Rebecca's family has different rules. We have taught Katy to call her friends' parents Mr. and Mrs. Whatever, but Rebecca calls us by our first names. Katy is not allowed to call anyone's home before ten o'clock in the morning on weekends, or between six and seven o'clock in the evening when they may be eating dinner. Rebecca calls our house at all hours. What can we do to keep our rules but also help Katy keep her friend?

• The first thing you might do is to meet Rebecca's parents and establish some sort of a relationship with them. Then it would be easy to mention that your family enjoys quiet mornings on the weekend and would prefer if Rebecca didn't call before ten.

•· Getting to know the parents of your child's friends is a good practice at any age. It gives you a look into the household where your child spends time, and a feeling for people who will influence your child. It also could give you someone to compare child-rearing notes with.

• You can't set rules for Rebecca, but you can set rules for what goes on in your home. We call these "house rules," and they can range from lofty principles ("We don't make fun of other peoples' religious beliefs in this house") to household chores ("Everyone who eats here is responsible for taking her own dishes to the sink").

• Don't worry about your daughter getting confused about different rules in the two households. Kids have been adjusting to that situation ever since there have been grandparents!

• When Rebecca does call during the times you designate as "mealtime" or "too early," tell her. "Hello, Rebecca. Katy is eating dinner right now, but I will have her call when she is through, or you can call back after seven."

• Friends are very important at your daughter's age. Think about how happy she is with Rebecca and then ask which of your rules are ironclad and which could be subject to change. You are certainly within your rights to insist that Rebecca calls you and your husband "Mr. and Mrs. Whatever" and that your daughter call Rebecca's parents by their formal titles, but is it really worth it? It seems to be an old-fashioned concept in our neighborhood these days. If she treats you with respect and affection, that should be good enough.

Split Personality

> I only have one question, but it's a big one. How can a seven-year-old boy be well behaved and quiet at home and be a loudmouthed hellion at school? My son's teacher sends me notes about his problem behavior and I wonder if she has him confused with another child. He's not perfect at home, but I find it hard to believe there's so much difference in our opinions. The teacher says that he is probably so disciplined at home that he has to "get it out of his system" when he is away from home.

• Children do have their ups and downs, but this is a little extreme. Either your idea of "well behaved" is unusual, or the teacher's idea of "problem behavior" is off the mark. In fact, your suggestion of the teacher confusing him with another child seems to be the most likely explanation.

• Find out from the teacher exactly what your son's problem behavior consists of. If that still doesn't sound like your child, ask for a conference with the school principal, guidance counselor, or school psychologist.

• There is a slight possibility that your son and this teacher have an immense personality conflict and she will be irritated by anything your son does and will interpret his behavior in the worst possible way. If so, you would be wise to get your son out of her class.

During the early school years, children become more independent, whether their parents like it or not. Friends become more important, and school becomes the major focus. As with any change, adjustments are necessary to keep family life running smoothly.

Children beginning school for the first time are certain to have some insecurities, to be uncertain about what is expected of them with the new people they're interacting with, and to be confused by the many changes involved. However, they are also likely to feel more independent, to want more time to spend with friends, and to insist that they know what is in their best interests.

Both the greater insecurities and independence of the early

school years are apt to present problems to parents. Conflicts will arise, but many will resolve themselves as children become more comfortable with their changed life-styles and as parents adapt as well. When dealing with children of any age, parents who recognize the changes that are going on in their children and in their lives will be able to anticipate many problem situations. Some can be avoided, others minimized, and all can be understood.

Index

A

Activity level
  discipline and, 108
  highly active child, 107–108
  low-activity child, 108–109
Adaptive child, 111
Aggression
  toward mother, 221–222
  toward new baby, 222
  toddler, 206
Air travel, infants, 183–184
Approach–withdrawal, 111
Argumentativeness, preschoolers, 257
Attachment
  assessment of, 138
  to baby-sitter, 172
  benefits of secure attachment, 139–140
  independence and, 136–138
  infancy, 62–64
  insecurely attached infants, 63, 135
  meaning of, 135
  parental sensitivity and, 62–63, 135–136
  securely attached infants, 62–63, 135, 138–140
  self-discipline and, 138–140
  stability over time, 139

B

Baby-sitters, 170–172
  attachment of child to, 172
  guidelines for use of, 170–171
  spoiling child, 193–194
Bathroom, nursery bathroom set-up, 253
Bathroom behavior, privacy and, 125, 253
Bath-time
  fear of tub-drain, 203–204
  infancy, 175
Bedroom, privacy and, 125–126
Bedtime
  bedtime fears, 251–252
  climbing out of crib, 192
  parental modeling of, 94
  sleeping in parents' bed, 164, 210–211

sleep problems, early childhood, 232–233
toddlers, 191–192
Bedwetting, preschoolers, 252
Behavior change
behavior modification, 39–41
punishment, 46–52
removing child from problem situations, 43
warnings, 43–44
Behavior modification, 39–41
limitations of, 40
love as reward, 41
Behavior problems
change and, 17–20
preventive approach to, 32–39
Birth order, social behavior and, 246–247
Breakfast-time problems, 212

C

Car travel, toddlers, 207–208
Cause/effect, learning of, 59
Challenging child. *See* Difficult child
Changes
adaptive child and, 111
behavior problem related to, 17–20
reactions to, 202
Childproofing, 33, 42
toddlerhood and, 68, 198, 204
Child rearing philosophy, 11–12
Cleaning own room, preschoolers, 256
Clinging to mother, terrible twos, 214–215
Cognitive development
early childhood, 76
infancy, 58–59
preschoolers, 78
toddlerhood, 64–65
Communication
foreign-speaking grandparents, 224–225
with infants, 176–177
listening to child, 116–118

to prevent problem behavior, 34–39
with toddlers, 185–186, 217
Consistency
importance of, 19–20
Control
choices/decision-making and, 28–30
development of child and, 28
versus giving in, 30
importance to children, 12
predicting child's behavior and, 109
Curiosity, toddlers, 186–187

D

Day care, 165, 167–170
activities, 196–197
clinging at drop off, 194
infancy, 165, 167–170
for infants, 170
options for, 167–168
toddlers and, 196–197
Deals, age and making deals, 54–55
Decision-making, by child, 28–30, 70–71
Defiance, terrible twos, 220–221
Dependent child, say "no" strategy and, 128
Development
discipline and, 6–7
early childhood, 74–78
infancy, 56–66
overestimating child's abilities, 54–55
parental behavior and, 55–56
preschoolers, 78–82
toddlerhood, 66–74
Diapering, infancy, 174–175
Difficult child, 113–115
discipline and, 114–115
parental resentment and, 113–114
Discipline
development of child and, 6–7
difficult child and, 114–115
disciplined life-style, 1–2

learning by example, 8
love/respect and, 7–8
meaning of discipline, 1–3
Disciplined life-style, 1–2, 27–31
control in, 28–31
rules, 231
Divorce
cooperation of ex-spouses,
143–144
discipline and, 143–144
new family members and, 148
noncustodial parent, 149–151
parent's behavior toward ex-
spouse, 144
rules of two-household family,
145–147
stepparents, 151–157
tips for relatives of divorced
couple, 148–149
use of chidren as messengers,
144–145
Dressing
infants, 173–174, 176
toddlers, 200–202

E

Early childhood, 74–78
bedtime, 233
birth order and social behavior,
246
cognitive development, 76
egocentricity, 76
fighting with friends, 244
following instructions, 236–
237
foul language, 240–241
habits, 241–244
humor, 74–75
imaginary friends, 242
independence, 235
language development, 75–76
lying, 243
motor-mouth syndrome, 245
playing alone, 238–239
security blanket, 233–234
sharing, 76–77
sleep problems, 232–233
social development, 76–78

thumb sucking, 234–235
toys, too many, 237–238
turn taking, 77–78
TV violence and, 247–248
Egocentricity, early childhood,
76
Emotions, intensity of reaction
and, 112
Exploration phase, toddlerhood,
66–68

F

Family life
divorce, 143–150
stability in, 142–143
stepparenting, 151–157
traditional families, 142
Fighting with friends
early childhood, 244
toddlers, 228–229
First year of life. *See* Infancy
Following instructions, early
childhood, 236–237
Food, playing with, 187–188
Foul language, early childhood,
240–241
Fussiness, infants, 163

G

Grandparents, 177–178, 180–182
advice from, 180–181
drop-in grandparents, 177–178
foreign speaking grandparents,
224–225
parent's resentment of, 178–
179
problem grandparents, 181
Grocery shopping
child's requests from grocery,
260–261
grocery-store mania, toddlers,
207
terrible twos, 227–228

H

Habits, early childhood, 241–244
Humor, early childhood, 75–76
Hyperactivity, 107

I

Imaginary friends, early childhood, 242
Independence, 54, 119–140
  attachment and, 134–140
  beginning for child, 134
  discipline problems and, 119–120
  "doing it themselves," 121–122
  early childhood, 236
  permissiveness and, 133–134
  preschoolers, 78–79, 255
  privacy, 124–126
  saying "no," 127–133
  self-discipline and, 120
  slow development approach, 123, 223
  toddlers, 200–201, 213, 215
Individuality of child
  in rate of development, 180
  respect for, 98–99, 101, 103
  siblings and, 104–106
  temperament, 105–116
Infancy, 56–66
  air travel, 183–189
  approach to early problem behavior, 158
  attachment, 62–64
  babysitters, 170–172
  bath-time, 175
  beginning of discipline, 173
  cognitive development, 58–59
  communication with baby, 176–177
  day care, 165, 167–170
  diapering, 174–175
  dressing/undressing of, 173–174, 176
  eating
    late night feedings, 159–160
    quality of food, 161–162
    schedules, 162
  father's participation in, 179
  fussiness, 163
  grandparents and, 177–179, 180–182
  language development, 60
  learning, 60–61
  motor development, 57
  parental disagreements and, 179
  parental socializing and, 182–183
  perceptual development, 59
  schedules, 56–57, 159, 162
  shampoo, 175–176
  sleeping, 57–58
  sleeping with parents, 164
  social development, 61–62
  working mothers, 166–169
Insecurely attached infants, 63, 135
Insensitive parents, 138
Isolation, as punishment, 50

L

Labeling children, cautions about, 115–116
Language development
  early childhood, 75, 76
  infancy, 60
  toddlerhood, 66
Learning
  infancy, 60–61
  methods of, 186
Life-style. *See* Disciplined life-style
Listening to child, 116–118
  difficulty of, 117–118
  effects of, 118
Love, as reward, 41
Lying, 130
  early childhood, 243

M

Mealtime
  eating strange food, 213–214
  family meals, 189
  fussy eaters, 189–190
  parental modeling of, 93–94
  playing with food, 187–188
  quality of food for infants, 161–162
  schedules for, 17–19, 159, 162
  toddlers, 187–190
Mood, quality of mood, 112

Morning routines, preschoolers, 250–251

Motor development
  infancy, 57
  toddlerhood, 64

Motor-mouth syndrome, early childhood, 245

Moving, reactions to, 202–203

N

Naps, nap-resistance, 190–191, 211

Natural consequences, 46–48
  value of, 47
  warning children about, 47–48

Negativity, toddlerhood, 65–66, 69

Nighttime feedings, infants, 159–160

Noncustodial parent, discipline and, 149–150

O

Outings
  terrible twos, 225
  toddlers, 204–205

Oversensitive parents, 136, 137

P

Parenting
  child rearing philosophy, 11–12
  different approaches to, 5–7
  freedom of, 95–96
  responsibility of, 11

Parents
  manipulation by child, 128
  united front discipline, 129

Parents as models
  about bedtime, 94
  about mealtimes, 93–94
  about sharing, 94
  informal education and, 91–92
  modeling socially inappropriate behavior, 87–89
  parental imperfection and, 84–86
  for social relationships, 89–91

Perceptual development, infancy, 59

Perfection
  myth of perfect parents/children, 9–10
  teaching children about parental imperfection, 84–86

Permissiveness
  independence and, 133–134
  versus respect, 102
  yes-sayers, 133–134

Personality. *See* Temperament

Piaget, Jean, 64

Playing alone
  early childhood, 238–239
  toddlers, 214–215

Possessiveness, terrible twos, 229–230

Power struggles, 200, 205

Preschoolers, 78–82
  argumentativeness, 257
  bedtime fears, 251–252
  bedwetting, 252
  child's requests at the grocery, 260–261
  cleaning own room, 256
  cognitive development, 78
  completing tasks on time, 80–82
  independence, 78–79, 255
  morning routines, 250–251
  nursery bathroom set-up, 253
  responsibility, 79–80
  rules and, 261–262
  school behavior problems, 263
  separation anxiety, 254
  temper tantrums, 257–259
  threats from child, 259–260

Privacy, 124–126
  bathroom behavior, 125, 253
  bedroom, 125–126
  respect for, 126

Privileges, removing privileges, 49

Punishment, 46–52
  isolation, 50
  natural consequences, 46–48
  removing privileges, 49

spanking, 50–52
time-out, 49–50

R

Reactions, intensity of, 112
Rebellious child, say "no" strategy and, 128–129
Removing child from problem situations, 43, 104
Respect for children, 7–8, 98–103
  child as individual and, 98–99, 101, 103
  child's need for, 100, 102, 106
  for child's privacy, 126
  consistency in, 101
  effect for child, 100, 101
  effect for parent, 102
  versus permissiveness, 102
Responsibility, children
  check-lists for kids, 79–80
  preschoolers, 79–80
  suggested tasks for children, 25–26
  teaching to children, 23–25
Rhythmicity/regularity of child, 109–110
  discipline and, 110
  irregular child, 110
  regular child, 110
Rules, 231
  child forgets rules, 204
  of divorced family, 145–147
  house rules, 12
  preschoolers and, 261–262

S

Safety in home, childproofing, 33, 42
Say "no" strategy, 127–133
  dependent child and, 128
  meaning "no," 130–131
  rebellious child and, 128–129
  saying "no," 127–128, 130
  saying "no" automatically, 131–132
Schedules, 12–18
  for adults, 18

feeding, for infants, 159, 162
importance of, 12, 19–20
infancy, 56–57
for meals, 17–19
more than one child and, 15–17
regularity and, 14–15
rhythmicity of child and, 109–110
for sleeping/napping, 13–15
School behavior problems, 263
Securely attached infants, 62–63, 135
Secure parents, characteristics of, 45
Security blanket
  early childhood, 233–234
  toddlers, 214
Self-discipline
  attachment and, 138–140
  independence and, 120
  permissive parents and, 133–134
Self-esteem, helping children feel useful, 20–23
Sensitive child, 103
Sensitivity to child
  attachment and, 63–64, 138–140
  insensitive parents, 138
  oversensitive parents, 136, 137
Separation, parent/child, 165
Separation anxiety
  preschoolers, 254
  toddlers, 194–195
Setting limits, toddlers and, 200–201
Shampoo
  fear of, 176
  infancy, 175–176
Sharing
  early childhood, 76–77
  parental modeling of, 94
  toddlers, 206
Sibling rivalry
  reducing, 23
  toddlers, 215–216

Siblings
   "fair" treatment by parents,
      105
   individuality of, 104–106
Sleeping
   infancy, 57–58
   schedule for, 13–15
Social development
   early childhood, 76–78
   infancy, 61–62
Social interaction
   birth order and, 246–247
   fighting with friends, 228–
      229
   toddlers, 205–206
Socializing, parental, 182
Social relationships, parental
      modeling of, 89–91
Spanking, 50–52
Special toy strategy, toddlerhood,
      68
Spoiling child, baby-sitters, 193–
      194
Stability, family life, 142–143
Stepparents, 151–157
   avoiding comparison to parent,
      154–155
   discipline and, 152
   influence of biological parents
      and, 153
   role of, 155
   tips for, 156–157
Supermom syndrome, 160

T

Table manners, teaching of,
      187
Telephone, attention-getting
      from baby and, 182–183
Temperament
   adaptive child, 111
   approach–withdrawal, 111
   difficult child, 113–115
   discipline and, 106
   highly-active child, 107–108
   intensity of reaction and, 112
   labeling children, 115–116
   low-activity child, 108–109

quality of mood, 112
   rhythmicity/regularity of child,
      109–110
   stability over time, 106, 115
Temper tantrums
   child's feelings about, 224
   options for handling of, 73–74
   preschoolers, 257–259
   prevention of, 223
   terrible twos, 223–224
   toddlers, 72–73
Terrible twos, 209–230
   aggression toward mother,
      221–222
   aggression toward new baby,
      222
   breakfast-time problems, 212
   clinging to mother, 214–215
   defiance, 220–221
   eating strange food, 213–214
   embarrassing comments, 226
   fighting with friends, 228–
      229
   grocery-store behavior, 227–
      228
   interruption of adult conversa-
      tions, 219–220
   nap resistance, 211
   outings, 225
   playing alone, 214–215
   possessiveness, 229–230
   resistance, types of, 216–217
   security blanket, 214
   sibling rivalry, 215–216
   sleeping in parents' bed, 210–
      211
   temper tantrums, 223–224
   threats from child, 220
   toddlerhood, 69
   whining, 218–219
   wild running, 227
Threats, parental, 38–39
Threats from child
   preschoolers, 259–260
   terrible twos, 220
Thumb sucking, early childhood,
      236
Time-out, 49–50

Toddlerhood, 66–74
  aggression, 206–207
  baby-sitter and, 193–194
  bedtime, 191–192
  car travel, 208
  childproofing, 198, 204
  childproofing and, 68
  cognitive development, 64–68
  communication with toddlers,
      185–186, 217
  day-care, 196–197
  decision-making by child, 70–
      71
  discipline and, 67, 68
  discipline for visiting toddlers,
      199
  dressing, 201–202
  exploration phase, 66–68
  fears of, 203–204
  forgetting rules, 204
  grocery-store mania, 207
  language development, 66
  mealtimes, 187–190
  moodiness during, 202–203
  motor development, 64
  nap-resistance, 190–191
  negativity, 65–66, 69
  outings, 204–205
  parental vacations without
      child, 195–196
  problems with toddlers, 71–72
  separation anxiety, 194–195
  setting limits, 200–201
  sharing, 206
  social interaction, 205–206
  special toy strategy, 68
  temper tantrums, 72–73
  terrible twos, 69, 208–230
  three-year-olds, 74–75
  toilet training, 197–198
  See also Terrible twos.
Toilet training, toddlers, 197–198
Toys, too many, 237–238
Turn taking, early childhood, 77–
    78

U
Usefulness, helping children feel
    useful, 20–23

V
Vacations, without children, 195–
    196
Violence, preschoolers reaction
    to, 247–248
Visiting children, discipline and,
    199

W
Warnings
    about misbehavior, 43–44
    in natural consequences ap-
        proach, 47–48
Whining, 218–219
Wild running, terrible twos, 227
Working mothers, 166–169
    decision-making about working,
        166–167, 192–193
    guilt and, 165
    options for, 167–168

Y
Yelling, parental, 39
''Yes'' times, 34

About the Authors

Barbara Bjorklund has a masters degree in developmental psychology from Florida Atlantic University and has done research on cognitive and social development at both Florida Atlantic University and the University of Miami Mailman Center for Child Development. She has taught child development classes at several south Florida colleges and universities.

David Bjorklund has a Ph.D. from the University of North Carolina at Chapel Hill and is Professor of Psychology at Florida Atlantic University, specializing in cognitive development, the study of children's thinking. He has published numerous articles on this topic in academic books and journals and serves on the editorial board of the *Journal of Experimental Child Psychology*. He is the author of *Children's Thinking*, which was published in 1989 by Brooks/Cole.

David and Barbara Bjorklund have conducted research on child development together and, from 1987 through 1989, co-authored a monthly column for *Parents Magazine*, "As They Grow—Seven to Ten Years." They continue to serve as contributing editors at *Parents* and write a number of feature articles each year on child development. They are currently writing a textbook titled, *Child Development: An Introduction to Child Appreciation*, which will be released by Brooks/Cole in 1991. The Bjorklunds live in Ft. Lauderdale, Florida. They have four children ranging in age from nine to twenty-eight and four grandchildren.

BRINGING UP BABY

A series of practical baby care and family living guides developed with the staff of *Parents*™ Magazine. Explains both the *whys* and *how-to's* of infant and child care.